Particle Swarm Optimization

Particle Swarm Optimization

Maurice Clerc

First published in France in 2005 by Hermes Science/Lavoisier under the title "L'Optimisation par essaims particulaires"
First published in Great Britain and the United States in 2006 by ISTE Ltd

Apart from any fair dealing for the purposes of research or private study, or criticism or review, as permitted under the Copyright, Designs and Patents Act 1988, this publication may only be reproduced, stored or transmitted, in any form or by any means, with the prior permission in writing of the publishers, or in the case of reprographic reproduction in accordance with the terms and licenses issued by the CLA. Enquiries concerning reproduction outside these terms should be sent to the publishers at the undermentioned address:

ISTE Ltd
6 Fitzroy Square
London W1T 5DX
UK

ISTE USA
4308 Patrice Road
Newport Beach, CA 92663
USA

www.iste.co.uk

© LAVOISIER, 2005
© ISTE Ltd, 2006

The rights of Maurice Clerc to be identified as the authors of this work has been asserted by them in accordance with the Copyright, Designs and Patents Act 1988.

Library of Congress Cataloging-in-Publication Data

Clerc, Maurice.
  [Optimisation par essaims particulaires. English]
  Particle swarm optimization / Maurice Clerc.
     p. cm.
  Includes bibliographical references and index.
  ISBN-13: 978-1-905209-04-0
  ISBN-10: 1-905209-04-5
  1. Mathematical optimization. 2. Particles (Nuclear physics) 3. Swarm intelligence. I. Title.
  QC20.7.M27C5513 2006
  539.7'2--dc22

2005037211

British Library Cataloguing-in-Publication Data
A CIP record for this book is available from the British Library
ISBN 10: 1-905209-04-5
ISBN 13: 978-1-905209-04-0

Printed and bound in Great Britain by Antony Rowe Ltd, Chippenham, Wiltshire.

Table of Contents

Foreword... 13

Introduction... 17

Part I. Particle Swarm Optimization 21

Chapter 1. What is a Difficult Problem? 23

    1.1. An intrinsic definition... 23
    1.2. Estimation and practical measurement..................... 25
    1.3. For "amateurs": some estimates of difficulty 26
        1.3.1. Function $\sum_{d=1}^{D} x_d$ 27
        1.3.2. Function $\sum_{d=1}^{D} x_d^2$ 27
        1.3.3. Function $\sum_{d=1}^{D} \sqrt{x_d |\sin(x_d)|}$ 27
        1.3.4. Traveling salesman on D cities...................... 28
    1.4. Summary.. 28

Chapter 2. On a Table Corner 29

    2.1. Apiarian metaphor.. 29
    2.2. An aside on the spreading of a rumor 30
    2.3. Abstract formulation.. 30
    2.4. What is really transmitted 34
    2.5. Cooperation *versus* competition............................. 35
    2.6. For "amateurs": a simple calculation of propagation of rumor...... 35
    2.7. Summary.. 36

Chapter 3. First Formulations 37

   3.1. Minimal version 37
       3.1.1. Swarm size. 37
       3.1.2. Information links 38
       3.1.3. Initialization 38
       3.1.4. Equations of motion 39
       3.1.5. Interval confinement 40
       3.1.6. Proximity distributions. 42
   3.2. Two common errors. 44
   3.3. Principal drawbacks of this formulation 45
       3.3.1. Distribution bias. 45
       3.3.2. Explosion and maximum velocity 48
   3.4. Manual parameter setting. 48
   3.5. For "amateurs": average number of informants. 49
   3.6. Summary 50

Chapter 4. Benchmark Set. 51

   4.1. What is the purpose of test functions? 51
   4.2. Six reference functions 52
   4.3. Representations and comments 52
   4.4. For "amateurs": estimates of levels of difficulty 56
       4.4.1. Theoretical difficulty. 56
           4.4.1.1. Tripod 56
           4.4.1.2. Alpine 10D 57
           4.4.1.3. Rosenbrock 57
       4.4.2. Difficulty according to the search effort 58
   4.5. Summary 58

Chapter 5. Mistrusting Chance. 59

   5.1. Analysis of an anomaly. 59
   5.2. Computing randomness. 61
   5.3. Reproducibility. 61
   5.4. On numerical precision 62
   5.5. The rare KISS 62
       5.5.1. Brief description. 63
       5.5.2. Test of KISS 64
   5.6. On the comparison of results 64
   5.7. For "amateurs": confidence in the estimate of a rate of failure. 65
   5.8. C programs 68
   5.9. Summary 69

Chapter 6. First Results 71

6.1. A simple program 71
6.2. Overall results 72
6.3. Robustness and performance maps 73
6.5. Theoretical difficulty and noted difficulty 80
6.6. Source code of OEP 0 80
6.7. Summary 85

Chapter 7. Swarm: Memory and Graphs of Influence 87

7.1. Circular neighborhood of the historical PSO 87
7.2. Memory-swarm 88
7.3. Fixed topologies 90
7.4. Random variable topologies 92
   7.4.1. Direct recruitment 92
   7.4.2. Recruitment by common channel of communication 92
7.5. Influence of the number of informants 93
   7.5.1. In fixed topology 93
   7.5.2. In random variable topology 95
7.6. Influence of the number of memories 95
7.7. Reorganizations of the memory-swarm 97
   7.7.1. Mixing of the memories 97
   7.7.2. Queen and other centroids 98
   7.7.3. Comparative results 98
7.8. For "amatheurs": temporal connectivity in random recruitment 99
7.9. Summary 101

Chapter 8. Distributions of Proximity 103

8.1. The random possibilities 103
8.2. Review of rectangular distribution 104
8.3. Alternative distributions of possibilities 105
   8.3.1. Ellipsoidal positive sectors 105
   8.3.2. Independent Gaussians 106
   8.3.3. Local by independent Gaussians 107
   8.3.4. The class of one-dimensional distributions 107
   8.3.5. Pivots 108
   8.3.6. Adjusted ellipsoids 112
8.4. Some comparisons of results 113
8.5. For "amatheurs" 116
   8.5.1. Squaring of a hypersphere 116
   8.5.2. From sphere to ellipsoid 117
   8.5.3. Random volume for an adjusted ellipsoid 117
   8.5.4. Uniform distribution in a D-sphere 118
8.6. C program of isotropic distribution 118
8.7. Summary 119

Chapter 9. Optimal Parameter Settings 121

9.1. Defense of manual parameter setting. 121
9.2. Better parameter settings for the benchmark set 122
   9.2.1. Search space 122
   9.2.2. To optimize the optimizer 123
   9.2.3. Analysis of results 125
      9.2.3.1. Rate of failure. 125
      9.2.3.2. Distribution 125
      9.2.3.3. Topology and the number of informants 125
      9.2.3.4. Informants K 125
      9.2.3.5. Coefficient φ 126
      9.2.3.6. Informants N and memories M. 126
9.3. Towards adaptation 127
9.4. For "amatheurs": number of graphs of information 127
9.5. Summary 128

Chapter 10. Adaptations 129

10.1. Demanding criteria. 129
   10.1.1. Criterion 1 129
   10.1.2. Criterion 2 129
10.2. Rough sketches. 130
   10.2.1. Weighting with temporal decrease 130
   10.2.2. Selection and replacement 131
   10.2.3. Parametric adaptations 132
   10.2.4. Nonparametric adaptations. 133
10.3. For "amatheurs" 135
   10.3.1. Formulas of temporal decrease 135
   10.3.2. Parametric adaptations 136
      10.3.2.1. Case 1 ($m_i \geq 0$). 137
      10.3.2.2. Case 2 ($m_i < 0$). 137
10.4. Summary 138

Chapter 11. TRIBES or Cooperatin of Tribes 139

11.1. Towards an ultimate program 139
11.2. Description of TRIBES 141
   11.2.1. Tribes 141
   11.2.2. The tribal relationships 141
   11.2.3. Quality of a particle 141
   11.2.4. Quality of a tribe. 142
   11.2.5. Evolution of the tribes 142
      11.2.5.1. Removal of a particle. 142
      11.2.5.2. Generation of a particle 144
   11.2.6. Strategies of displacement 145

11.2.7. Best informant 146
    11.2.7.1. Direct comparison, general case 147
    11.2.7.2. Comparison by pseudo-gradients, metric spaces 147
11.3. Results on the benchmark set 147
11.4. Summary 149

Chapter 12. On the Constraints 151

12.1. Some preliminary reflections. 151
12.2. Representation of the constraints 152
12.3. Imperative constraints and indicative constraints. 153
12.4. Interval confinement. 154
12.5. Discrete variable 154
    12.5.1. Direct method 155
        12.5.1.1. List not ordered (and not orderable) 155
        12.5.1.2. Ordered list 155
    12.5.2. Indirect method 155
12.6. Granularity confinement 156
12.7. "all different" confinement. 156
12.8. Confinement by dichotomy. 157
12.9. Multicriterion treatment. 158
12.10. Treatment by penalties. 161
12.11. C source code. Dichotomic search in a list 162
12.12. For "amatheurs" 162
12.13. Summary 165

Chapter 13. Problems and Application 167

13.1. Ecological niche 167
13.2. Typology and choice of problems 168
13.3. Canonical representation of a problem of optimization 169
13.4. Knapsack 169
13.5. Magic squares 170
13.6. Quadratic assignment 171
13.7. Traveling salesman 172
13.8. Hybrid JM 173
13.9. Training of a neural network 174
    13.9.1. Exclusive OR. 175
    13.9.2. Diabetes among Pima Indians 176
    13.9.3. Servomechanism. 176
    13.9.4. Comparisons 176
13.10. Pressure vessel 177
    13.10.1. Continuous relaxed form 179
    13.10.2. Complete discrete form 180
13.11. Compression spring 182
13.12. Moving Peaks 185

13.13. For "amatheurs": the magic of squares 188
13.14. Summary. 188

chapter 14. Conclusion 189

14.1. End of the beginning. 189
14.2. Mono, poly, meta. 189
14.3. The beginning of the end? 190

Part II. Outlines 193

Chapter 15. On Parallelism 195

15.1. The short-sighted swarm 195
15.2. A parallel model 195
15.3. A counter-intuitive result 196
15.4. Qualitative explanation 197
15.5. For "amatheurs": probability of questioning an improved memory . . . 198
15.6. Summary 199

Chapter 16. Combinatorial Problems 201

16.1. Difficulty of chaos 201
16.2. Like a crystal 202
16.3. Confinement method 203
16.4. Canonical PSO 204
16.5. Summary 210

Chapter 17. Dynamics of a Swarm 211

17.1. Motivations and tools 211
17.2. An example with the magnifying glass 212
   17.2.1. One particle 212
   17.2.2. Two particles 214
17.3. Energies 217
   17.3.1. Definitions 217
   17.3.2. Evolutions 218
17.4. For experienced "amatheurs": convergence and constriction 220
   17.4.1. Criterion of convergence 220
   17.4.2. Coefficients of constriction 221
   17.4.3. Positive discriminant 222
17.5. Summary 224

Chapter 18. Techniques and Alternatives 225
    18.1. Reprise. 225
    18.2. Stop-restart/reset 226
        18.2.1. A criterion of abandonment 226
        18.2.2. Guided re-initialization. 227
    18.3. Multi-swarm 227
    18.4. Dynamic optimization. 228
    18.5. For "amatheurs" 229
        18.5.1. Maximum flight and criterion of abandonment. 229
        18.5.2. Dilation 230
    18.6. Summary 230

Further Information 231

Bibliography 233

Index 239

Foreword

Goal and limits

This book is the first to deal exclusively with particle swarm optimization. In his *Swarm Intelligence* [KEN 01], originally entitled *Particle Swarm Optimization* (PSO), my friend Jim Kennedy has devoted three chapters out of eleven to this subject, above all as an illustration of the more general concept of collective intelligence without dwelling on the details of practical implementation.

For this book, my goal was simpler: to give you the concepts and tools necessary and sufficient for the resolution of problems of optimization, including the codes of various programs.

After having assimilated the contents of the first and more important part, you should be able to apply PSO to practically any problem of minimization of an assessable function in a continuous, discrete or mixed search space. You will also be able to deal with multi-objective problems, either as such, or as methods of taking into account complex constraints of a mono-objective problem.

PSO is in constant and fast evolution, but the corpus of techniques presented here is already sufficiently reliable and particularly effective, even though, as we shall see, many and interesting ways of research are yet to be explored, particularly regarding adaptive PSO. An important international collaboration, XPS (eXtended Particle Swarms), led by the University of Essex in Great Britain, began at the end of 2004. It should lead to major breakthroughs both theoretical and practical. As the promoters of the project put it:

"[The goal is] to include strategies inspired by a broad range of collective behavior, in biology and particle physics, to deal with many problems in engineering and to establish solid theoretical and mathematical bases [. . .]".

In spite of its brief history, PSO has already entered into science fiction: Michael Crichton, in his novel Prey [CRI 03], has explicitly referred to it, in particular using the concept of constriction . . . albeit in a form that is very different from the original one!

Organization of the book

The book is structured in two parts. The first describes PSO in detail, from a very simple primitive parametric version to an adaptive version that does not require the user to supply parameters. The discussion thread is a benchmark set of six test functions which enable us to compare the influence of the parameters and search strategies. The final chapter of this part focuses on some more realistic problems.

The second part is entitled "Outlines", indicating that the items discussed are not dealt with in detail, as this would go beyond the scope of this book. It is primarily about parallelism, the canonical PSO (a basis, among others, of the combinatorial PSO) and the dynamics of the swarms. The final chapter very briefly presents some techniques and alternatives such as the stop-reset, the multi-swarm and the dynamic PSO (optimization of a function changing during the very process of search). The interested reader will be able to refer to the documents cited.

Many chapters end with a more mathematical part. This part specifies or justifies some of the assertions made in the body of the text but is by no means necessary for the comprehension of those ideas. It can thus be comfortably skipped if you do not have the taste or the time for it.

Various versions of PSO are studied, some in a very thorough manner, others very briefly. The diagram below shows the links between them and the levels of detail of the presentations. In particular, the significant field of specific implementations of PSOs is only skimmed through. It would be, in itself, worth a later work, particularly as the methods implemented are very often hybrid, i.e. use several methods of optimization jointly, in particular for difficult combinational problems.

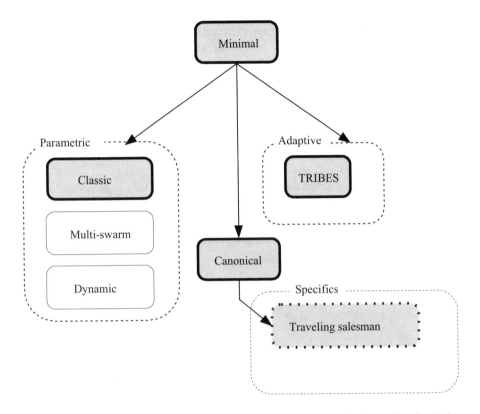

Figure 1. *Various versions of PSO considered. Those with a gray background and a thick continuous outline are really detailed. The outline is dotted if there is presentation without implementation. The versions indicated in the white zone are only mentioned*

On the source codes

The programs used were developed under Linux and deliberately written in pure ANSI C to be easily compilable under any operating system. There is consequently neither graphic interface, nor specific memory management.

For certain small programs, the source codes are given explicitly. The others are available on the Internet, starting from the following link: http://www.hermes-science.com/clerc/oep.zip. More generally, the portal of PSO is Particle Swarm Central: http://www.particleswarm.info/.

On technical terms

Normally the essence of each chapter (including some rather delicate reasoning) may be read without any deep mathematical knowledge. Nevertheless some specialized terms are used here and there, particularly for the sake of conciseness, but these are easily comprehensible. For example, "hypersphere in a space with D dimensions" will often be replaced by "D-sphere", and "hyperparallelepiped in a space with D dimensions" will be replaced by "D-rectangle".

To contact the author

If you wish to send comments, point out errors or make suggestions, you can contact Mr Maurice Clerc:
- by email, at maurice.clerc@writeme.com;
- *via* the author's website, http://www.mauriceclerc.net;
- *via* the editor.

Introduction

On some types of optimization

Iterative optimization is as old as life itself. Even very primitive beings act according to a simple impulse that can be summarized in a few words: "To improve their situation". Hence, many strategies are conceivable, but those we see every day in action in nature, and prove their effectiveness by the persistence of the species that practice them, already offer a broad range of solutions. It is therefore not surprising that, explicitly or implicitly, several mathematical models of optimization take as a starting point biological behaviors and make an abundant use of metaphors and terms originating from genetics, ethology, and even from ethnology or psychology.

Among these models, one can distinguish those corresponding to individual behavior and those using collective behavior. In the first case, the most obvious strategy is to seek to benefit permanently from any obvious immediate improvement. If the objective is to reach a summit, at every crossroads one will systematically take the route that seems to go up more; for example, by testing them all over a small length. Obviously, by doing this, one may well end up on a secondary summit, which could be only a very poor local optimum.

To compensate for the limitations of this primitive gradient strategy, it would be necessary to make a real conceptual leap and allow the situation to more or less deteriorate for a long time, in the hope that it would improve eventually. Since this behavior could be suicidal, it is advisable to be protected by a safeguard, i.e., in practice, to remember the best position already found, in order to be able return to it if necessary. At the same time, the individual can afford to explore on the basis of a wider variety of rules, even straightforwardly randomly, or, more intelligently, according to a chance "guided" by gradually acquired knowledge.

In the second case, i.e. collective optimization, this maintenance of the asset can be done quite naturally, since it is enough that the individual who has the best position does not move, leaving others to explore the environment. But now, two new parameters come into play: the size of the group and its structure.

The structure relates to the way in which information is transmitted between individuals. To what is each individual related? Are these links constant or variable? Are the exchanges bidirectional or not? Is there a hierarchy? Sub-groups? The basic problem is that of the use of knowledge. One rightly feels that the more the search space is sampled by successively evaluated positions, the better one should be able to predict the areas that are interesting to explore, by making certain assumptions about the regularity of the search space. However, these forecasts have a price. Is it worthwhile?

Not always. The most obvious academic case is that of a function to be optimized completely at random: the best strategy is the most stupid and very cheap, since it simply consists in generating equally random positions. Generally, the more progressive sampling of the studied function presents a higher degree of randomness, the more the strategy of research must itself call for randomness.

The size of the group can be fixed at the beginning or be variable during the research. In the second case, it is necessary to define mechanisms of selection or generation, or, more often, both. Moreover, even in the first case, such mechanisms can be used, the constant size being preserved by a dynamic equilibrium, any selection being compensated by a generation.

On PSO

Particle swarm optimization (PSO), in its historical version, is a collective, anarchic (in the original sense of the term), iterative method, with the emphasis on cooperation; it is partially random and without selection. The goal of the early chapters will be to detail these characteristics and formalize them to obtain an exploitable model that is particularly effective for strongly nonlinear problems.

We will see initially why and how this model can treat continuous and heterogeneous (i.e. in which some of the variables are continuous and others discrete, possibly coding combinational aspects) optimizations in a uniform way. Then we will study some alternatives. The goal here is not to make an exhaustive survey, but to work on a selection of those which either have already proved to be of interest, or seem most promising. In other words, their choice is necessarily subjective. We will look in particular at the versions known as adaptive, whose "ultimate" form, called TRIBES, does not require any parameter other than those defining the problem.

The few problems with accompanying notes should then allow you to become familiar with PSO, to better determine its domain of competence and hopefully to use it yourself later with profit, perhaps even to make improvements upon it.

PART I

Particle Swarm Optimization

Chapter 1

What is a Difficult Problem?

1.1. An intrinsic definition

As regards optimization, certain problems are regarded as more difficult than others. This is the case, *inter alia*, for combinatorial problems. But what does that mean? Why should a combinatorial problem necessarily be more difficult than a problem in continuous variables and, if this is the case, to what extent is it so? Moreover, the concept of difficulty is very often more or less implicitly related to the degree of sophistication of the algorithms in a particular research field: if one cannot solve a particular problem, or it takes a considerable time to do so, therefore it is difficult.

Later, we will compare various algorithms on various problems, and we will therefore need a rigorous definition. To that end, let us consider the algorithm for purely random research. It is often used as a reference, because even a slightly intelligent algorithm must be able to do better (even if it is very easy to make worse, for example an algorithm being always blocked in a local minimum). Since the measurement of related difficulty is very seldom clarified (see however [BAR 05]), we will do it here quickly.

The selected definition is as follows: the difficulty of an optimization problem in a given search space is the probability of not finding a solution by choosing a position at random according to a uniform distribution. It is thus the probability of failure at the first attempt.

Consider the following examples. Take the function f defined in [0 1] by $f(x) = x$. The problem is "to find the minimum of this function nearest within ε". It is easy to calculate (assuming that ε is less than 1) that the difficulty of this problem, following the definition above, is given by the quantity (1 − ε). As we can see in Figure 1.1, it is simply the ratio of two measurements: the total number of acceptable solutions and the total number of possible positions (in fact, the definition of a probability). From this point of view, the minimization of x2 is twice as easy as that of x.

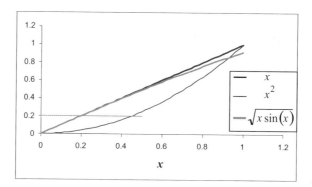

Figure 1.1. *Assessing the difficulty. The intrinsic difficulty of a problem of the minimization of a function (in this case, the search for an item x for which f(x) is less than 0.2) has nothing to do with the apparent complication of the formula of the function. On the search space [0 1], it is the function x^2 that is by far the easiest, whereas there is little to choose between the two others, function x being very slightly more difficult*

It should be noted that this assessment of difficulty can depend on the presence of local minima. For example, Figure 1.2 represents part of the graph of a variant of the so-called "Alpine" function, $f(x) = |x\sin(x) + 0.1x|$. For $\varepsilon = 0.5$ the field of the acceptable solutions is not connected. Of course, a part contains the position of the global minimum (0), but another part surrounds that of a local minimum whose value is less than ε. In other words, if the function presents local minima, and particularly if their values are close to that of the global minimum, one is quite able to obtain a satisfactory mathematical solution, but whose position is nevertheless very far from the hoped for solution.

By reducing the tolerance level (the acceptable error), one can certainly end up selecting only solutions actually located around the global minimum, but this procedure obviously increases the practical difficulty of the problem. Conversely, therefore, one tries to reduce the search space. But this requires some knowledge of the position of the solution sought and, moreover, it sometimes makes it necessary to define a search space that is more complicated than a simple Cartesian product of intervals; for example, a polyhedron, which may even be non-convex. However, we will see that this second item can be discussed in PSO by an option that allows an imperative constraint of the type $g(position) < 0$ to be taken into account.

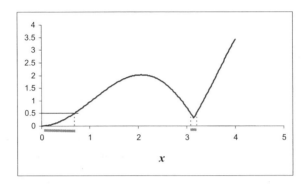

Figure 1.2. *A non-connected set of solutions. If the tolerance level is too high (here 0.5), some solutions can be found around a local minimum. Two different methods of avoiding this problem when searching for a global minimum are to reduce the tolerance level (which increases the practical difficulty of research) or to reduce the search space (which decreases the difficulty). But this second method requires that we have at least a vague idea of the position of the sought minimum*

1.2. Estimation and practical measurement

When high precision is required, the probability of failure is very high and to take it directly as a measure of difficulty is not very practical. Thus we will use instead a logarithmic measurement given by the following formula:

$$difficulty = -\ln(1 - failure\ probability) = -\ln(success\ probability)$$

In this way one obtains more easily comparable numbers. Table 1.1 presents the results for four small problems. In each case, it is a question of reaching a minimal value. For the first three, the functions are continuous and one must accept a certain margin of error because that is what makes it possible to calculate the probability of success. The last problem is a classic "traveling salesman problem" with 27 cities, for which only one solution is supposed to exist. Here, the precision required is absolute: one wants to obtain this solution exactly.

Problem	Search space	Value to be reached	Admissible error	Logarithmic difficulty
$\sum_{d=1}^{10} x_d$	$[0\ 1]^{10}$	0	0.01	61.2
$\sum_{d=1}^{10} x_d^2$	$[0\ 1]^{10}$	0	0.01	29
$\sum_{d=1}^{10} \sqrt{x_d} \lvert \sin(x_d) \rvert$	$[0\ 1]^{10}$	0	0.01	Estimate 63
Traveling salesman	$\{1,2,...,10\}^{27}$	C	0	61.26

Table 1.1. *Difficulty of four problems compared. When the probabilities of success are very low, it is easier to compare their logarithms. The ways of calculating the difficulty are given at the end of the chapter. For the third function, it is only a rather pessimistic statistical estimate (in reality, one should be able to find a value less than the difficulty of the first function). For the traveling salesman problem (search for a Hamiltonian cycle of minimal length), it was supposed that there was only one solution, of value C; it must be reached exactly, without any margin of error*

We see, for example, that the first and last problems are of the same level of intrinsic difficulty. It is therefore not absurd to imagine that the same algorithm, particularly if it uses randomness advisedly, can solve one as well as the other. Moreover, and we will return to this, the distinction between discrete/combinatorial problems and continuous problems is rather arbitrary for at least two reasons:

– a continuous problem becomes necessarily discrete, since it is treated on a numerical computer, hence with limited precision;

– a discrete problem can be replaced by an equivalent continuous problem under constraints, by interpolating the function defining it on the search space.

1.3. For "amateurs": some estimates of difficulty

The probability of success can be estimated in various ways, according to the form of the function:

– direct calculation by integration in the simple cases;

– calculation on a finite expansion, either of the function itself if it is derivable around the optimum several times (Taylor's formula), or of a Padé approximation (ratio of two polynomials);

– statistical estimate.

For Table 1.1, the probabilities of success were calculated as indicated below.

1.3.1. Function $\sum_{d=1}^{D} x_d$

Let us call p the probability of success and ε the required precision. One has successively:

$$p = p\left(\sum_{d=1}^{D} x_d < \varepsilon\right) = \int_0^\varepsilon p\left(\sum_{d=1}^{D-1} x_d < \varepsilon - u\right) du = \frac{\varepsilon^D}{D!}$$

the last equality being obtained easily by recurrence. But this is valid only if all the components are picked at random from the interval $[0\ 1]$. If the real interval is $[0\ R]$, this result must be multiplied by $(1/R)^D$. Finally, we obtain:

$$difficulty = \ln(D!) - D\ln(\varepsilon) + D\ln(R) = \sum_{d=1}^{D} \ln(d) - D\ln(\varepsilon) + D\ln(R)$$

1.3.2. Function $\sum_{d=1}^{D} x_d^2$

Here, calculation is even simpler ... provided its formulae are known! Effectively we want the probability of $\sum_{d=1}^{D} x_d^2 < \varepsilon$ for $0 \le x_d \le 1$. It is therefore enough to work out the ratio of the volume of the hypersphere of dimension D and radius $\sqrt{\varepsilon}$ and of the volume of the hypercube of edge 2. It is given by the traditional formula:

$$\begin{cases} \dfrac{\pi^{D'}}{D'!} \sqrt{\varepsilon}^D \dfrac{1}{2^D} & \text{si } D = 2D' \\ \pi^{D'} \dfrac{2^D}{D!} \sqrt{\varepsilon}^D \dfrac{1}{2^D} & \text{si } D = 2D'+1 \end{cases}$$

As before, if the hypercube is of edge $2R$, it is necessary to multiply by $(1/R)^D$.

1.3.3. Function $\sum_{d=1}^{D} \sqrt{x_d |\sin(x_d)|}$

Here direct analytical determination is tricky. It would certainly be possible to use an expansion of a finite series, but let's take a lazier method of estimation, which nevertheless requires the use of a computer.

We take a very small search space $[0\ r]^D$, such that there are nevertheless points in which the function has a greater value than the tolerance level, ε. For $D = 10$, one can take $r = 0.005$.

We can at random draw a great number of items (10^8 in the example), each time we evaluate the function, in order to see whether we obtain a value less than ε or not. We deduce an estimate from the success rate, τ. In the example, one obtains $\tau = 0.999732$. Note that it is necessary to use a good pseudo-random number generator. For example, the function *rand* in the programming language C is not always appropriate (see Chapter 5).

One then calculates that on the search space $[0\ r]^D$, the success rate would be only $\tau' = \tau \left(\dfrac{r}{R} \right)^D$. The measurement of corresponding difficulty is thus:

$$\textit{difficulty} = -\ln(\tau) - D\ln(r) + D\ln(R)$$

Note that this estimate is a little pessimistic as soon as $R \geq \pi$, since there are then several global minima (every point where $\sin(x_d) = 0$, for all x_d). The number of these points is $n = (1 + Ent(R/\pi))^D$, but the further one moves from the origin of the coordinates, the more the corresponding minimum is "pointed" and the less, therefore, its existence reduces the difficulty of the problem. The fact is, moreover, that PSO never finds them before the origin of the coordinates itself (as long as, of course, this is in the search space).

1.3.4. *Traveling salesman on D cities*

One can always fix the town of departure. There then remain $(D-1)!$ possible combinations for the others. It is assumed that there is only one solution. The probability of success while choosing randomly is thus $1/(D-1)!$ and so one obtains the formula:

$$\textit{difficulty} = \sum_{d=1}^{D-1} \ln(d)$$

1.4. Summary

A problem is regarded as easy if the probability of finding a solution by chance is large. Thus the intrinsic theoretical difficulty can be quantified by the inverse of the logarithm of the probability of success. Some examples are given, showing that extremely different, continuous, discrete or combinatorial *a priori* problems have, in fact, the same level of difficulty.

Chapter 2

On a Table Corner

2.1. Apiarian metaphor

The bee dances. While humming, she describes a kind of slightly tilted oblate eight. Undulating quickly, she crosses once, twice, ten times, the same closed curve, followed by her sisters who pass very close to her, scenting her and listening to her. And her dance is a message, which says to them: "15° relative to the sun; 300 meters; lavender; much".

About 1927, Karl von Frisch discovered that bees brought back to the hive not only nectar and pollen, but also information [FRI 84]. He patiently decoded their language and the attentive observer can now understand them to some extent. It is even possible today, thanks to tiny robots, "to speak to them". Thus, we know rather well now why and how, once a good site is located by a worker, it is quickly and effectively exploited by others. The transmitted direction and distance incorporate inaccuracies; interpretation is prone to small errors; and, finally, the flight itself towards the site indicated undergoes slight deviations. The net result is that the many workers who answer the call of their colleague will finally distribute themselves at random around the initial site. Thus, if there is a better site nearby, it will very probably also be located.

But that does not explain how an interesting site that is far from those already known can also be found. As Karl von Frisch noted, this kind of discovery must be the work of an "original", but he did not propose a model explaining the search strategy of such dissidents. Is this happening at random? Or systematically according to a preset plan? Moreover, one bee must sometimes combine information from several different sources: its own knowledge of the ground and information from one or more nectar-gathering bees. The way it does this remains a mystery, but to learn something from the behavior of our bees, we will nevertheless have to model it; therefore, in fact, to invent an entirely new method.

2.2. An aside on the spreading of a rumor

It is rather natural, and traditional, to model a network of information between individuals by a graph, sometimes called an influence graph. Each node of the graph represents an individual, and an arc, *an information link*, between two individuals A and B means "A informs B". These links are not necessarily constant. In particular, in our swarm, they change at every moment (with each time increment, if time is discrete, which we will accept from now on). Complex studies, highlighting phenomena of avalanche and the influence of phenomena of training have been made [DER 03], but we will be satisfied here with a simplistic model.

With each time increment, each particle randomly chooses a certain given number of other particles to inform. One can then calculate (see section 2.6) various elements, for example the minimal value of this number, varying according to the size of the swarm, to be almost sure that any information was received at least once by everyone after a certain time.

The interesting point is that the number informed by a given particle can remain very small. For example, if we want quasi-certainty (probability of 0.9999) that any individual can be informed by any other after 10 time increments, it is enough that each one informs two at each increment, and this is valid for a broad range of swarm sizes, from 10 to 300, approximately.

2.3. Abstract formulation

In PSO, an "interesting site" corresponds to at least a local optimum of a certain function defined in a search space. This function can be given by a mathematical formula or, failing this, by an algorithm, or even by the outcome of a process, real or simulated. The main thing is that one can calculate its value at each point.

For a first simple version, we do not seek all the interesting sites, but only the most interesting, i.e. the global optimum of our function. With this intention, PSO takes as a starting point the cooperative behavior described in our metaphor: each particle is able to communicate to some others the position and quality of the best site it knows, a quality that one can interpret as its "value". Let us call this set of particles connected to a given one by the descending information links the group of information receivers. Conversely, at every moment, a given particle can belong simultaneously to several informant groups and thus has a certain number of informants, who inform it about various more or less good sites. It is up to it to take advantage of this information in order to define its next displacement. This operation of synthesis of information for an action has not yet been elucidated in biological reality, but has been the subject here of a very simple formalization (linear). This formalization does not claim to model the real behavior of bees or any other living organism. It simply proves to be effective for the resolution of many mathematical problems of optimization.

If one wants to continue to develop the metaphor, particle = bee, it would actually be necessary to speak of these bees as mutant or, at least, equipped with mobile phones! However, since a real bee must return to the hive to deposit the pollen or nectar it has collected, the fact that transmission of information is done only here is not a handicap. By contrast, in PSO there would be no advantage in each particle returning systematically to the same initial point before carrying out a new trip. Consequently, the communications are made remotely. This assumption made, we can now outline an algorithm of optimization taking as a starting point what we have just seen.

First of all, it is necessary to define a swarm in the search space. Of what size? The simplest thing to do, for the moment, is to give it a fixed size. We will see later that it is possible to be more astute and vary it automatically according to the results obtained. Whereas real swarms of bees typically number 20,000 individuals, we will be satisfied with sizes of about 20 to 40. While anticipating a little, it turns out that in PSO these sizes are very often sufficient. Of course, in a genuine hive, the vast majority of bees do not bring new information at all, being satisfied with exploiting, in the material sense of the term (nectar, pollen, etc.) a site already found. In PSO, it is certainly useful to exploit a known site, but only from the viewpoint of the theory of optimization, i.e. by checking the neighborhoods to find out if there is a better one. A multitude of purely nectar-gathering workers is not necessary.

In accordance with our metaphor, initially all the particles of the swarm should be at the same place. But, after the first time increment, they will be dispersed randomly, because, in the absence of any information, this is still the best method. Therefore, to simplify, let us say that this random distribution is the initial position of the swarm. Let us note that this also relates to the rates of travel of the particles, which we will also initialize randomly, over a reasonable range of values, as a function of the size of the search space.

It is also necessary for us to define, for each particle, which are its informants. Always by analogy with what (apparently) occurs in a hive, we can randomly define for each particle its group of information receivers, which, automatically, also determines the informants of each particle, since, formally, we establish a graph of relation between the particles.

How many information receivers, and how many informants? On the one hand, if all the particles are informed by each one, all information acquired is disseminated immediately, which may seem favorable. But, on the other hand, it is highly risky to have behavior that is too uniform: with the same information, all the particles will act in the same way. For difficult research, this is not effective. Conversely, if each particle has too few informants, we will be able to obtain more diversified behaviors, but then there is the risk that the information is badly transmitted. However, it is important that if a particle finds a good site, all the others can become aware of it more or less directly, in order to take advantage of it.

We thus have two criteria: diversity, which increases as the number of informants per particle decreases, and propagation, which becomes faster and more complete as this number increases. A priori, the relation "being informant of" is not symmetrical, but, as we shall see, it is the case in almost all current versions of PSO. To simplify, we will thus say that the information links are symmetrical: any informant is also informed.

Under these conditions, as we saw, if the choice is made randomly with each time increment, taking two or three information receivers for each particle seems a good compromise. Another method, which will be clarified in the chapter on topologies of the graphs of information (Chapter 7), is not to choose informants randomly once and for all, but according to a rule taking into account our two criteria, for example according to a circular diagram. A third method, about which we will also speak, is the possibility of making a permanent and judicious automatic selection of informants. The whole set of informants of a given particle will be called its I-group.

The nature of the transmitted information is obviously significant, but the more information there is, the more time-consuming and difficult it will be for a particle to deal with it. Therefore, rather than complicating matters we will say that each informant is able to transmit only two pieces of data that, in brief, we will call the overall best performance: the position of the best site it knows and the quality of this site. Translated into the language of optimization of a mathematical function, that means: a point in the search space and the value at this point of the function to be optimized.

Most difficult to model is the way in which an informed particle calculates its next displacement. First, let us note that it is in general already moving: it thus has a certain velocity. Then, since it is a possible informant in respect of other particles, it knows its own best performance. Lastly, therefore, it knows all the best performances of its informants. Let us simplify matters by keeping only the best. There thus remain three elements to be combined: proper velocity, proper best performance, and the best of the better performances of informants.

Let us imagine three extreme cases. In the first case, the particle is adventurous and intends to follow only its own way. Then it will allot a null confidence to received information and even to its own explorations: it will be satisfied with following more or less the already followed direction, i.e. the next displacement will be made with approximately the same velocity (intensity and direction) as the preceding one. In the second case, it is very conservative: it will grant great confidence to its best performance and will tend to return to it unceasingly. In the third case, it does not accord any confidence to itself, but instead moves according to the guidance of its best informant.

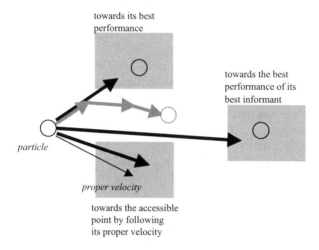

Figure 2.1. *Three fundamental elements for the calculation of the next displacement of a particle: according to its own velocity, towards its best performance and the best performance of its best informant. The way in which these three vectors are combined linearly via confidence coefficients is the basis of all the versions of the "classic" PSO. The three gray arrows represent such a combination, which will give the next position of the particle*

We thus have three fundamental displacements, shown in Figure 2.1 according to its current velocity; towards its own best performance; and towards that of its best informant. It is significant to note that "towards" in fact means "towards a point located not far from", a concept that will be clarified by defining *random proximities* (to be exact, random distributions). In the same way, "according to its velocity" means "towards the point that would be reached by continuing with the same velocity vector". The simplest way to calculate the true displacement starting from these three basic vectors is to make a linear weighting of it, thanks to *confidence coefficients*. All the skill of the first versions of PSO consists of the judicious definition of these coefficients.

2.4. What is really transmitted

After having detailed why and how a simple model of propagation of rumor can ensure the fast propagation of information, we are going to explain now that in PSO, this information is not always transmitted and that, when it is, it can be quite distorted . . . and that this is a good thing!

Everything depends on the fact that a particle transmits only its best performance. Let's take the case of a particle A which announces to a particle B: "My best performance is . . ." In general, particle B has other informants. In the first case, A is not the best of them. Then, as we saw, B does not take it into account at all and thus, obviously, its own best performance, i.e. the information which it will itself transmit, does not reflect in any way the information coming from A.

In the second case, A is the best of B's informants. Then, B modifies its position according to this information and we have two possibilities again. Either, by doing this, B does not improve its best performance and thus, again, what it will transmit does not contain anything coming from A. Or, on the contrary, the new position of B is better than its previous best performance and replaces it. In this single case, when B informs another particle, we can say that that information contains something resulting from A, but in a degraded form, since it is simply the result of a calculation having jointly used it with other elements.

Why is this process finally more effective, at least with regard to our objective of finding the global optimum, than a complete and perfect diffusion of information collected? It is undoubtedly because it models Karl von Frisch's intuition concerning the role of "original" individuals, in the sense of those who "wander away from the standard", in such a way that all the particles are more or less, precisely, original. Thus it makes for much diversity. If you have a little experience of other methods of iterative optimization, for example genetic algorithms, you can already infer from them what the experiment confirmed: PSO is particularly interesting for difficult problems. That does not mean, of course, that it cannot solve easy problems, but for the latter, there are often specific methods that are more effective. For example, PSO is not at all the best tool for the resolution of linear systems.

2.5. Cooperation *versus* competition

Since we have invoked the genetic algorithms, this may be the occasion to note a significant characteristic of PSO, at least in its classic versions: it does not practice any selection. The idea is that today's less successful particles are perhaps the tomorrow's successful ones. The particles with poor performance are preserved, with the hope that it is precisely among them that the "originals" are to be found, the dissenters that will make it possible to discover the best site in the search space. Moreover, the experiments have entirely justified this hope.

Naturally, researchers in optimization have found it very tempting to try to amalgamate qualities of PSO with those of other methods. And this is why versions with selection have seen the light of day. Contrary to what one might believe, this has shown that their principal quality is not to be more effective, but primarily to open the way for an autonomous PSO, without parameters defined by the user, and particularly not the size of the swarm. An example of this will be given later (see Chapter 11).

2.6. For "amatheurs": a simple calculation of propagation of rumor

Following the guidance of our apiarian metaphor, let us suppose that with each time increment a certain number K of information links are established randomly by each particle. Also let us suppose, for the sake of simplicity, that this number is constant. Also, by assumption, any individual receiving information at time T will retransmit it at time $T + 1$. What is the maximum number of increments T after which an individual C will almost certainly have received the information from A? Or, conversely, what must be the value of K such that any individual has almost certainly received information coming from A after T increments?

Let us answer the second question, which is the more interesting here. At the first increment, individual A disseminates its information. That amounts to choosing K individuals among N, including perhaps itself, i.e. to make K draws randomly, with replacement. The probability for a given individual C not to be selected is $1-1/N$, and the probability that it is still not selected after K draws is thus $(1-1/N)^K$.

With the second increment, the diffusion is made on K^2 individuals chosen randomly, and so on. Generalizing, the probability for an individual still not to be reached after the tth increment is $(1-1/N)^{K^t}$. Consequently, the probability $pr(t)$ of it being reached at least once is given by the complement of this formula:

$$pr(t) = 1 - \left(1 - \frac{1}{N}\right)^{K^t} \qquad [2.1]$$

This probability increases very quickly with t. Conversely, therefore, K does not need to be large for propagation to occur quickly. From the above formula one derives that, if one wants a near certainty with small ε (i.e. a probability equal to $1-\varepsilon$):

36 Particle Swarm Optimization

$$K = \left(\frac{\ln(\varepsilon)}{\ln\left(1-\frac{1}{N}\right)} \right)^{1/t} \qquad [2.2]$$

Figure 2.2 shows the evolution of $pr(t)$ for $K = 2$ and some sizes of swarm.

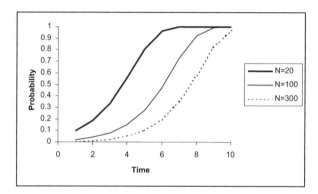

Figure 2.2. *Propagation of a rumor. Here, with each time increment, each particle informs another two at random. Even for a swarm of size $N = 300$, it is almost certain that any particle receives information from another at least once after at most 10 time increments*

2.7. Summary

The basic model of PSO is defined in an informal way, following quite freely the example of information exchanges between bees. Each particle combines in a linear fashion three elements to decide on its next movement: its current velocity, the best position it has found up to now and the best position found by its informants.

Informants are selected at random with each time increment. At this stage, their number is a parameter of the algorithm, just like the size of the swarm. Even if the swarm is large compared to the number of informants per particle, one can show that propagation of information occurs very quickly.

Chapter 3

First Formulations

3.1. Minimal version

3.1.1. *Swarm size*

Let us recall that for the moment the size of the swarm is fixed once for all. Intuitively, we feel of course that, the more particles, the faster the search will be in terms of the number of iterations. But, this iteration count is not really a relevant criterion. Rather, what counts is the number of times that the function to be minimized must be evaluated, because in the majority of real problems, this evaluation requires a considerable time. And, obviously, for an iteration, the number of evaluations is equal to the number of particles. Therefore, if we want to reduce the total number of evaluations needed to find a solution, we are tempted to decrease the size of the swarm. But too small a swarm is likely to take longer to find a solution or even not to find it at all.

In short, a compromise must be reached. Empirically, the experimenters proposed sizes of about 20 to 30 particles, which, indeed, proved entirely sufficient to solve almost all classic test problems. Note how small this value is, compared with those usually used, for example in the genetic algorithms (GA), a fact which does not facilitate comparisons. Those who are for GA say "Since I use 100 genes in my algorithms, I will take 100 particles for a comparison with PSO". At once, obviously, they find that PSO, although finding a solution at least as often as the genetic algorithms, is not very effective in terms of number of evaluations, since this number of particles is rather too large and there is no selection. Conversely, if those who are for PSO use GA with only 20 genes, they will observe that the algorithm finds the solution less often, which is quite normal as well. In fact, and we will return to this later, like any algorithm, PSO has its "field of competence", its "ecological niche", where it turns out to be the best choice [EBE 98, GUD 03, JEN 96, SET 03].

In the examples below we will systematically use a swarm of 20 particles, eventually showing that even this small number is sometimes larger than necessary. But we will also see later, in the chapter on performance maps, that a slightly greater number is more comfortable, in the sense that for a wide range of test problems it increases the average probability of success. Anyway, we must now make a move through the search space, first by defining their initial positions and velocities, then by specifying the equations of motion.

3.1.2. *Information links*

The information links are redefined randomly with each iteration: each particle informs K others chosen randomly. We note that it means that the group of informants corresponding to a particle has an average size slightly less than K, owing to the fact that the same information receiver can be selected several times. In the same way, it means that the average size of the groups of informants is also slightly less than K, though that is a little less obvious. The exact formula and the manner of finding it are given at the end of the chapter, for the benefit of mathematical amateurs.

It is enough for us here simply to note that the smaller the swarm, the lower the average number of informants of a given particle in respect of K. For example, for a swarm of 20 particles, with K = 3 one finds that the average size of the group of informants is 2.85, whereas it is 2.71 for a swarm of 10 particles.

This is relevant when one decreases the size of the swarm in the hope of reducing the total number of evaluations needed to achieve the goal. With fewer particles, the swarm is certainly a little less ready to explore the search space, but there is a kind of automatic partial offsetting by the correlative reduction of the average size of the groups of informants. As we have seen and will examine further, this reduction actually encourages exploration by increasing diversity.

3.1.3. *Initialization*

Note that, for the moment, we are interested only in continuous problems with real variables. A search space is defined, for example, classically, like one (hyper)cube of the form $[x_{min}, x_{max}]^D$. We will see, in Chapter 12, how it is possible to define much more general search spaces (with discrete variables and more complex forms) without changing the guiding principles of the method.

Initialization simply consists of initially randomly placing the particles according to a uniform distribution in this search space. This is a stage that one finds in virtually all the algorithms of stochastic iterative optimization.

But here, moreover, the particles have velocities. By definition, a velocity is a vector or, more precisely, an operator, which, applied to a position, will give another position. It is in fact a displacement, called velocity because the time increment of the iterations is always implicitly regarded as equal to 1.

In practice, it is not desirable that too many particles tend to leave the search space as early as the first increment, or for that matter later. We will see below what occurs in this case, but, for the moment, let us be satisfied with deriving at random the values of the components of each velocity, according to a uniform distribution in:

$$\left[(x_{min} - x_{max})/2, (x_{max} - x_{min})/2\right]$$

3.1.4. *Equations of motion*

The dimension of the search space is *D*. Therefore, the current position of a particle in this space at the moment *t* is given by a vector *x(t)*, with *D* components. Its current velocity is *v(t)*. The best position found up to now by this particle is given by a vector *p(t)*. Lastly, the best position found by informants of the particle is indicated by a vector *g(t)*. In general, we will write simply *x*, *v*, *p*, and *g*. The dth component of one of these vectors is indicated by the index *d*, for example x_d. With these notations, the equations of motion of a particle are, for each dimension *d*:

$$\begin{cases} v_d \leftarrow c_1 v_d + c_2 (p_d - x_d) + c_3 (g_d - x_d) \\ x_d \leftarrow x_d + v_d \end{cases} \qquad [3.1]$$

The confidence coefficients are defined in the following way:

– c_1 is constant (confidence in its own movement);

– c_2 and c_3 (respectively confidence in its best performance and that of its best informant) are randomly selected with each step of time according to a uniform distribution in a given interval [0, c_{max}].

This is why equation [3.1] can be rewritten in a more explicit way, by highlighting the random elements:

$$\begin{cases} v_d \leftarrow c_1 v_d + c_{max} alea(0,1)(p_d - x_d) + c_{max} alea(0,1)(g_d - x_d) \\ x_d \leftarrow x_d + v_d \end{cases} \qquad [3.2]$$

40   Particle Swarm Optimization

To use this model, the two parameters c_1 and c_{max} must be defined. The latter can be regarded as the maximum confidence granted by the particle to any performance transmitted by another. For each problem, "the right" values can be found only by experiment, with the help, however, of two empirical rules, made available after many tests.

The first rule stipulates that c_1 must have an absolute value less than 1. It is understood intuitively if one considers what occurs in the course of several successive time increments, in the specific case where the particle is and remains itself its best informant. We then have $p_d = x_d = g_d$ and, with each increment, velocity is simply multiplied by c_1. If its absolute value is greater than 1, velocity increases unceasingly and convergence is impossible. Note that, in theory, nothing prevents this coefficient being negative, the behavior obtained being strongly oscillatory, but this is never the case in traditional PSO. So, we will assume it to be positive.

In practice, this coefficient should be neither too small, which induces a premature convergence, nor too large, which, on the contrary, can slow down convergence excessively. The authors of the first work on PSO recommended that it be equalized to 0.7 or 0.8.

The second rule states simply that the parameter c_{max} should not be too large, a value of about 1.5 to 1.7 being regarded as effective in the majority of cases. When it was originally stated, this rule did not have a justification, even an intuitive one. It was purely experimental.

In fact, the recommended values are very close to those deduced later from mathematical analyses showing that for a good convergence the values from c1 and c_{max} should not be independently selected [CLE 02, TRE 03, VAN 02]. For example, the pairs of values (0.7 1.47) and (0.8 1.62) are indeed correct. The first experimenters, James Kennedy and Russel Eberhart, with the possible addition of Yuhui Shi [SHI 9a], did good work! The existence of this relation between these two parameters will help us later establish performance maps in only two variables: a parameter φ and the size of the swarm.

3.1.5. *Interval confinement*

During the first experiments of PSO, the test functions used were defined for all values. For example, the function:

$$f(x) = \sum_{d=1}^{D} x_d^2$$

(historically called Sphere, but which is in fact a paraboloid) in any point of real space R^D can be calculated. During the evolution of the swarm, it may have happened that a particle left the search space as initially defined, but that was of no importance, since the value of its position could in fact still be calculated without "crashing" the data-processing program. Nevertheless, obviously, that is not always the case. For example, in the majority of programming languages and with the majority of compilers, the evaluation of a function such as:

$$f(x) = \sum_{d=1}^{D} \sqrt{x_d}$$

returns an error message as soon as one of the coordinates x_d is negative.

More generally, a number of functions have a space of definition that is not infinite. Consequently, it was necessary to add very quickly a mechanism to prevent a particle leaving the search space. The simplest is the *interval confinement*. Let us always assume, for the sake of simplicity, that the search space is $[x_{min}, x_{max}]^D$. Then this mechanism stipulates that, if a coordinate x_d calculated according to equations of motion [3.2] leaves the interval $[x_{min}, x_{max}]$, one allots to it the nearest value of the border point. In practice, therefore, it amounts to replacing the second line of [3.2] by:

$$x_d \leftarrow MIN\left(MAX\left(x_d + v_d, x_{min}\right), x_{max}\right) \quad [3.3]$$

However, this simple form, while giving correct results, has a disadvantage. Indeed, we are in a scenario where the proper velocity of the particle tends to make it leave the search space. Confinement [3.3] certainly brings back the particle to the border of the search space, but does not change its velocity. This is calculated again and thus in general is modified next time, but it is not uncommon for it to remain oriented more or less in the same direction. Thus the particle will tend to cross the border again, be brought back to that point by confinement, and so on. In practice, it will be as though it "were stuck" to this border.

That is why one must supplement the mechanism of confinement with a velocity modification. One can replace the component that poses a problem by its opposite, possibly balanced by a coefficient less than 1, or one can simply cancel it. If cancellation is chosen, the complete mechanism is then described by the following operations:

$$x_d \notin [x_{min}, x_{max}] \Rightarrow \begin{cases} v_d \leftarrow 0 \\ x_d < x_{min} \Rightarrow x_d \leftarrow x_{min} \\ x_d > x_{max} \Rightarrow x_d \leftarrow x_{max} \end{cases} \quad [3.4]$$

The adaptation is immediate in case the intervals defining the search space are different for each dimension. But what is to be retained above all is the very principle of confinement, which stipulates that "if a particle tends to leave the search space, then bring it back to the nearest point in this space and consequently modify its velocity". We will see in particular that this principle can be used to define confinements necessary to problems in non-null granularity (positions with integer values, for example) or to problems (typically combinatorial) whose solutions must have all coordinates different.

3.1.6. *Proximity distributions*

What is the consequence of introducing random coefficients into equations of motion? For a better understanding, let us consider all the possible displacements obtained while varying independently c_2 and c_3 between 0 and c_{max}. Let us call $\tilde{p}$ the vector whose d^{th} component is:

$$alea(0, c_{max})(p_d - x_d)$$

and $\tilde{g}$ the one whose d^{th} component is:

$$alea(0, c_{max})(g_d - x_d)$$

It is easy to see that if one places the origin of $\tilde{p}$ (respectively $\tilde{g}$) in x, its end then traverses a D-parallelepiped whose two opposite tops are x and $c_{max}p$ (respectively $c_{max}g$). This D-parallelepiped is called the *proximity* of p (respectively g). It is an example of formalization of what we described in the preceding chapter by using the expression "towards ...".

The distribution of the possible points in the proximities of p and g is uniform. On the other hand, the distribution of the new possible positions for the particle, even if its field is also a hyperparallelepid, is not itself uniform. Indeed, for a given dimension d, the random variable whose occurrence is the dth component of the new velocity is the sum of two random variables having each one a density of constant probability on an interval. To clarify these ideas, let us suppose that one has $p_d < g_d$ and $v_d = 0$. Then the probability density of the sum of these two variables has a trapezoidal form. It increases linearly on $[0, c_{max} p_d]$, from 0 to p_d/g_d, preserves this last value in the interval $[c_{max}p_d, c_{max}g_d]$ then decreases linearly to 0 on the interval $[c_{max}g_d, c_{max}(p_d + g_d)]$. The resulting distribution thus makes it a "truncated pyramid", whose center is at the point $(c_{max}(p_1 + g_1)/2, c_{max}(p_2 + g_2)/2)$. It is uniform on a rectangle and decreases linearly beyond the edges of this rectangle. Figure 3.1 shows a sample of 1,000 points in the proximity of *p*, 1,000 points in that of *g* and 1,000 next possible positions which result from this by linear combination.

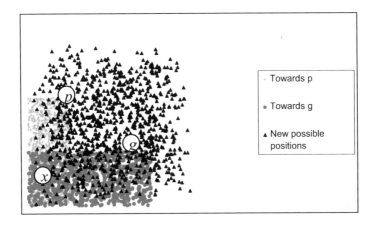

Figure 3.1. *Example of proximities in two dimensions. The proximity of p (the best position found up to now by particle x) is a rectangle of which one of the tops is x and the other $c_{max}(p - x)$ and the distribution of possibilities is uniform there. Similarly for g (the best position found by informants of x). By linear combination, one obtains the next possible positions of the particle. Their envelope is also a rectangle, but the distribution is not uniform there (less dense on the edges). To clarify the Figure, the velocity of the particle was assumed to be null and for each distribution only a sample of 1,000 points was represented*

Let us emphasize this concept of the distribution of the next possible positions or, briefly, the *distribution of the possibles*. This is the basis of all the algorithms of iterative optimization calling for randomness (stochastic). With each time increment, certain positions are known and starting from this information, it is a question of choosing the next position(s) for it (or them). Whatever the method used to work out the answer, the result is always of the same type: a set of candidate positions, each one being assigned a probability of being selected.

This is why it is so important, for any method of this type, to examine carefully the distributions obtained with each increment and to ask whether they can be made more effective. For PSO, we will see that this step easily induces interesting improvements. *A contrario*, let us quickly mention two rather common errors that impoverish the distributions of the possibles.

3.2. Two common errors

The equations of motion [3.2] are sometimes written in vectorial form:

$$\begin{cases} v \leftarrow c_1 v + alea(0, c_{max})(p-x) + alea(0, c_{max})(g-x) \\ x \leftarrow x + v \end{cases} \quad [3.5]$$

In this case, in accordance with the definition of the multiplication of a vector by a coefficient, it means that all the components, for example vector $p - x$, are multiplied by the same random number. This is an error in the sense that it corresponds to an algorithm different from that of PSO, but we can also regard this form as an alternative. It should, however, be noted that the best parameter settings for c_1 and c_{max} bypass the use of a constriction coefficient (see Chapter 6) and that this alternative is then much less effective than the classic form.

The proximity of p (respectively g) is a simple segment here and the distribution of possibles for the next displacement is a D-parallelepiped located "between" p and g (these two points are on its surface), which restricts exploration, in particular because an entire set of points located close to p (respectively g) has no chance of being selected.

The other error, or alternative, consists of carrying out a factorization in the first equation of motion:

$$v_d \leftarrow c_1 v_d + alea(0, c_{max})(p_d + g_d - 2x_d) \quad [3.6]$$

or:

$$v_d \leftarrow c_1 v_d + alea(0, 2c_{max})\left(\frac{p_d + g_d}{2} - x_d\right) \quad [3.7]$$

In this form, we see that the next position will then be taken randomly according to a uniform distribution in a hyperparallelepid whose edge for dimension d is length $c_{max}|p_d + g_d|$ and whose center is found by adding to vector x the vector $c_1 v + c_{max}(p+g)/2$. Actually, one could simply describe this as an alternative rather than an error, because this distribution is almost as rich as the original.

3.3. Principal drawbacks of this formulation

The repeated experiments using the version of PSO defined by equations [3.2] and [3.4] (the version that, for brevity, we will name OEP 0) highlight certain insufficiencies or anomalies that can also be seen as ideas for improvements in subsequent versions.

3.3.1. *Distribution bias*

We saw that, with each time increment and for each particle, the distribution of possibles is non-uniform and of (hyper-)rectangular envelope. In itself, it would not be a defect if it corresponded at least to an empirical rule, aiming, for example, to favor a certain area of the search space. For example, one might think of searching "preferentially" around one of the two best-known positions of the particle (p and g) or "around" a point located between p and g, but closer to g than p, etc.

However, this is not the case. There is no reason why the median point of the distribution obtained should be at the center of a "promising" area. Actually, the very particular form of this distribution is an artifact resulting only from the simple choice of coding of random elements. Since the majority of data-processing languages have only the function *alea* (0,1), one immediately has *alea* (0, c_{max}) = c_{max} *alea* (0,1). However, coding a distribution of different envelope (spherical, for example) is appreciably more difficult, at least if the computing time is not to increase exponentially with the number of dimensions. We will see examples of this later.

Moreover, it should be noted that this distribution depends on the coordinate system (see Figures 3.2 and 3.3). If by bad luck the point p is on a coordinate axis, the D-rectangle of its proximity loses a dimension. For a problem with two dimensions, for example, it is reduced to a segment. A simple rotation of the coordinate system completely modifies the whole ensemble of next possible positions and thus strongly influences the behavior of the particles. Convergence is as likely to be accelerated as slowed down, but, again, in an unforeseeable way.

This phenomenon is often concealed, because the majority of traditional test functions are symmetrical around the origin of the coordinates.

46 Particle Swarm Optimization

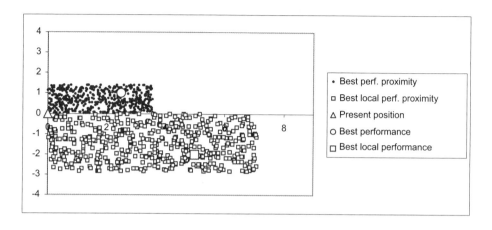

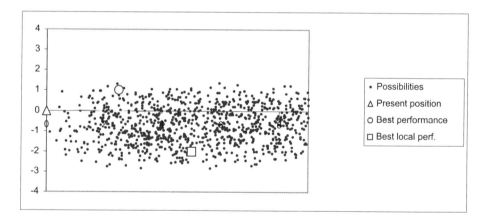

Figure 3.2. *Distribution of the next possible positions. The upper diagram shows each of the two elementary distributions and the lower their combination (sample of 1,000 points)*

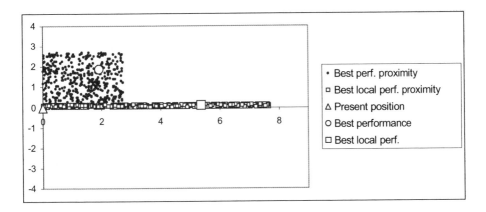

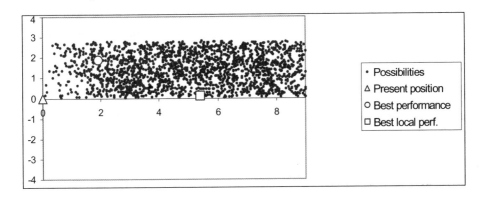

Figure 3.3. *Depending on the coordinate system chosen, the distribution of the next possible positions can be very variable. Here, a rotation of the coordinate axes was carried out, one of the axes practically aligning itself on the vector $g - x$*

The second bias led to alternatives privileging distributions with a center of symmetry (spheres, Gaussian, etc.) or whose form depends only on the respective positions x, p, and g (Gaussian "distorted"). To mitigate the first bias at the same time, these distributions are placed in a way that is *a priori* wiser. For example, by centering them on the segment $p - g$ and a little closer to g than p, one can hope to take advantage of a possible favorable "gradient effect" from p towards g.

3.3.2. *Explosion and maximum velocity*

If one does not want to subject oneself to a parameter c_1 less than 1, to support exploration, then it is necessary to face the phenomenon of the "explosion" of the swarm. Indeed, *roughly speaking*, as we saw, with each time increment velocity is multiplied by c_1. If this coefficient is greater than 1, then it will tend to increase more and more. That is why certain authors introduce an additional parameter, in the form of a maximum velocity: any velocity tending to exceed it is brought back to it. This maximum velocity v_{max} is a real number, which can be different for each dimension. An empirical rule requires that, for a given dimension, one takes it to be equal to half the range of possible values for the search space. Any larger value would ensure that the particles are made to leave the search space too often.

For example, if for a dimension d the search space is the interval [0.5], one will take a maximum velocity of 2.5 for this dimension. It means that if the first calculation of equation [3.2] gives a velocity v_d greater than 2.5, one will take it instead to equal 2.5. If the values are discrete, for example $\{0,1,...,5\}$, the greatest extent covered by the possible values remains from 0 to 10, but the maximum velocity could be selected as being 2 or 3.

Unfortunately, whoever says "additional parameter" says also "choice of this parameter", which still complicates the task of the user a little, since, in OEP 0, all the parameters are up to him.

3.4. Manual parameter setting

Table 3.1 recapitulates the various parameters of the model which have to be defined and the few empirical rules which could be worked out to guide the choice. These rules are very approximate and, for a given problem, we are faced with the strong possibility of searching at length before finding a "good" set of parameters. The good news, nevertheless, is that PSO is very robust, in the sense that broad variations in the parameters do not prevent convergence, even if, of course, it can be more or less rapid.

In this respect, in the majority of the problems, the informant group size is the parameter to which the behavior of the swarm is the least sensitive. One can take it systematically equal to 3 without much risk. Even if this is not the best value for your precise problem, the performances, in general, are not seriously degraded as a result. Nevertheless, if you are sure that the function to be minimized does not present local minima, you will probably find it beneficial to increase this value, to even consider that each particle informs all the others and thus to take it equal to N.

Parameter	Title and nature	Empirical rule of choice and comment
c_1	Self-confidence; real number	In]0,1[. Suggestion: 0.7
c_{max}	Confidence in others; real number	About 1.5. Suggestion: 1.43
N	Swarm size; integer	From 20 to 40. Suggestion: 20
K	Group size of informed; integer	From 3 to 5. To N for the simple problems without local minima. Suggestion: 3
v_{max}	Maximum velocity; real number	Essential only if c_1 is greater than 1. Value about half of $x_{max} - x_{min}$. Possibly different for each dimension.

Table 3.1. *Parameters of OEP 0. The fifth, maximum velocity, is useful only if one wants to force a greater exploration of the search space by balancing velocity by a "self-confidence" greater than 1*

The number of evaluations of the function to be minimized is equal, with each time increment, to the number of particles. Consequently, the degradation of the performances according to this criterion is at most proportional to the size of the swarm. Actually it is often much less, since the increase in the number of particles also increases the probability of finding a solution more quickly. That is why the recommended values 20 to 40 are very generally satisfactory.

For the two parameters of confidence, precise values are suggested. As indicated previously, they form a pair initially found in experiments but subsequently confirmed mathematically. Other values are naturally possible and it is even possible, by choosing them judiciously, more or less to induce a given behavior of the particles, in particular oscillating or not around a solution [TRE 03, VAN 02].

3.5. For "amatheurs": average number of informants

One supposes that each particle of a swarm of total size N randomly chooses, with putting back, K particles to be informed. The probability that a particle is not selected is $p = (1 - 1/N)^K$ and the probability that it is selected is $q = 1 - p$.

Let s be the number of informants of a given particle. The probability that s is null is the probability that it is chosen by nobody, i.e. neither by particle 1, nor by particle 2 . . . nor by particle N. This probability is thus p^N.

In the same way, for s to equal 1, it must be chosen by one particle (N possibilities) and not chosen by all the others. Its probability is thus $Np^{N-1}q$. More generally, for an unspecified value of s between 0 and N, the probability is $C_N^s p^{N-s} q^s$, where C_N^s is the number of combinations of s elements among N.

Thus, finally, by taking the sum of the possible values weighted according to their probability, the average value of the number of informants is:

$$\sum_{s=0}^{N} sC_N^s p^{N-s} q^s = \sum_{s=0}^{N} sC_N^s \left(1-1/N\right)^{K(N-s)} \left(1-\left(1-1/N\right)^K\right)^s$$

From a graph theory point of view, it is the average number of ancestors by node when, in a graph of size N, the arcs are built by randomly taking K downward for each node. Figure 3.4 shows, for $K = 3$, the evolution of this value according to N.

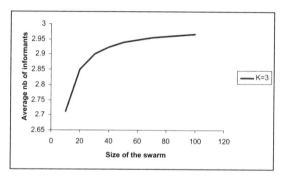

Figure 3.4. *Average number of informants by particle when each particle informs K others at random, according to the size of the swarm.*
Here K = 3. This number is all the less than K as the swarm is small

3.6. Summary

From the basic principles presented in the preceding chapter, we propose a first simple formulation, called OEP 0, which specifies the rules of displacement of the particles. The information links between particles are randomly selected with each iteration. The equations of motion combine linearly, thanks to confidence coefficients, vectors of position randomly drawn according to non-uniform distributions whose supports are (hyper-)rectangles in the search space.

The various parameters (size of the swarm, coefficients, number of informed particles chosen at random, etc.) depend entirely upon the user for the moment and some semi-empirical rules are given to guide these choices.

Certain insufficiencies of this first version are noted here. Highlighting them will guide the improvements brought about later on.

Chapter 4

Benchmark Set

4.1. What is the purpose of test functions?

To test, of course! But to test what? We have seen so far only the principles of a primitive version of PSO, which leaves most of the work to randomness, not only for displacements but also for the establishment of information links. In the next chapter we will see the exact way in which these random choices are simulated on computers; then, finally, in the following chapter, we will examine the results obtained with this primitive version.

Because we will later study more effective alternatives, we must use the same set of problems throughout, in order to give a better comparison of the results, hence the benchmark set defined here, which includes several traditional scenarios, from a simple function with a single minimum to one having a considerable number of local minima of very similar values. Note that, for the moment, we deal only with continuous or semi-continuous functions. When we examine the variants of PSO appropriate for dealing with discrete (and, more generally, heterogeneous) problems, it will obviously be necessary to enrich this benchmark set with adequate examples.

If you have experience of another method of optimization, you should apply it to this benchmark set, in order to form your own opinion. The reader interested in a rigorous approach to the comparison of iterative stochastic methods will be able to consult [DRE 03], in particular Chapter 8.

52   Particle Swarm Optimization

Name Difficulty	Formula	Search space	Objective
Tripod 33	$p(x_2)(1+p(x_1))$ $+\|x_1+50p(x_2)(1-2p(x_1))\|$ $+\|x_2+50(1-2p(x_2))\|$ with: $\begin{cases} p(u)=1 \text{ si } u \geq 0 \\ =0 \text{ si } u < 0 \end{cases}$	$[-100,100]^2$	0 ± 10^{-5}
Alpine 10D 121	$\sum_{d=1}^{D} \|x_d \sin(x_d)+0,1x_d\|$	$[-10,10]^{10}$	0 ± 10^{-5}
Parabola 30D 273	$\sum_{d=1}^{D} x_d^2$	$[-20,20]^{30}$	0 ± 10^{-5}
Griewank 30D 335	$\dfrac{\sum_{d=1}^{D}(x_d-100)^2}{4000}$ $-\prod_{d=1}^{D} \cos\left(\dfrac{x_d-100}{\sqrt{d}}\right)+1$	$[-300,300]^{30}$	0 ± 10^{-5}
Rosenbrock 30D 370	$\sum_{d=1}^{D-1}(1-x_d)^2+100(x_d^2-x_{d+1})^2$	$[-10,10]^{30}$	0 ± 10^{-5}
Ackley 30D 470	$-20e^{-0,2\sqrt{\frac{\sum_{d=1}^{D} x_d^2}{D}}} - e^{\frac{\sum_{d=1}^{D} \cos(2\pi x_d)}{D}}$ $+20+e$	$[-30,30]^{30}$	0 ± 10^{-5}

Table 4.1. *Summary of the benchmark set. The theoretical levels of difficulty were calculated or considered as indicated previously. This sample of traditional test functions was selected to cover a broad range of difficulties. None of these functions is discrete (this case will be studied later), but one of them (Tripod) presents brutal discontinuities*

4.2. Six reference functions

Table 4.1 specifies the formulae for six functions that are more or less difficult to deal with. In each case, the known minimal value is zero and one wishes to reach it with a margin of 10^{-5}.

4.3. Representations and comments

For each function, one or more three-dimensional graphical representation is given below, with, for each figure, a comment explaining the type of difficulty that an algorithm for finding the minimum value can encounter. However, as you have undoubtedly noticed, almost all the problems of the benchmark set are actually in 10 or 30 dimensions. So, one should not lose sight of the fact that restriction to the three-dimensional case, which is moreover almost always represented in two dimensions (on screen or printed), gives only a very vague idea of the real problem.

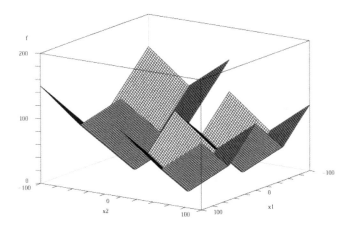

Figure 4.1. *Tripod. Minimum 0 is at point (0 – 50). Theoretically easy, this problem misleads many algorithms, which are easily trapped in one or other of the two local minima. Note that the function is not continuous, which, however, does not obstruct PSO in any way. This problem was first proposed in [GAC 02]*

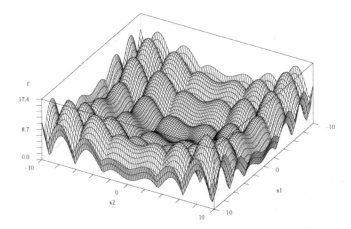

Figure 4.2. *Alpine. Many local and global minima (of zero value). Surface is not completely symmetrical compared to the origin. Nevertheless, this problem remains rather easy and may be viewed as a kind of pons asinorum for optimization algorithms in continuous variables*

54 Particle Swarm Optimization

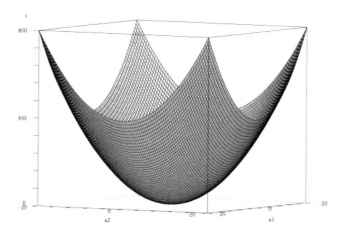

Figure 4.3. *Parabola. Only one minimum. Because of its stochastic character, PSO might not be as effective as a specific deterministic algorithm (e.g. gradient descent), but the various alternatives could be more or less adapted to solve this problem. This function, which, in two dimensions, is a paraboloid, is sometimes called "Sphere" in the literature, undoubtedly because of its equation*

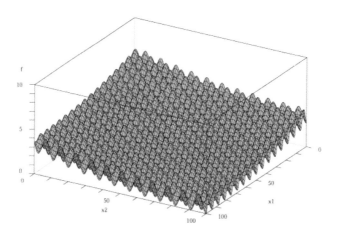

Figure 4.4. *Griewank. Already more difficult. The global minimum 0 is at (100 100) and is almost indistinguishable from many closely packed local minima that surround it. On the one hand, that tends to increase the difficulty of the problem, but, on the other hand, because the local minima are very close together, it is rather easy to escape from them, at least for stochastic algorithms*

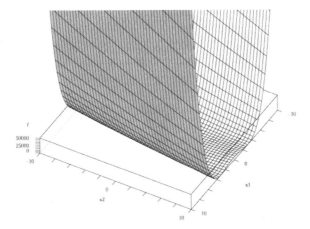

Figure 4.5. *Rosenbrock. Represented here on $[-10\ 10]^2$. There is a barely noticeable global minimum at (1,1). For the majority of optimization algorithms it is difficult to find, and PSO in its initial version is no exception. The graph lies mostly beyond the limits of the diagram (maximum value of about 1.2×10^6)*

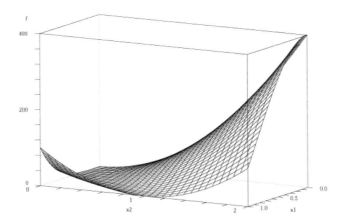

Figure 4.6. *Rosenbrock again, but on $[0\ 1] \times [0\ 2]$, in order to highlight the minimum. In two dimensions, the problem is easy, but the difficulty increases very quickly with the number of dimensions of the search space*

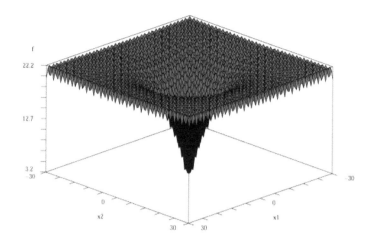

Figure 4.7. *Ackley. Apparently a little like Alpine, but actually more difficult, even with the same dimensionality. The "basin of attraction" of the global minimum is narrower, which decreases the effectiveness of random displacements*

4.4. For "amatheurs": estimates of levels of difficulty

4.4.1. *Theoretical difficulty*

Let us recall that it is calculated by the formula $-\ln(\sigma)$, where σ is the probability of success by randomly choosing a position in the search space.

4.4.1.1. *Tripod*

Direct calculation is very simple here. Let ε be the required precision. It is assumed to be less than 1, in order to deal only with the global minimum. The acceptable portion of surface is thus a reversed pyramid with height ε and whose base is a square of diagonal 2ε. The surface of this square is thus $2\varepsilon^2$. Since the search space is $[-100 \ 100]^2$, the level of difficulty is given by:

$$\textit{difficulty} = -\ln\left(\frac{2\varepsilon^2}{200^2}\right) = 2\ln(200) - 2\ln(\varepsilon) - \ln(2)$$

For $\varepsilon = 10^{-5}$, one thus finds a difficulty of approximately 33.

4.4.1.2. Alpine 10D

The estimate of difficulty was made only statistically, by supposing initially that the only solution is the origin of the coordinates. Then one finds a level of difficulty of about 132. But any point whose coordinates are either 0 or $\mathrm{asin}(-0,1)$ is also a solution. On $[-10,10]^{10}$ there are 3^{10} such points and, therefore, the real level of difficulty is closer to $132 - 10\ln(3)$ or 121.

4.4.1.3. Rosenbrock

Here also, the estimate was made only statistically and thus remains rather rough. It is interesting to note that the evolution of the difficulty according to the dimensionality of the problem, indicated in Table 4.2, is almost linear. However, we must not forget that the measure is logarithmic. The true difficulty thus increases exponentially.

Out of curiosity, one can also make an analytical estimate by using Taylor's formula. Around the position $\bar{1} = (1,...,1)$ corresponding to a minimum of 0, the first and second partial derivatives are null (which explains why the function is so "flat"). Stopping with the second order, it is found that the function is approached by the formula $f(\bar{1}+h) = h^2(1+(D-1)101)$. If we want this value to be less than ε, that gives us the edge of the cube of dimension D in which the solution points are $h = 2\sqrt{\varepsilon/(1+(D-1)101)}$.

Dimension	Difficulty
2	20
5	60
10	120
20	245
30	370

Table 4.2. *Rosenbrock Function. Theoretical difficulty according to the number of dimensions*

Thus, in our example, with $\varepsilon = 10^{-5}$ and $D = 30$, and the search space $[-10 \ 10]^{30}$ of volume 20^{30}, the theoretical difficulty is given by:

$$difficulty = -\ln\left(\left(\frac{2\sqrt{10^{-5}/2930}}{20}\right)^{30}\right) \cong 362$$

By construction, this value is less than the actual value. It is thus seen that the statistical estimate of 370 found previously is completely acceptable.

4.4.2. Difficulty according to the search effort

Obviously the theoretical difficulty decreases if one is allowed to draw several positions at random. Let T be the number of such choices. Since the probability of success for a single draw is σ, the probability of failure is $(1-\sigma)$ and the probability of still not having found a satisfactory position after T draws is $(1-\sigma)^T$. By contrast, the probability of having found a solution with a maximum of T draws is its complement with 1. Finally, in passing to the logarithm, one obtains the theoretical difficulty as a function of the search effort T

$$\textit{difficulty}(T) = -\ln\left(1-(1-\sigma)^T\right) \cong -\ln(T\sigma)$$

When the probability of success with only one choice is very low, which is normally the case for the interesting problems, the last expression gives a good approximation.

4.5. Summary

To clarify these ideas and to compare later on the influences of the various parameters and strategies, a benchmark set of six traditional test functions is defined. The functions are continuous or semi-continuous, but the theoretical difficulty of finding their minimum in the search space varies several orders of magnitude from one function to another.

Chapter 5

Mistrusting Chance

5.1. Analysis of an anomaly

Originally, this book was not intended to include a chapter devoted specifically to randomness. All the versions published of PSO used language C's *rand* function or the equivalent in other languages and that did not seem to pose any problem. However, one day, during the treatment of the example of the Ackley function with an already old version, an obvious anomaly appeared.

The principle of the test was very simple. One gave oneself a maximum number of evaluations of the function, for example 40,000, one launched the program 100 times and counted the number of executions that, under the constraint of these 40,000 evaluations at most, had still not found a solution. One thus deduced from it an estimate of the rate of failure of the algorithm on this problem.

A limit of 40,000 evaluations gave a failure rate of 53% (the version of PSO used was very rudimentary). On increasing the limit to 60,000 evaluations, the rate of failure went up to 63%! After analysis of the possible causes of this anomaly, it turned out that it was due to the poor quality of the pseudo-random number generator normally used in ANSI C. Let us take a look at a very simple example which is even more obvious.

On the interval [–1 1], T numbers are generated randomly, hoping to find one of absolute value less than $\varepsilon = 10^{-5}$. Obviously the probability of failure pr(T) decreases as T increases, according to the formula:

$$pr(T) = (1-\varepsilon)^T \qquad [5.1]$$

For example, for $T = 10^6$, one finds a probability of failure of 0.000045. However, when one carries out the experiment with a little program in C consisting of some lines using the function *rand* (see program 5.1), the rate of failure is in fact 100% whatever the permitted search effort, i.e. the value of *T*. Indeed, it turns out that the pseudo-random number generator is unable to produce an absolute value less than 0.0000305 in the interval [–1 1], as is explained further.

Let us note that the opposite situation is also possible. If one makes the same test on the interval [0, 1], the probability of theoretical failure is again given by equation [5.1]. However, this time the program in C gives appreciably lower rates of failure. Figure 5.1 shows how large the variations can be, relative to true randomness. It is clear that we cannot trust a pseudo-chance of such poor quality, at least to carry out the programs of stochastic optimization we are studying here.

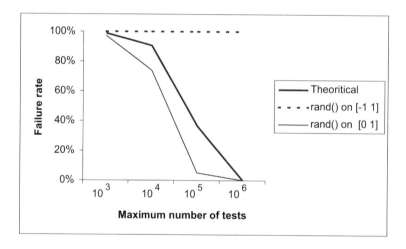

Figure 5.1. *Poor quality of classical pseudo-randomness. Even on a very simple example (in this case the random search for a number of absolute value less than 10^{-5} in a given interval), the rand function in ANSI C can give, with certain compilers and on certain machines, rates of failure very different from the theoretical rates*

Thus when we use the term "to take randomly" it is necessary to distinguish between the mathematical description which recommends, for example, a law of probability to constant density, and the practical realization in data processing, which delivers only one pseudo-chance, sometimes too regular to be honest. Let us see more precisely why, and how it is possible to remedy it.

5.2. Computing randomness

When one asks a computer to provide a random number according to a uniform distribution in an interval [a b], the generated number is in fact often initially an integer N between 0 and M, which is then reduced to the interval by a linear transformation. In C, the number M is the internal constant RAND_MAX. Normally, it is equal to 32,767 ($2^{15} - 1$) and the first two generated numbers are 41 and 18,467. You can check this using program 5.2 at the end of the chapter.

Even by neglecting the statistical fluctuations inherent in the initial generation process (these are always present), it means that you will in any case obtain only numbers of the form $a+(n/M)(b-a)$. The distribution obtained is thus far from being uniform, since it concentrates on $M + 1$ values in [a b]. None of the points between these values can be reached. This is why, for example, it is impossible to find in this way, a number between $-1/32767$ and $1/32767$ on the interval [–1 1], i.e. of absolute value less than $\varepsilon = 0.0000305$. Conversely, on the interval [0 1], it is enough to draw $N = 0$ and the probability of failure is thus $(1-1/M)^T$, lower than the theoretical probability as soon as ε is less than $1/M$.

The larger your search space is, the more this situation introduces a significant bias. For example, to generate an initial position "randomly" between 0 and x_{max}, one is often satisfied with initially generating a value on [0 1], then multiplying it by x_{max}. If this last is not negligible relative to M, this means that large intervals of value are in fact inaccessible, at least at the beginning of the process and that, on the contrary, the numbers which delimit them are unduly favored.

Lastly, one might think that for the same standardized language, all the compilers define a given function in the same way, but that is not always the case (one might add, in passing, that the originators of compilers do not always respect the standard).

In the same way, one can also ask to what extent the numerical inaccuracy inherent in the computing can modify, from one machine to another, the behavior of a PSO algorithm. We will therefore ask ourselves the question of the reproducibility of the results taking into consideration these two potential sources of error: the quality of the pseudo-randomness and maximum numerical precision.

5.3. Reproducibility

"With the stochastic algorithm A, whose code is given below, the rate of failure for the problem P is $x\%$." You have all seen statements of this kind. You may even have gone to the extent of programming the famous algorithm A, and then carrying it out in accordance with the given instructions. But you have probably not found the published failure rate, but another, possibly rather different rate. However, the very basis of the experimental scientific method is precisely that published experiments can be reproduced and the same results found within well-defined margins of error. With regard to PSO, and for that matter the majority of iterative stochastic algorithms, the experiments are executions of computer programs, and the differences noticed have two sources: the numerical precision of the pair machine/compiler and the mode of generation of the pseudo-random numbers. For better reproducibility of the results, it is desirable to be, as far as possible, free from them and we will see how that is possible.

5.4. On numerical precision

A calculator necessarily carries out numerical rounding-off. A simple test allows you to get some idea of the possible level of precision of your machine. The small program 5.3 will enable you to know from which value of n the number 10^{-N} is treated as equal to zero.

On a 32-bit computer, one finds in general that 10^{-323} is regarded as zero. That is why the results given in this book correspond to calculations made internally with this level of precision. It is very much better than what is necessary for all practical problems. So this factor is not generally to blame for the non-reproducibility of the experiments. However, we have already seen that the quality of the generated pseudo-randomness is very significant. So let us examine another mode of generation, which gives more usable results than those provided by the majority of the algorithms of the standard compilers.

5.5. The rare KISS

We wish to proceed in such a way that by carrying out a given algorithm on a given problem, we obtain the same result, whatever the language of coding, whatever the compiler, and (almost) whatever the machine used. We have seen that the intrinsic numerical precision of the computer is not really a problem, being largely sufficient today even on current machines.

But, on the other hand, we must give up the idea that the generation of the pseudo-random numbers is only a standardized black box. A detailed study of the possible abolition of chance would be beyond the scope of this work, but one stage is in any case useful: inclusion in the algorithm itself of the deterministic generation of pseudo-random numbers, in order to be less dependent on data-processing languages and compilers.

In any case, in practice, that can amount precisely to detailing one of the methods that fulfills functions such as rand in C, random in PASCAL, or ran in OCCAM, but, as we saw in the case of C, the result is likely to be unusable for our purposes. Thus we shall explore another method, called KISS, which has interesting characteristics.

5.5.1. *Brief description*

This algorithm, easily downloadable from various Internet sites, is based on a different principle. It seeks to generate the most realistic possible randomness, while remaining reproducible. It is based on three fast generators, already individually rather good, and it composes them in an astute way. It is cyclic, but the period exceeds 2^{123}. Even if each generation of a number took only an attosecond (10^{-18} s), to find the same number twice you would have to be very patient! Figure 5.2 tries to visualize the generated randomness.

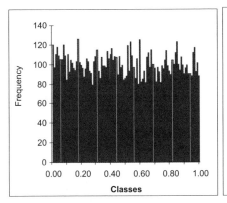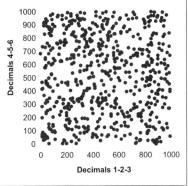

Figure 5.2. *Pseudo-randomness of KISS. On the left-hand diagram, each point represents one of the the first 1,000 values. Its abscissa is the number formed by the first three decimals of the value and its ordinate is the number formed by the fourth to sixth decimals. The right-hand diagram, a traditional histogram of the first 10,000 values, confirms and specifies this distribution. The pseudo-randomness is very realistic here, which is confirmed by statistical tests*

Even visual inspection suggests that this pseudo-randomness is of good quality. This is confirmed by checking various criteria (Kolmogoroff, χ^2, Weil, etc. [MAU 75]). KISS passes all the traditional tests easily but, more concretely, we shall see its results for our little example of random search.

5.5.2. *Test of KISS*

As before, we seek "randomly" in the interval $[-1\ 1]$ a number of absolute value less than 10^{-5}. The pseudo-randomness is now generated with KISS, and this for various values of the maximum number of allowed tests. In each case the rate of failure is calculated after 10,000 executions of the program. This already gives us a good estimate of the rate of real failure very near to the theoretical rate of failure (see Table 5.1).

Maximum number of tests	Probability of theoretical failure	KISS Probability of failure estimated on 10,000 executions
1,000	99%	98.79%
10,000	90.48%	90.73%
100,000	36.79%	36.29%
1,000,000	0.0045%	0%
	Distance	0.006

Table 5.1. *Test of KISS. On the small problem of random search for a number of absolute value less than 10^{-5} in the interval $[-1\ 1]$, it cannot be distinguished significantly from true randomness, as the calculation of the difference between the estimated probability and the theoretical probability for some values of the number of tests shows*

5.6. On the comparison of results

One sometimes comes across assertions of the kind "I launched algorithm A and algorithm B 100 times each on the same problem. The failure rate of B is 4% less than that of A. This algorithm is thus a little better." Is such an assertion justified? Actually, not really, and we will now examine why (for a more detailed mathematical explanation, see section 5.7).

The result of an execution, under the constraint of a maximum number of evaluations, is binary – success or failure – with a probability of failure characteristic of the algorithm. But the rate of failure calculated after 20, 100, and 1,000 executions is only one estimate, accurate to within δ. Naturally, this δ is becomes smaller as the number of executions is increased, but it should be evaluated.

Table 5.2 gives us, for confidence thresholds of 95% and 99%, the interval of probable values for the rate of failure, once this was estimated after T executions.

After a number of executions equal to	If the rate of estimated failure is $\hat{\tau}$, there is 95% chance that the real rate is in the interval	Same thing, with 99% chance
20	$\hat{\tau} \pm 11.0\%$	$\hat{\tau} \pm 14.4\%$
100	$\hat{\tau} \pm 4.9\%$	$\hat{\tau} \pm 6.4\%$
1,000	$\hat{\tau} \pm 1.5\%$	$\hat{\tau} \pm 2.0\%$
10,000	$\hat{\tau} \pm 0.5\%$	$\hat{\tau} \pm 0.6\%$

Table 5.2. *Confidence to be granted to a stochastic search algorithm*

Thus, for example (and this will help us to establish at least approximate performance maps), with 100 executions, we have a 95% chance of knowing the rate with a margin of less than 5%. In many cases, it is largely sufficient to compare algorithms or the influence of a modification of parameters for a given algorithm, but precisely on condition that the variation of the rates of failure is greater than 5%.

Hereafter, unless otherwise stated, KISS will be used to generate pseudo-random numbers. Naturally, in your own applications, it can be replaced by any other good quality generator. In fact, even certain C compilers, such as that under Linux used for this book, provide an almost acceptable *rand* function, with a RAND_MAX equal to $2^{31} - 1$ instead of $2^{15} - 1$. Note, in passing, that if the theories postulating the quantization of space-time are justified, no real problem requires, on a given dimension, a precision better than 10^{-34} or 10^{-35}, the order of magnitude of Planck's constant [SMO 04].

5.7. For "amatheurs": confidence in the estimate of a rate of failure

The rates of failure that one can calculate by carrying out the search algorithm several times are only estimates made after *T* executions with, for each execution, a given maximum number of tests. As one might expect, the estimate becomes increasingly precise as it is calculated on a growing number of executions (see Figure 5.3). But the question is what confidence one can grant to an estimate.

Let *X* be the random variable whose occurrence is returned by each execution: 1 if there is failure, with a probability τ, 0 if not, with a probability $1 - \tau$. This rate characteristic of failure of the algorithm for the problem under discussion is not known. After *T* executions, we have an estimate of it without skew $\hat{\tau}$, which is given by the following formula, where *t* is the rank of the execution:

$$\hat{\tau} = \frac{1}{T}\sum_{t=1}^{T} X_t \qquad [5.2]$$

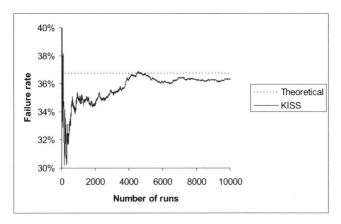

Figure 5.3. *Evolution of the rates of failure with pseudo-randomness KISS. For each execution, the maximum number of tests is 100,000. The estimated rate of failure converges towards the theoretical value*

With a good quality pseudo-randomness, the X_t are random independent Bernoulli variables and $\hat{\tau}$ a binomial random variable of average τ. Therefore, its characteristic function φ is defined by $\varphi(u) = (1-\tau) + \tau e^{iu}$. The values at 0 of its successive derivatives give us the moments, in this particular case all equal to τ.

$$E(\hat{\tau}) = \frac{d\varphi}{du}(0) = \tau$$

$$E(\hat{\tau}^2) = \frac{d^2\varphi}{du^2}(0) = \tau$$

The variance σ^2 is given by the classic decomposition formula: $\sigma^2 = E(\hat{\tau}^2) - E(\hat{\tau})^2 = \tau - \tau^2$. It is worth adding that, in practice, as soon as $T > 30$, the theorem of the central limit enables us to define a random variable Y_T which almost follows a reduced centered normal law:

$$Y_T = \frac{\hat{\tau} - \tau}{\sigma}\sqrt{T}$$

With these elements, one can then estimate T to have a given confidence interval, or the converse. Let us suppose, for example, that one wants an estimate of the rate of failure to within a confidence interval of $\pm\delta$ (let us say 1%), with a degree of confidence c (e.g. 95%). One can write successively:

probability $\left(|\hat{\tau} - \tau| < \delta\right) = c$

probability $\left(|Y_T| < \delta\dfrac{\sqrt{T}}{\sigma}\right) = c$

One can deduce from this that $T = \left(u \dfrac{\sigma}{\delta}\right)^2$, where u is given either by calculation or by consultation of a table like that below, giving the probability for Y_T being between $-u$ and u.

Degree of confidence	90%	95%	99%
u	1.645	1.96	2.576

Table 5.3. *A tabulation of the distribution reduced centered normal law*

To say that $c = 0.95$ amounts to saying that Y_T is between -1.96 and 1.96. Hence the estimate of T for $\delta = 1\%$ is 0.01.

$$T = \left(1.96 \dfrac{\sigma}{0{,}01}\right)^2 = 38416\sigma^2$$

In our example, for 100,000 evaluations, the theoretical rate of failure is 36.79% and variance 0.23. One deduces from this that T must be worth at least 8,934.

However, in fact, one does not know the variance σ^2 but only its estimate, $\hat{\sigma}^2 = \hat{t} - \hat{t}^2$. This does not pose a problem, because we find an acceptable value very quickly (8,537 as of the sixth execution in our small example, by using KISS). In practice, therefore, one carries out ten executions. Thereafter, after each execution of rank t, one calculates the estimate $\hat{\sigma}^2$. One stops as soon as t is greater than $\hat{\sigma}^2$. Or, more simply, one is pessimistic and careful by always taking the maximum variance to be 0.25 (which corresponds to a failure rate of 50%). One finds then that $T = 9{,}604$.

Conversely, one can ask how much confidence to grant to the rate of failure estimated after, say, 100 executions, always with a threshold of 95%. Let δ be the variation with the true value of the rate of failure which it is then necessary to accept. One has immediately:

$$\delta = 1.96 \dfrac{\sigma_{max}}{\sqrt{T}} = 1.96 \dfrac{0.25}{10} = 0.049 = 4.9\%$$

One can thus learn that the practical formula to use is:

$$T = 0.25 \left(\dfrac{u}{\delta}\right)^2 \qquad [5.3]$$

where u is given by Table 5.3.

5.8. C programs

PROGRAM 5.1. – Random search using the function *rand*

```
//In the interval [a b], one seeks a number of absolute value lower than
eps double A, B, T, T, X;
int        n_echec, n_exec, n_exec_max;
= 1;b -= 1 has; //Interval of research
eps = 0.00001; //desired Precision
n_exec_max = 1000; //a Number of executions
T = 10000; //a maximum Number of evaluations for each execution
n_echec = 0;
for (n_exec = 0;n_exec < n_exec_max;n_exec++)

for (T = 0;t < T;t++)

X = has + (b-a)*(double)rand()/RAND_MAX;
if (fabs(x) < eps) goto exec;

n_echec = n_echec + 1;
exec: ;

printf("Failure rate%f", n_ failure /(double)n_exec_max);
```

PROGRAM 5.2. – Checking of the function *rand*

```
//Base of the equal distribution and first values
printf("RAND_MAX%i", RAND_MAX);
srand(1);
for (N = 0;n < 2;n++) printf("%i", rand());
```

PROGRAM 5.3. – Evaluation of the precision of execution of a computer

```
//Below a certain value (1/10)^p, a number is treated as zero
init = 0.1; precision = 0; value = init;
while (value > 0) value = value*init; precision = precision + 1;
printf("Null value for 10 power -%.0f", precision);
```

PROGRAM 5.4. – Deterministic Pseudo-Randomness KISS:

```
/ * It passes the majority of the tests of checking of randomness, while
remaining reproducible
The three components of KISS are:
```

$X_N = (aX_{N-1} + 1) \bmod 2^{32}$

$Y_N = Y_{N-1} (I + L^{13}) (I + R^{17}) (I + L^{5})$

$Z_N = 2z_{N-1} + Z_{N-2} + retenue \bmod 2^{32}$

```
y is a shift register on vectors of 32 bits, of period 2^32 -1.
Z is a simple sequence of multiplications with reserves, of which the
period is 2^63 + 2^32 -1.
The total period of KISS is thus 2^32 (2^32 -1)(2^63 + 2^32 -1). It is higher than
2^127
*/
# define ulong unsigned long
# define RAND_MAX_KISS ((unsigned long) 4294967295)
ulong     rand_kiss();
void      seed_rand_kiss(ulong seed);

static ulong kiss_x = 1;
static ulong kiss_y = 2;
static ulong kiss_z = 4;
static ulong kiss_w = 8;
```

```
static ulong kiss_carry = 0;
static ulong kiss_k;
static ulong kiss_m;
...
void main()

...
seed_rand_kiss(1); //Initialization of seed. The value can be changed
...

void seed_rand_kiss(ulong seed)
  kiss_x = seed | 1;
  kiss_y = seed | 2;
  kiss_z = seed | 4;
  kiss_w = seed | 8;
  kiss_carry = 0;

ulong rand_kiss()
// R = (double)rand_kiss()/RAND_MAX_KISS; //a number gives on [0 1]
  kiss_x = kiss_x * 69069 + 1;
  kiss_y ^ = kiss_y < < 13;
  kiss_y ^ = kiss_y > > 17;
  kiss_y ^ = kiss_y < < 5;
  kiss_k = (kiss_z > > 2) + (kiss_w > > 3) + (kiss_carry > > 2);
  kiss_m = kiss_w + kiss_w + kiss_z + kiss_carry;
  kiss_z = kiss_w;
  kiss_w = kiss_m;
  kiss_carry = kiss_k > > 30;
  return kiss_x + kiss_y + kiss_w;
```

5.9. Summary

The standard pseudo-randomness generator provided with certain compilers is not good quality. Thus, on a very simple random search problem, it can be shown that the *rand* function in ANSI C can give a rate of failure of 100%, whereas the theoretical rate is almost zero. We therefore propose using a random number generator, KISS, available in the public domain, which, while also giving reproducible sequences (important for comparison of algorithms), simulates true randomness much better.

One recalls some rules concerning the estimate of the rate of failure of a stochastic algorithm on a problem, in particular the relation between the number of executions and the confidence which one can grant to the estimated rate. This will make it possible to give a precise meaning to assertions like "this algorithm (or this set of parameters) is better than this other for such and such a problem".

Chapter 6

First Results

6.1. A simple program

We now have to hand all the elements needed to write a program for OEP 0.

In its source code in C (see program 6.1) all the parameters are "hard coded", but, naturally, they could be picked interactively or be read from a file. The subroutine *ma_fonction* contains the six functions of our benchmark set. You can easily add the one corresponding to your problem, but if this problem is difficult, it will undoubtedly be more judicious to use one of the more elaborate and more effective versions that we will look at later. Here it is simply a question of establishing reference results, precisely to be able to quantify the improvements made by the following versions.

The values retained for the parameters are as follows:

– size of the swarm $N = 20$;
– number of informed particles chosen randomly by each particle $K = 3$;
– confidence coefficients $c_1 = 0.689343$ and $c_{max} = 1.42694$. These rather mysterious values were selected to facilitate the comparison with later versions that use one coefficient. Some complementary explanations are given in section 6.3.

6.2. Overall results

To compare two algorithms on the treatment of a given problem, we will need a criterion of effectiveness or, more precisely, inefficiency. It is defined as follows:
– initially one compares the rates of failure;
– if they are equivalent but less than 100%, one compares the numbers of evaluations;
– if they are also equivalent, the found values are compared.

The two concepts of equivalence used are to be defined by the user in statistical terms, as was discussed in Chapter 5. They could be, for example, the probabilities of equality greater than 95%. Nevertheless, in any case, if the best values obtained are both less than the acceptable error, it should be regarded as equivalent.

In fact, this composite and hierarchical criterion is especially interesting for the development of algorithms on benchmark sets for which the desired objectives are known. With a given search effort (in practice here the number of evaluations) one wants initially the highest possible probability of finding a solution; then, when the rate of failure is less than 100%, that it be found as soon as possible. It is only if the rate of failure is 100% that one is satisfied with the best value found.

For real problems, it is generally the reverse. The maximum search effort is often given, but one does not know the value of the minimum to be reached. Then one sets as one's objective a value that is definitely lower and, therefore, one is always in the last scenario: the comparisons of algorithms could be made only on the best values that they are able to find.

When the rate of failure is less than 100%, it is also possible to calculate the total number of evaluations to be carried out (while launching the program several times) to succeed at least once with a given probability, and to take this number as a criterion. Indeed, if the rate of failure is p, then p^T is the probability of having never succeeded even after t executions. It decreases quickly with t.

For example, for a rate of failure of 50%, four or five executions are enough to have a 95% chance to find a solution. Besides, it is the basis of the Stop/Restart strategy that we will look at in the second part of this work.

Table 6.1 presents some results on our benchmark set of six functions, for various values of the search effort, in terms of a maximum number of evaluations. In order to have a rough but more practical single numerical indicator to handle, the average of six rates of failures is also indicated. Thus, in a very artificial way, we can retain "OEP 0 → 45.7%".

Name	The number of evaluations per execution (average on 100 executions)	Result
Tripod	40,000	39%
Alpine 10D	15,000	28%
Parabola 30D	15,000	27%
Rosenbrock 30D	40,000	100% average 39.026
Griewank 30D	40,000	55%
Ackley 30D	40,000	25%
Average rates of failure		45.7%

Table 6.1. *Some results with OEP 0. As envisaged, the minima of the Rosenbrock, Griewank and Tripod functions are difficult to find. The size of the swarm is 20 and the number informed particles chosen at random by a given particle is 3. The rates of failures are an estimate after 100 executions. In the event of a failure rate equal to 100%, one gives the average value of the 100 found results*

Obviously, these results are modified if one changes the values of the parameters, particularly the size of the swarm and the confidence coefficients. In the ideal case, it would be necessary to test all the possible combinations. In practice, one is satisfied with plausible fields of values in order to establish performance maps.

6.3. Robustness and performance maps

As we have already indicated, it is possible to show that a good convergence can be ensured by making the two coefficients (c_1 for confidence in the current tendency and c_{max} for confidence in informants) dependent. This is demonstrated in [CLE 02], but let us just remember that the relation between them can be written using an intermediate parameter φ:

$$\begin{cases} c_1 = \dfrac{1}{\varphi - 1 + \sqrt{\varphi^2 - 2\varphi}} \\ c_{max} = \varphi c_1 \end{cases}$$

Naturally, other pairs of values are possible, but by using these relations we can make a study of simplified robustness, by varying only the size of swarm N and the parameter φ. Note that for φ the above formula imposes values greater than 2, the coefficient c_1 having to be a real number. Incidentally, the values of the coefficients used in OEP 0 to draw up Table 6.1 correspond to $\varphi = 2.07$.

Our study of robustness will be simultaneously very simple and very tiresome. It is simply a question of considering a great number of pairs of value (N, φ) and examining how the algorithm behaves on our test functions for each pair. Of course, it is necessary to limit the space of the possible values. For the swarm, we will take from 5 to 40 particles. For the coefficient φ, we saw that it must be greater than 2. In addition, the experiment shows that c_{max} must be greater than 1. These two remarks lead us to vary φ in the interval [2.01 2.4]; for example, with an increment of 0.1. For each function the result is a surface of performance, (N, φ, h) where h can be, for example, an estimate of the rate of failure, obtained after 100 tests.

In practice, the representation used is a *performance map* whose colors or levels of gray code the different ranges of value of h. The Figure s below are such maps for our test functions, except for the Rosenbrock function, which has a rate of failure too close to 100% for all the examined pairs of values. In such a case, the best value obtained after a given number of tests (here 100) remains an interesting criterion and one can still use it to establish a performance map, after normalization (see Figure 6.5).

The examination of these maps teaches us that the fields of "good" values can be very broad (Parabola, Alpine, Rosenbrock), rather narrow (Ackley), or even sparse (Tripod, Griewank). It also teaches us that a swarm size of 20 particles is sometimes "high-risk", insofar as, for certain functions, we obtain good results only for one small interval of values of φ. The question which then arises is concerned with knowing whether bigger swarm sizes, inducing greater robustness, are not on the other hand exacting a penalty in terms of a number of evaluations (and thus of time calculation).

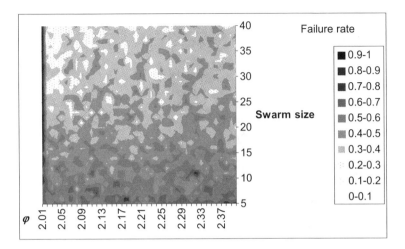

Figure 6.1. *Performance map for the Tripod function. The good pairs of parameters are sparse. It is difficult to locate a more favorable zone for rather large size swarms and rather small φ coefficients*

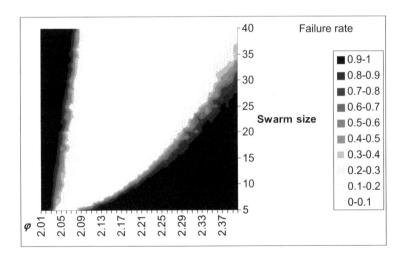

Figure 6.2. *Performance map for the function Alpine 10D. All pairs of values (size of the swarm, coefficient φ) that give null or very low rates of failure are acceptable. They correspond to the broad white portion of the Figure. This zone cannot be infinite and "is closed again" beyond a certain size of swarm (approximately 90 particles)*

76   Particle Swarm Optimization

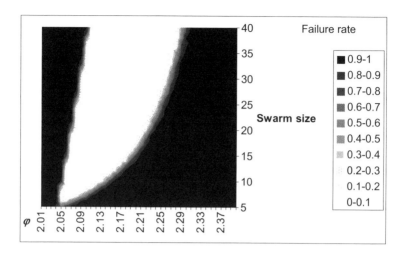

Figure 6.3. *Performance map for the function Parabola 30D. Here, the zone of null rate of failure would not go beyond approximately 70 particles. While the morphology of the function is very different from that of Alpine (only one minimum instead of many local minima), the structure of the performance map is very similar*

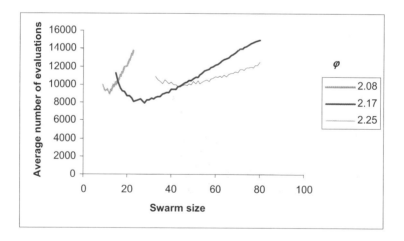

Figure 6.4. *Parabola 30D. Average number of evaluations. While restricting oneself to the field where the rate of failure is almost zero, one can carry out some cuts with φ constant. In fact, the smallest swarms necessarily converge most quickly. The performance surface makes a "basin" and the optimum is around 25 particles. Thus, with 9 particles and $\varphi = 2.08$, the average number of evaluations is approximately 9,800. But with another pair of values (e.g. 20 particles and $\varphi = 2.17$) one finds a smaller average number of evaluations, about 8,600*

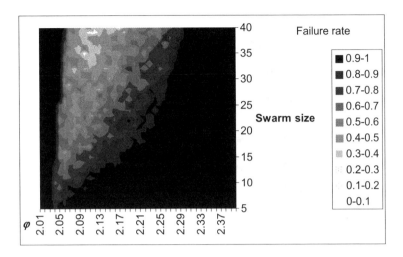

Figure 6.5. *Performance chart for the Griewank function. It is seen immediately that the problem is more difficult to solve. Nevertheless, one notices that even with this primitive version of PSO, it is possible to go below a 25% failure rate, provided that good parameters are found (here, one needs a rather large size of swarm, about 35 to 40 particles)*

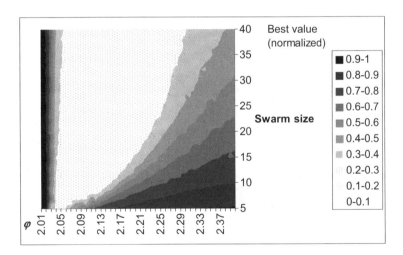

Figure 6.6. *Performance chart for the Rosenbrock function. With the search effort agreed (with more than 40,000 evaluations), there is never "success", i.e. of value less than 10^{-5}. That is why the map is established according to the best value reached, after transformation to remain in the interval [0, 1]*

78 Particle Swarm Optimization

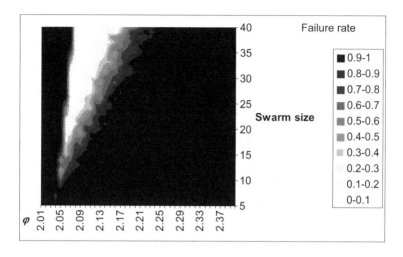

Figure 6.7. *Performance chart for the Ackley function. The interesting zone is very narrow, even if the general form is the same as for the preceding functions. Here still, it is less risky to use rather large swarms*

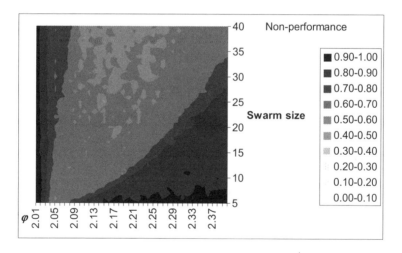

Figure 6.8. *Average performances on the benchmark set. One notices that a coefficient φ of about 2.17 and a swarm size greater than 30 give the best results*

The answer is not obvious, because, on the one hand, a small swarm carries out few evaluations to each iteration but, on the other hand, it often needs more iterations to find a solution. Detailed analysis of the results of the executions which were used to establish the performance maps shows that there is generally no simple relation between the average number of evaluations and the size of the swarm, but that one can sometimes find such a relation when one restricts oneself to a single value of φ.

On Figure 6.9 we can see the example of the Ackley function for the pairs of values (swarm size, coefficient φ) which lead to a zero rate of failure. Note that the average numbers of evaluations have a rather large dispersion. However, with φ constant, the average number of evaluations increases quasi-linearly with the size of the swarm, which remains all the lower when φ is large. Therefore, in such a case, the reduction in the size of the swarm, within certain limits, for example from 40 to 30, increases the effectiveness of the algorithm, since the number of evaluations decreases for an unchanged or almost unchanged failure rate.

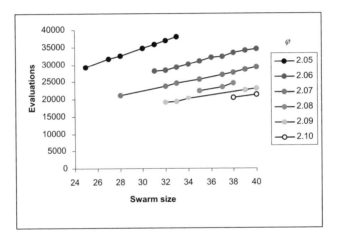

Figure 6.9. *Ackley function with zero rate of failure. The performance map of this function indicates that one can obtain such a rate of failure for certain sizes of swarm between 25 and 40 and certain values of φ between 2.05 and 2.1. The average numbers of evaluations are rather dispersed between 20,000 and 40,000. With φ constant, they are in increasing quasi-linear relationship to the size of the swarm*

However, this is not the case for all the problems. With the Tripod function, for example, such a relation is not obtained at all, as examination of the performance map suggests. This is one of the reasons it was introduced into the benchmark set. We will see that it is also atypical regarding the influence of parallel calculation for the evolution of the swarm.

6.4. Theoretical difficulty and noted difficulty

A synthetic way of using the performance maps is quite simply to take the average of the rates of failure on all the pairs of parameters (N,φ) that are taken into account. Using this approach, if the values of the parameters that are taken into account are sufficiently representative of all the possible values, one obtains a number that should be larger for problems whose theoretical difficulty is high.

Function Search effort	Average Rate of failure	Measured difficulty −ln(success rate)	Theoretical difficulty according to search effort
Tripod 40,000	42%	0.22	22
Alpine 10D 15,000	43%	0.33	111
Parabola 30D 15,000	64%	1.02	264
Griewank 30D 40,000	84%	1.61	325
Rosenbrock 30D 40,000	100%		360
Ackley 30D 40,000	89%	2.21	460

Table 6.10. *Comparison between theoretical difficulty and average rate of failure (with OEP 0). The classification obtained is of course the same in both cases, with the notable exception of the Rosenbrock function. But note that the algorithm is much better than pure chance (it is the least that can be done, but it was advisable to check it). Moreover, the progression of difficulty noticed is much less than that of the theoretical difficulty: in general PSO is more effective for more difficult problems*

6.5. Source code of OEP 0

```
# define D_max 100          //Maximum of the search space (dimensions)
# define N_max 100          //Maximum swarm size
# define two_pi 6.283185307
# define E 2.718281828
# define ulong unsigned long   //For  generation  of  pseudo-random
numbers
# define RAND_MAX_KISS ((unsigned long) 4294967295)

//Structures
struct    position int size;double x[D_max]; double F; ;
```

```
struct     vector int size;double v[D_max]; ;

//Subroutines
double     alea(double has, double b);
int        alea_ whole(int has, int b);
double     ma_ function(struct position X, int function);
ulong      rand_kiss();
void       seed_rand_kiss(ulong seed);

//Aggregate variable
int        nb_eval; //a total Number of evaluations

//main Program
void main()
{
double     c1, cmax;        //Confidence coefficients
int        D;         //Dimension of the search space
int        D;         //current Dimension
double     eps;       //desired Precision
double     eps_moyen;       //average Precision on several executions
int        eval_max;        //Parapet. Max of evaluations of the function numbers
double     eval_moyen;      //an average Number of evaluations
double     fmin;      //Objective to reach
int        function;        //Code of the function to be minimized
int        G;         //Row of best informant
int        K;
int        K;         //maximum Size of the groups of informed
int        LIENS[N_max][N_max]; //Links of information
int        m;
struct     better position;         //Memorizing of the very best position
struct     P[D_max position];// Positions
struct     P_m[D_max position]; //Better found positions
double     min_f; //Objective to reach
_ int      N;         //Size of the swarm
int        N;         //Row of the current particle
int        n_echec;         //a Number of failures
int        n_exec, n_exec_max; //Numbers of executions
struct     V[D_max vector];// Velocities
double     xmin, xmax;      //Interval for the search space

seed_rand_kiss(1); //Initialization of the generator of random numbers
//Parameters of adjustment
c1 = 0.689343; cmax = 1.42694;     //Correspondent with phi = 2.07 in the versions
//later
N = 20; K = 3;    //Size of the swarm, numbers informants/particle

//Problem to be treated (to be changed according to the problem, of course)
function = 10;    //Code of the function. Cf ma_fonction()
xmin = -100; xmax = 100; D = 2; //Search space
eps = 0.00001;    //desired Precision
fmin = 0; //Objective to reach
n_exec_max = 100; //a Number of executions
eval_max = 40000; //a maximum Number of evaluations

//Initialization of the informative variables
n_exec = 0; eval_moyen = 0; eps_moyen = 0; n_echec = 0;

init: //Initializations of the positions and velocities
n_exec = n_exec + 1;
for (N = 0;n < N;n++)

P[n].taille = D; for (D = 0;d < D;d++)P[n].x[d] = alea(xmin, xmax);
```

82   Particle Swarm Optimization

```
V[n].taille = D;
for (D = 0;d < D;d++) V[n].v[d] = alea((xmin-xmax)/2, (xmax-xmin)/2);


//initial Evaluations
nb_eval = 0;

for (N = 0;n < N;n++)

  P[n].f = fabs(ma_fonction(P[n], fonction)-fmin); //Evaluation of the
position
P_m[n] = P[n]; //Better position = initial position


//Memorizing the best result reaches up to now
better = P_m[0];
for (N = 0;n < N;n++) if (P_m[n].f < meilleure.f) better = P_m[n];

loop:
//Defines partially randomly which informs which
for (N = 0;n < N;n = n++)// Initialization

for (m = 0;m < N;m = m++) LIENS[m][n] = 0;
LIENS[n][n] = 1; //Each particle gets information itself


for (m = 0;m < N;m = m++)// Other links. With more K particles informed per m

for (K = 0;k < K;k++)n = alea_entier(0, N-1);LIENS[m][n] = 1;


//Displacement of the swarm
for (N = 0;n < N;n++)// For each particle...

// research of best informant

for (G = 0;g < N;g++) if (LIENS[g][n] - - 0) continuous; goto continuation;
continuation:      min_f = P_m[g].f;
for (m = G + 1;m < N;m++)

if (links [m][n] = = 0) continuous;
if (P_m[m].f < min_f) G = m;min_f = P_m[m].f;

/ calculation the new velocity
for (D = 0;d < D;d++)


V[n].v[d] = c1*V[n].v[d] + alea(0, cmax)*(P_m[n].x[d]-P[n].x[d]);
V[n].v[d] = V[n].v[d] + alea(0, cmax)*(P_m[g].x[d]-P[n].x[d]);

// displacement
for (D = 0;d < D;d++) P[n].x[d] = P[n].x[d] + V[n].v[d];

/ interval confinement
for (D = 0;d < D;d++)

if (P[n].x[d] < xmin) P[n].x[d] = xmin;V[n].v[d] = 0;
if (P[n].x[d] > xmax) P[n].x[d] = xmax;V[n].v[d] = 0;


// evaluation of the new position
P[n].f = fabs(ma_fonction(P[n], fonction)-fmin);

// updated of the best position
```

```
if (P[n].f < P_m[n].f) P_m[n] = P[n];

// memorizing of the best result reached up to now
if (P_m[n].f < meilleure.f) better = P_m[n];


//Test of end
if (meilleure.f > eps && nb_eval < eval_max) goto loop;
if (meilleure.f > eps) n_echec = n_echec + 1;

//Posting of the best found result
printf("%i. Eval =%i. Value%f. Position:): ", n_exec, nb_eval, meilleure.f);
for (D = 0;d < D;d++) printf("%f", meilleure.x[d]);

//Calculation and posting of various information
eval_moyen = eval_moyen + nb_eval;
eps_moyen = eps_moyen + meilleure.f;
if (n_exec < n_exec_max) goto init;

eval_moyen = eval_moyen/(double)n_exec;
eps_moyen = eps_moyen/(double)n_exec;
printf("average Eval =%f", eval_moyen);
printf("average Eps =%f", eps_moyen);
printf("Failure rate =%f", n_echec/(double)n_exec);
}

//=========================================================================
double    alea(double has, double b)
{
  //Gives a random number between a and b
//according to a pseudo-uniform distribution
double r;
r = (double)rand_kiss()/RAND_MAX_KISS;
return a + r*(b-a);
}
//=========================================================================
int     alea_entier(int a, int b)
{
// Gives an integer at random between a and b
int     ir;
double  r;
r = alea(0,1); ir = (int)(a + r*(b + 1-a)); if (ir > b) ir = b;
return ir;
}
//=========================================================================
double ma_ function(struct position x, int function)
{
// Evaluates the value of the function to be minimized at position x
//ADD your own function
int D,d;
double f, p, som1, som2, xd;
double    x1, x2;

nb_eval = nb_eval + 1;
D = x.taille;

switch (function)
{
case 1: //Sphere
f = 0; for(d = 0;d < D;d++) f = f + x.x[d]*x.x[d];
break;

case 2: //Square oot. To use a xmin > = 0
```

```
f = 0; for(d = 0;d < D;d++) f = f + sqrt(fabs(x.x[d]));
break;
case 3: //Alpine. Min 0 in (0,0... 0)
//alternative 1
//       f   =    0;for(d   =   0;d   <   D;d++)    f   =   f   +
sqrt(fabs(x.x[d]*sin(x.x[d])));
//alternative 2
f = 0;for(d = 0;d < D;d++) f = f + fabs(x.x[d]*(sin(x.x[d]) + 0.1));
break;

case 4: //Rosenbrock, Banana function. Min 0 in (1... 1)
f = 0;
for (D = 0;d < D-1;d++)

xd = 1-x.x[d]; f = f + xd*xd; xd = x.x[d]*x.x[d]-x.x[d + 1];
f = f + 100*xd*xd;

break;

case 5: //Ackley
som1 = 0;som2 = 0;
for (D = 0;d < D;d++)

xd = x.x[d]; som1 = som1 + xd*xd; som2 = som2 + cos(two_pi*xd);

f = (-20*exp(-0.2*sqrt(som1/(double)D))-exp(som2/(double)D) + 20 + E);
break;

case 6: //Griewank
f = 0;
p = 1;
for (D = 0;d < D;d++)

xd = x.x[d]-100;
f = f + xd*xd;
p = p*cos(xd/sqrt(d + 1));

f = f/4000 -p + 1;
break;

case 10: //Tripod function (Louis Gacogne)

//on [- 100, 100], min 0 at (0, -50)
x1 = x.x[0];
x2 = x.x[1];

if(x2 < 0) f = fabs(x1) + fabs(x2 + 50);
else

if(x1 < 0) f = 1 + fabs(x1 + 50) + fabs(x2-50);
else f = 2 + fabs(x1-50) + fabs(x2-50);

break;

return f;
}

//= = = = = = = = = = = = = = = = = = = = = = = = = = = = = = = = =
= = = = = = = = = = = = = = = = = = = = = = = = = = = = = = = KISS
... (generator already seen)
```

6.6. Summary

While varying the parameters of algorithm OEP 0 systematically, it is possible to establish performance maps for the functions of the benchmark set. They show that for almost all the functions there are many values of the parameters for which convergence is excellent (rate of failure zero or almost zero).

This does not mean to say that the parameter setting is always easy to find, but that, at least, the algorithm is potentially effective.

Chapter 7

Swarm: Memory and Graphs of Influence

7.1. Circular neighborhood of the historical PSO

The first articles presenting PSO (*Particle Swarm Optimization*) under its original name were published in 1995 [EBE 95, KEN 95]. This primitive version is practically no longer used. Nevertheless, it opened the way for the study of graphs of influence with fixed topology, because the information links between particles were defined once for all, generally according to a "circular" diagram.

N particles of the swarm are laid out virtually on a circle, then numbered sequentially from 1 by traversing this circle. Each particle has a set of informants of fixed size K, historically called its *neighborhood*. The neighborhood of size K of a particle is obtained from the virtual circle by recruiting alternately on the right and on the left of its position, until a total of $K - 1$ neighbors is obtained. Moreover, the particle itself is also included.

On Figure 7.1 we can see the result for a swarm of seven particles for two sizes of neighborhood (3 and 4). The program used (OEP 5) is available *via Particle Swarm Central* [PSC]. Note that for the definition of the neighborhoods, no concept of distance between particles in the search space is taken into account: it is about a *social* neighborhood rather than *a geographical* neighborhood, which, on the contrary, would use a metric and for which the neighborhood of size K of a particle would be formed of the K particles closest (including itself). This alternative would be more expensive in calculation time and, moreover, does not seem to have a significantly higher effectiveness by itself. On the other hand, it is a condition necessary to the use of the technique of multicentroid reorganization of memories, which we will discuss later.

The moment *K* is greater than 3, the relation may not be symmetrical for certain particles. On the right-hand side of Figure 7.1, we see clearly that, for example, particle 1 informs particle 6 without the reverse being true. That is why the term "neighborhood", which evokes ideas of symmetry, is in the end not very apt. As we have seen, it is replaced here by the term "(group of) informants".

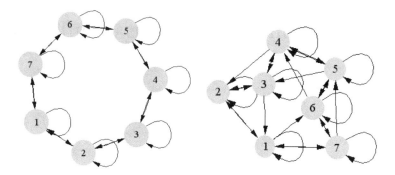

Figure 7.1. *Regular graphs of influence of a swarm of seven particles. For each arc, the particle origin influences (informs) the end particle. On the graph on the left, each particle has 3 informants, including itself. For particle 1, they are 1, 2 and 7. On the right-hand side, there are 4 informants (1, 2, 7 and 3)*

7.2. Memory-swarm

From this idea, it is tempting to imagine other configurations. What happens, for example, if the virtual arrangement of the particles is a square grid mapped onto a torus or if the graph of the relations is hierarchical or of the type "small world" like an Internet network, for example? The study of these questions leads us to differentiate properly the two functions provided by the particles: exploration of the search space and memorizing of the best position found during this search.

From the outset, we have postulated that each particle was ready to fulfill these two functions. That led us to quite convoluted formulations, like "the best of the best positions found until now by informants". Moreover, the data memorized by the particle itself are processed separately from that brought by the others, whereas nothing in their nature distinguishes them. Also, that demands that we memorize as many positions as there are particles, neither more, nor less. Lastly, it could be desirable to connect directly the positions memorized in order to deduce from them some interesting new displacements. However, one can certainly study various topologies, (see, for example, [CLE 99, KEN 99]), but without all the desirable flexibility.

That is why it is interesting to change the point of view slightly and consider that the functions of exploration and memorizing are carried by distinct particles. That will also enable us to define more easily various kinds of groups of informants.

Thus we will have as before, an *explorer-swarm* composed of turbulent particles, moving with each time increment, but we will also have a *memory-swarm*. Its particles, which we will call simply *memories* and which we can imagine heavy, slow and wise, move only occasionally and definitely, towards the best positions announced by the *explorer* particles. Thus, the association of a memory and explorer corresponds to a particle according to the historical terminology.

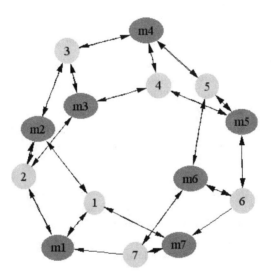

Figure 7.2. *Graph of influence with memory-swarm (N = 7, M = 7, K = 3). It is formally similar to that of the left of Figure 7.1, but the explorer-swarm (particles in pale gray) and the memory-swarm (particles in dark gray) have been differentiated. This more complicated representation offers more freedom of configuration, for example by modifying the number of memories or by making them communicate directly with each other*

Figure 7.2 shows an example of information links according to this second point of view, which is strictly equivalent to the historical circular diagram with 3 informants per particle. Previously, each particle informed some others, including itself. Moreover, it memorized its best performance. Now, the explorers do not memorize anything but instead inform the memories, which, in return, guide them in their exploration. The advantage of this new representation is that it allows new structures of information. For example, the memory-swarm and the explorer-swarm need not be the same size. Likewise, one can make the memories communicate directly between themselves, reworking memorized information and drawing from the results consequences in terms of new displacements with probable improvement.

7.3. Fixed topologies

Let us consider initially the case where the graph of information, as in the historical PSO, is defined once and for all before the process of iteration. We will not recapitulate here the results obtained with a particular topology, but will merely retain the following three principal empirical rules:

– rule 1: a fixed topology must be regular (the same number of links for each particle), because one does not know *a priori* which particles will be the best;

– rule 2: for each regular topology and each problem, there is an optimum number of links (number of informants), but if one does not have any information on the difficulty of the problem, it is better to define fewer possible links, while keeping the connexity of the graph of influence;

– rule 3: one can sometimes increase the effectiveness of the algorithm by making the particles of the memory-swarm communicate directly among themselves.

For the first two points, note that these conclusions are valid only if the topology is fixed once and for all. We will see that in adaptive PSO the situation is quite different. Also, note that the application of rules 1 and 2 in fixed topology leads automatically to the circular diagram. It is, in effect, the connected regular graph for which the nodes can have fewest possible arcs (two per node, plus an arc on itself).

Table 7.1 illustrates how much the performances can differ according to whether fixed topology is regular or randomly selected before the beginning of the process. For one of the test functions (Alpine), random topology gives a better result, but it is precisely a stroke of luck. Regular topology is more robust and the total average performance is better.

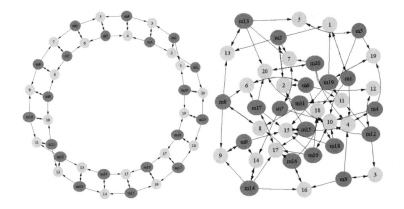

Figure 7.3. *Regular versus irregular in fixed topology (N = 20, M = 20, K = 3). Graphs of information. The two graphs are more similar than they appear. In both cases, each explorer particle informs only one memory and each memory is informed by just one explorer. The number of arcs per particle is exactly 3 in the regular diagram on the left, it is 2 to 4 (with an average of 3) in the right-hand diagram. This small difference is enough to modify the results obtained appreciably*

Function (search effort)	Circular topology (N = 20, M = 20, K = 3) Rate of failure	Fixed random topology (N = 20, M = 20, K = 3) Rate of failure
Tripod (40,000)	7%	25%
Alpine 10D (15,000)	17%	5%
Parabola 30D (15,000)	0%	0%
Griewank 30D (40,000)	42%	57%
Rosenbrock 30D (40,000)	100% 38.3	100% average result 37.5
Ackley 30D (40,000)	40%	94%
Average of the rates of failure	34%	47%

Table 7.1. *Regular versus irregular in fixed topology (N = 20, M = 20, K = 3). Results on the benchmark set, with OEP 5. Circular topology is on the whole more effective, even if, obviously, it can happen by chance that an irregular topology is more appropriate for a given problem (see Alpine). To facilitate the comparisons, the same parameters are used as for Table 6.1 carried out with OEP 0*

7.4. Random variable topologies

After fixed topologies, let us explore those that vary during iterations. More precisely, we will consider here only those that are modified randomly, hardly taking account, if at all, of the information collected during the process, i.e. certainly in a rather stupid way, but very economic in terms of computing times. The case of more intelligent modifications will be studied in the chapters on adaptation.

Again, one can imagine thousands of ways of doing this, but not all are effective. In all cases, however, it is a question of how a memory recruits an explorer to inform and vice versa. To illustrate the principle, let us compare two methods: that which was already presented for version OEP 0 and another which gives sometimes better results.

7.4.1. *Direct recruitment*

The principle of this direct random recruitment, but distinguishing between memories and explorer, can be summarized briefly as follows:
– a number K less than or equal to the size of the swarm is defined at the beginning;
– with each time increment, each memory draws randomly K explorer particles and establishes an information link towards them;
– in the same way, with each increment, each explorer establishes a link towards at least one memory.

Moreover, in practice, if the number of memories is different from the number of explorer, one "cheats" a little, in order to guarantee that each explorer has a link towards a memory and vice versa. Note that this is only an empirical rule, which seems more effective than pure chance.

7.4.2. *Recruitment by common channel of communication*

The metaphor underlying this method is that of synchronization by sharing a channel of communication with the same frequency. According to your preferences, you can imagine, for example, populations of neurons which join to carry out a certain task or many newsgroups in real time on the Internet (*chatting groups* or *chats*).

It is supposed that there are F possible frequencies. With each time increment:
– each explorer chooses a frequency randomly;

– each memory chooses a frequency randomly;

– only the explorers and memories that have chosen the same frequency can communicate.

As above, the situation is arranged so that every explorer can transmit its information to at least one memory and vice versa.

At every moment, the corresponding graph of information is non-connected, but as it changes constantly, there is nevertheless a kind of temporal connectivity. In practice, with swarms of about 30 particles of each type and 10 frequencies, at the end of 20 time increments it is almost certain that any information could have been disseminated everywhere (see probability calculus at the end of the chapter).

7.5. Influence of the number of informants

7.5.1. *In fixed topology*

Let K be the number of informants per particle and let us treat our benchmark set by varying it. The results obtained with a circular fixed topology are summarized in Figure 7.4. In order to highlight better what occurs, the maximum number of evaluations was changed to 100,000 and swarm size to 40. The Rosenbrock function does not appear there, because even then the rate of failure remains 100%.

Then one highlights three types of variation of the effectiveness when K increases:

– average improvement, then stagnation, with possibly light deterioration for the greatest values (see Alpine and Parabola);

– practically no change (see Griewank);

– improvement at the beginning, then strong deterioration (see Tripod and Ackley).

A partial qualitative explanation is possible. First of all, there is a discontinuity of the topology of the graph of influence between the values $K = 2$ and $K = 3$. For the first, the graph is a one-way circle; for the second, it is bidirectional. For N particles, it means that the average time of transfer of information decreases abruptly from $N/2$ to $(N+1)/4$: it is practically divided by 2. That it frequently results in greater effectiveness is therefore not surprising.

94   Particle Swarm Optimization

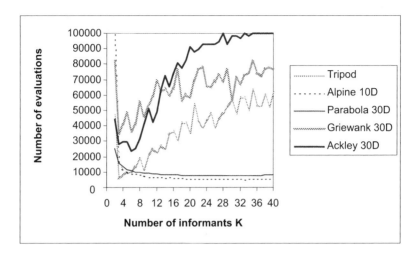

Figure 7.4. *Influence of the number of informants K. Results with a fixed circular topology (N = M = 40). It is noticed that on the whole it would be wiser to choose a rather small value, even if it is not completely optimal for certain problems (like here Alpine and Parabola)*

Indeed, the larger the value of K, the denser the graph of influence and, therefore, the more rapidly information on a promising position will be transmitted to all the particles. Those will then tend to gather more quickly (in addition, one can show that the velocity of decrease of the diameter of the swarm increases with K). However, if this phenomenon takes place too quickly (i.e. if K is too large), the swarm quite simply does not have time to seek elsewhere, because, according to the equations of motion, the velocity of each particle is on average decreasing, and this all the more quickly as the particles are closer.

If there are no local minima, the promising position has every chance to be closer and closer to the global minimum and the fact that many particles explore in the neighborhood is beneficial (see Parabola). If there are local minima close in value but distant in search space, the reverse is true: the swarm is extremely likely to be trapped (see Tripod, Griewank, Ackley). Lastly, in an intermediate situation, there are certainly local minima, but if those that are far away from the global minimum are also much worse (to be more precise, if the ratio of the variation of values at the distance is sufficiently large) the swarm manages to be unaware of them (Alpine).

Similar results are obtained in random fixed topology. The significant point is the lesson that can be learnt from such analyses: it is definitely more advisable to choose a small value for the number of informants. That is why the choice $K = 3$ is a good compromise. Nevertheless, if one can afford, in terms of search effort, to test also *a contrario* the extreme value $K = N$ is interesting, since for certain problems it is the optimal value. In particular, if one knows in advance that there are no local minima, it is probably the best choice.

7.5.2. *In random variable topology*

We can make the same kind of study when the graph of influence is randomly modified with each iteration. As we can see in Figure 7.5, the results are very similar. The only notable difference is that there is no discontinuity between the values $K = 2$ and $K = 3$. That can be understood, since it is now only a matter of one maximum value. Actually, for $K = 2$ the graph contains nodes with one or two arcs and, for $K = 3$, nodes with one, two or three arcs. It is normal that the difference is less marked.

Finally, the conclusion remains the same: in the absence of other information, a small value is the best choice; but, for certain types of problems, one can improve a little by taking, quite to the contrary, the greatest possible value.

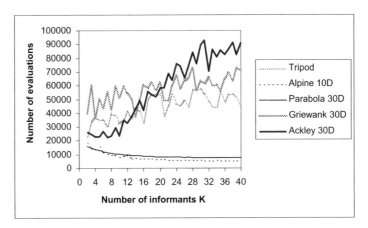

Figure 7.5. *Influence of the number of informants K. Results with a variable random topology. In this case also, the choice of a low value is the wisest. It will be noted, however, that there is no discontinuity between values 2 and 3*

7.6. Influence of the number of memories

Since we dissociated explorers and memories, we can vary their number independently. It is then interesting to wonder whether it is better to have more explorers than memories or the reverse. Here, intuition is rather misleading. For example, for a problem without local minima, like Parabola, one might believe that it is more effective to have just a few memories, perhaps only one, informed by many explorers, as in the graphs at the top of Figure 7.6.

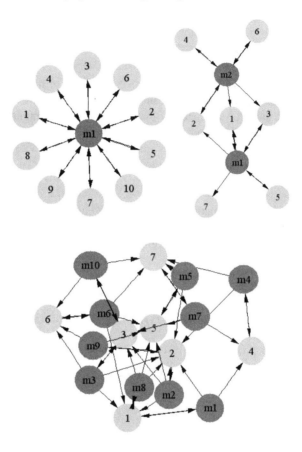

Figure 7.6. *Graphs of influence with $N \neq M$. For more clarity, the numbers of particles selected were relatively small. On the graphs on the top, there are fewer memories than explorers ($N = 10$, $M = 1$ and $N = 7$, $M = 2$). On the bottom, it is the reverse ($N = 7$, $M = 10$)*

It is not at all like this, as Figure 7.7 shows. However, it is true for the Alpine function: the star graph with only one memory is most effective. This indicates that there is no obvious link between the form of the function and the optimum number of memories to treat it. What is obvious is that in general it is preferable to make this a rather large number, and even a little greater than that of the explorers. There is certainly the risk that in certain cases the performances are degraded, but not much. Incidentally, this shows that the implicit "choice" imposed by the traditional PSO, to have as many memories as explorers, is a good compromise. Finally, as before, only extreme values are interesting: *a priori* large values and, in certain exceptional cases, very small ones.

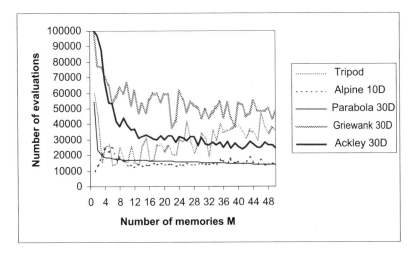

Figure 7.7. *Influence of the number of memories (N = 40, K = 3, T = 100,000). The graph of information is here in variable random topology with each iteration. Contrary to intuition, even for a problem with just one global minimum and without local minima, like Parabola, it is more effective to have many memories, and even a number greater than that of explorers. One will note the exceptional case of Alpine, for which only one memory (star graph) is the best configuration*

7.7. Reorganizations of the memory-swarm

As announced earlier, it is sometimes possible to make better use of the information collected during the process, by making the memories communicate directly between themselves and reorganizing their contents. To illustrate this point, we will test two types of reorganization: according to a mixing of the memories and a centralized diagram (calculation of a "queen"). In both cases, there is no, or very little, reduction in the diversity of memorized information (whereas we will have some systematically in the adaptive techniques), but the fields of application are different.

7.7.1. *Mixing of the memories*

What is interesting in the random modification of the links between particles is that it accelerates the diffusion of information. Indeed, a memory in possession of a promising position has a better chance of passing the good word directly to the explorers. The reverse is also true but, in fact, the situation is not symmetrical if this mixing of the memories is not too frequent. Indeed, if an explorer is informed by a memory that is worse than its own position, it will take account of it on only one time increment.

Nevertheless, it is done without control, i.e. chance (or bad luck!) perhaps plays too significant a role. Hence the idea, on the contrary, of carrying out a mixing of more or less the same type, but according to precise rules. The simplest way – but one can of course imagine many others – consists of two stages:

– search of the best memory and the worst,

– exchange of these two memories.

Obviously, on the contrary, the links should not be randomly modified, under penalty of losing the benefit of the operation.

7.7.2. *Queen and other centroids*

Here the idea is that when the memory-swarm really starts to converge, its "center of gravity" has a good chance of being better than any single particle. In the original version ([CLE 99]), this center of gravity is called *queen* and calculated as a new temporary particle and assuming that the particles each have a mass inversely proportional to their performance (i.e. larger as the position is better).

In fact, since then, it has been shown that to adopt equal masses is on the whole equally effective, while being less arbitrary (no additional function to define). The method is particularly interesting when coupled with the Stop/Restart technique, which we will examine later, or, which amounts to the same while being more difficult to program, by defining not one but several centroids, which, to be effective, also requires the size of the swarm to be increased ([KEN 00]).

7.7.3. *Comparative results*

Table 7.2 shows the average results for 100 tests. Let us recall that with this number of tests, the percentages are estimated only with a margin of approximately 5%, but that will be enough for us to highlight the differences in behavior.

The first column restates the values obtained initially with OEP 0, to facilitate comparison. It is noted that simple mixing (exchange of worst and best memory) improves all the results and, for some, in a very significant way (Parabola, Ackley). The use of a queen degrades some slightly (Tripod, Ackley), but improves others in an even more marked way (Alpine, Parabola).

It is therefore tempting to couple the two methods in order to see whether the improvements override deteriorations. Unfortunately, this is not always the case. More precisely, it is often true for relatively easy problems (like the first three of our examples), while the performances for more difficult problems become frankly bad (for example, 83% failure rate for Ackley).

Name	Variable random graph (OEP 0)	with mixing	with queen
Tripod	39%	39%	43%
Alpine 10D	28%	24%	8%
Parabola 30D	27%	0%	0%
Griewank 30D	55%	49%	49%
Rosenbrock 30D	100% average 39.026	100% average 35.07	100% average 27.76
Ackley 30D	25%	6%	34%
Average of the rates of failure	44.5%	37.7%	39%

Table 7.2. *Influence of the direct reorganization of memories. This type of method does not reduce diversity and can, in certain cases, be very effective. The results are averages of 100 executions, with N = M = 20 particles, K = 3 and φ = 2.07*

For the parameters number of informants and number of memories, it has been possible to develop rules for empirical and robust choices. However, it is not the same for the techniques of reorganization of memories. After many tests, which obviously go well beyond those presented here, only rather vague recommendations can be proposed for the moment: use mixing, it will most probably improve the performances, and, if possible, try a queen/centroid(s) method, since very significant gains can sometimes be obtained by using it.

7.8. For "amatheurs": temporal connectivity in random recruitment

We have seen that the random assignment of channels of communication generates, with each iteration, subgraphs of information links that are disconnected. However, as precisely this structure is modified with each time increment, information can nevertheless be transmitted everywhere with a non-null probability: over a certain period, all happens as if the graph were connected.

Let m be a memory carrying information and n an unspecified explorer. What is the probability that n can receive information coming from m after at the most t time increments? Let N be the number of explorers, M the number of memories and F the number of channels (implied, the number of different frequencies). At moment 0, memory m drew channel c at random. The probability that n also drew c is simply $p = 1/F$. It is the probability that there is a link between m and n and, therefore, that n can be informed in just one time increment.

So that n cannot be informed at the first increment, but only at the second, the following events need to happen:
 – at time 0, n did not draw the channel c (probability $1-p$);
 – either m draws c_1 with time 1, and n also (probability p).

Or then:
 – n draws c_1 at time 1 (probability p);
 – and at least 1 explorer drew c (probability $1-(1-p)^N$) at time 0 receiving information thus from m;
 – and at least 1 memory drew c at time 0 (being then informed by at least one of the previous explorers) and c_1 at time 1 (thus informing n). Note that the transfer of explorer information towards memory is not counted as a "time" (it is included in the iteration of displacement). The probability of this ensemble of two events is easy to calculate by considering its opposite (either no c with the first draw, or at least c with the first draw and any c_1 with the second). One thus finds $1-2(1-p)^M +(1-p)^{2M}$.

Thus, for the second time increment, the probability is (by posing $q = 1-p$):

$$p_2 = qp\left(1+(1-q^N)\right)\left(1-2q^M q^{2M}\right)$$

Thus, the probability that information can be transmitted either at the first increment or at the second is:

$$p_{\leq 2} = 1-q(1-p_2)$$

Beyond this, the exact formula becomes complicated, but if p is not too small (let us say greater than 15%), it can be approached by $p_{\leq t} = 1-q^t$, which gives us the evolution of the Figure below, which shows us that the quasi-complete temporal connexity is then ensured after 20 iterations. Note that the growth is moderate, which is an asset for difficult problems, because too rapid transmission of information harms the exploration of the search space.

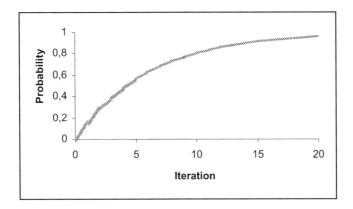

Figure 7.8. *Temporal connexity in recruitment by common channels. At every moment the graph of information is not connected, but since the links vary in the course of time, all happens more or less as if it were: the probability that information carried by a given particle can be known by any other increases in the course of time*

7.9. Summary

In traditional PSO, the particles have a double role: to explore and memorize. It is interesting to separate these functionalities and distinguish between purely explorer particles and purely memory particles, the latter moving only definitely.

The information links between these two groups of particles form a graph which can be regular or random, fixed at the beginning of process or modified during its course. The results obtained with these various topologies suggest rules of choice for the number of links per particle and the number of memories.

Moreover, it is then possible to make the memories communicate between themselves directly, in order to reorganize themselves or to synthesize information, operations which can sometimes appreciably accelerate convergence.

Chapter 8

Distributions of Proximity[1]

8.1. The random possibilities

As we saw, in particular, in the chapter "First formulations", the process of iterative stochastic optimization primarily rests on the definition, with each stage, of the next possible positions in the search space of dimension D, together with their probabilities of being selected. In PSO, this can be summarized, for a given particle, by the vectorial equation giving the next vector displacement (called velocity for historical reasons):

$$v(t+1) = c_1 v(t) + \mathbf{A}(p(t) - x(t)) + \mathbf{A}'(g(t) - x(t))$$

where $\mathbf{A}$ and $\mathbf{A}'$ are matrices $D \times D$ with random diagonal, the other elements being null (the general case is beyond the scope of this book). For the traditional PSO studied until now, each one of these matrices can be written:

$$\begin{bmatrix} alea(0, c_{max}) & \ldots & 0 \\ \ldots & alea(0, c_{max}) & \ldots \\ 0 & \ldots & alea(0, c_{max}) \end{bmatrix}$$

the function $alea(0, c_{max})$ returning a random value between 0 and c_{max} according to a uniform distribution. As we have noticed, this results in the distribution of

---

1. This somewhat technical chapter may only be skimmed through on first reading. To understand the chapters that follow, it is enough to know of the existence of the various distributions described here.

possibles associated with **A** being a uniform D-rectangle whose diagonal is the vector $p(t)-x(t)$. Similarly for that associated with the matrix **A'**, with the diagonal $g(t)-x(t)$. After a short review of the characteristics of this kind of distribution, we will see that it is sometimes more judicious to use others, based on isotropy, such as spheres or more or less deformed Gaussians. In fact, we will see that actually a good strategy consists of using several of them in alternation during the search process. In passing, to simplify their later referencing, we will allot a number to them.

8.2. Review of rectangular distribution

Let us point out the equations of the traditional PSO, just to keep in mind that each random element corresponds to a uniform distribution of possible positions in a D-rectangle.

Distribution 1

$$\begin{cases} v_d \leftarrow c_1 v_d + alea(0, c_{max})(p_d - x_d) + alea(0, c_{max})(g_d - x_d) \\ x_d \leftarrow x_d + v_d \end{cases}$$

We have already noted that the combination by summation of the two uniform D-rectangles is no longer uniform, but that, nevertheless, its support remains itself a D-rectangle. The experiment shows that it is not very satisfactory, owing to the fact that certain positions can then be selected in the "corners", without justification or necessity.

In addition, as already remarked, the distribution depends on the coordinate system and not only on the relative positions of the three points concerned $x(t)$, $p(t)$, and $g(t)$. We had noted that this was no longer very satisfactory from a theoretical point of view, but it is now advisable to make the matter more nuanced. A significant element is the evolution of the total volume of the distribution during the process. At a given moment and for a given particle, the distribution of related possibles can lose one or more dimensions if, by bad luck, one or more coordinates are null or almost null and this, by definition, depends on the coordinate system. But that changes according to moments and particles, and one often notes a phenomenon of compensation: if, for example, $p(t)$ is on one of the coordinate axes and thus the dimensionality of the associated distribution is reduced by one, the volume of the distribution associated with $g(t)$ is often larger, and vice versa. Hence, the combination of both is more robust than each one separately. Thus, even if there is an undeniable bias, on average its influence on the effectiveness of the algorithm is seldom notable. It is just necessary to keep its existence in mind, because if the algorithm seems to converge badly a simple rotation of the axis of coordinate can sometimes improve things.

On the other hand, the "rectangular" form of the final distribution has a clear influence. Indeed, it results from time to time in placing near the top of a D-rectangle particles that are pure artifacts having nothing to do with the structure of the problem. When that does not happen too often, there is no need to worry and it can even be beneficial (because, as we have seen, to have some dissenting particles is desirable). However, when the dimension of the problem is large, that becomes much more frequent (for simple geometrical reasons) and the outcome is less favorable. Hence, the interest in using distributions that are a little less "jagged".

8.3. Alternative distributions of possibilities

To mitigate the defects of the rectangular distribution, a simple method is to start from an isotropic distribution, for example spherical or Gaussian. A small program delivering a position according to such a distribution is given in an appendix (section 8.6). It is, in any case, an excellent exercise in statistics! From there, one can imagine many alternatives. We will examine some of them.

8.3.1. *Ellipsoidal positive sectors*

This is a method very close to the original PSO. The uniform random choices are replaced by choices resulting from a spherical distribution or, more precisely, resulting from a distribution whose support is a positive spherical sector.

Distribution 2

$$\begin{cases} v_d \leftarrow c_1 v_d + c_{\max} \left| alea\_sphère(0,\rho)_d \right| (p_d - x_d) \\ \quad + c_{\max} \left| alea\_sphère(0,\rho)_d \right| (g_d - x_d) \\ x_d \leftarrow x_d + v_d \end{cases}$$

The function $alea\_sphère(0,\rho)$ returns a point chosen randomly according to a uniform distribution in the D-sphere centered on the origin of the coordinates and whose radius is ρ. In Figure 8.1, this radius was calculated so that the volume of the sphere is equal to 1, in order to remain closer to the traditional equations. The final distribution then is concentrated (which is not always an advantage). It will also be noted that it remains dependent on the coordinate system. Nevertheless, it gives better results in general than the rectangular distribution.

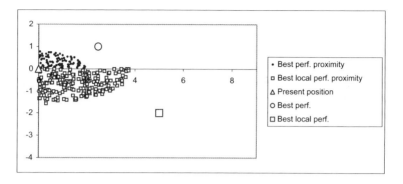

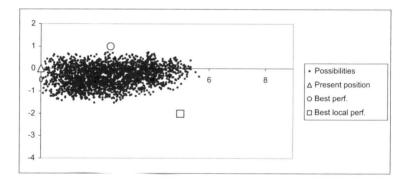

Figure 8.1. *Distribution of possibilities starting from deformed positive spherical sectors. If one seeks to be closer to the traditional equations, as here, the resulting distribution is concentrated. The results are in general better than with the rectangular distribution of the traditional PSO*

8.3.2. *Independent Gaussians*

This is rather similar to the preceding method. For each dimension, instead of calling upon a uniform distribution on an interval, a normal distribution is used. The equations of motion thus become those below.

Distribution 3

$$\begin{cases} v_d \leftarrow c_1 v_d + alea\_normal(\mu,\sigma)(p_d - x_d) \\ \quad + alea\_normal(\mu,\sigma)(g_d - x_d) \\ x_d \leftarrow x_d + v_d \end{cases}$$

This alternative introduces *a priori* two additional parameters, the average μ and the standard deviation σ of the distribution. If one wants to remain rather close to the traditional version (rectangular distributions), it is enough to take $\mu = c_{max}$ and $\sigma = c_{max}/4$, which ensures that more than 95% of the distribution is in the interval $[0, c_{max}]$. This method is effective enough for more or less combinatorial discrete problems, but not so effective for continuous problems such as those of our benchmark set.

8.3.3. *Local by independent Gaussians*

One might call this an alternative of the preceding alternative. The idea is to seek only locally "around" the best-known position of the particle, that is to say *g*. Thus, for each dimension *d*, a coordinate more or less close to g_d is drawn randomly according to a Gaussian law, which gives the following equation of displacement if the distribution is centered on *g*:

$$x_d \leftarrow g_d + alea\_normal(0, \|g_d - x_d\|)$$

The Gaussian law can be replaced by a uniform law on $\left[-\|g_d - x_d\|, \|g_d - x_d\|\right]$ but, in any case, the effectiveness of this type of distribution varies considerably according to the problem. For example, on our benchmark set, the failure rate is 100% for Griewank and 0% for Ackley. On the other hand, we will use it jointly with others in adaptive PSO TRIBES later on. For this particular use, experiment shows that a distribution centered no longer on *g* but a little beyond it compared to *x* is very slightly more robust. We will refer to this as 3', and, more precisely, to the following equation of displacement:

Distribution 3'

$$x_d \leftarrow g_d + alea\_normal(g_d - x_d, \|g_d - x_d\|)$$

8.3.4. *The class of one-dimensional distributions*

We have just seen two alternatives that have in common the independent use of random distributions for each dimension. On the same principle, many others have been imagined (see, for example, [MIR 02B, SHI 98B, XIE 02]). There is no question of presenting an anthology of them here; we merely note that the corresponding equations of motion have the following general form:

$$\begin{cases} v_d \leftarrow alea_1(c_1,\tau_1)v_d + alea_2(c_2,\tau_2)(p_d - x_d) \\ \quad + alea_3(c_3,\tau_3)(g_d - x_d) \\ x_d \leftarrow x_d + v_d \end{cases}$$

where each function $alea_i$ depends on two parameters and returns a real number according to a probability distribution to specify. We have seen examples of deformed positive spherical sectors and of Gaussians. Log-normal laws of the type $c_i(\log N(0,1))^{\tau_i}$ sometimes also give good results.

Nevertheless, used as such, these alternatives are on the whole neither better nor worse than those here detailed. As usual, all depends on the problem being tackled. However, some of them do appear rather effective when the parameters themselves are modified in a relevant way during the process. We will therefore speak about it again in the chapter devoted to adaptive PSO.

In the meantime, it is nevertheless possible to give some qualitative advice, which can guide your choice if you plan to carry out your own alternative for a precise type of problem. These indications are primarily empirical and relative to the values of the averages and standard deviations of the distributions $alea_i$.

For $alea_1$, i.e. consideration of the particle's own velocity:

– average less than 1 (risk of divergence if not, unless adding a constraint maximum velocity);

– low standard deviation. You will have noted that, in traditional PSO, it is null.

For $alea_2$ and $alea_3$, i.e. consideration of two good known performances of the particle:

– average of about 0.7. In traditional PSO, it is approximately from 0.5 to 1;

– deviation type greater with increasing difficulty of problem. In traditional PSO, it is approximately 0.6 to 1.15 ($2.\text{average}/\sqrt{3}$, owing to the fact that the distribution is uniform).

8.3.5. *Pivots*

The original pivot method [SER 97], retranscribed in the vocabulary of PSO, would consist of having with each iteration only an even number of particles, pairing them and, in each pair, taking as pivot the better of the two. The pivot does not move and the new position of the other particle is randomly selected according to an isotropic (e.g. Gaussian) distribution centered on the pivot.

Here, one proceeds a little differently. For each particle one considers two more points of the search space, but they are its best performance *p* and the best performance of its informants, *g*. One defines then two hyperspheres, H_p and H_G, centered on these points and of the same radius equal to their distance. Then, in each sphere, one randomly chooses a point according to a uniform distribution. One assigns to this point a weight in decreasing proportion to the value of the function to be minimized, evaluated in the center of the sphere. Finally the new position is calculated as the barycenter of these the last two points (see Figure 8.2).

It is interesting to note that this method no longer explicitly calls for the speed of movement. The equation of motion can be written, in condensed vectorial form:

Distribution 4

$$x \leftarrow c_2 alea(H_p) + c_3 alea(H_g)$$

To help understand and calculate variables of state like the kinetic energy, it is always possible to posit that the "velocity" is the difference between the position at moment *t* + 1 and that at moment *t*:

$$v(t) = x(t+1) - x(t)$$

First, the assignment of a weight has a rather awkward *a priori* arbitrary aspect. But, in fact, the method is extremely robust with respect to the choice of weighting function, provided that this observes some very general conditions: strict decrease and finite value for a zero value of the function to be minimized (presumed to be positive, a case to which one can, in practice, always return). For example, one can take as weighting coefficients $\dfrac{f(p)}{f(p)+f(g)}$ and $\dfrac{f(g)}{f(p)+f(g)}$.

Second, it seems that the current position of the particle is not taken into account in calculating the future position, contrary to the formula of the traditional PSO. This may seem curious, but, in fact, it is only an impression. If this position is bad, there is rarely any interest in using it. In a manner of speaking, one can thus say that it is taken into account precisely by being unaware of it! In addition, if it is good, then it actually coincides with its best performance *p* and so it rightly intervenes in the calculation.

110   Particle Swarm Optimization

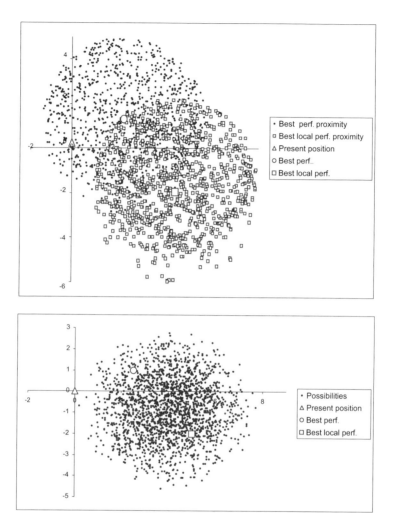

Figure 8.2. *Distribution of the possibilities by the method of pivots. The basic uniform distributions are here two hyperspheres which one combines linearly. The distribution of the new possible positions is still in a hypersphere, but it is no longer uniform, as one can see on the sampling of 2,000 points in the second Figure. One will note the greater extension compared to preceding methods, certainly penalizing for easy problems, but interesting for functions whose sought minimum has a narrow basin of attraction*

Pivots with noise

This second strategy starts exactly like the preceding one. Simply, once the new position determined, it is still modified according to Gaussian random noise effects, of null average and with the standard deviation becoming smaller as the best performance of the particle approaches that of its informants. For example, if f is the function to be minimized, one will be able to take as standard deviation:

$$\sigma = \frac{f(p)-f(g)}{f(p)+f(g)}$$

Here still, the exact formula is not very significant. It is enough that the result is at the most equal to 1 and strictly decreasing with the difference of the performances, $f(p)-f(g)$.

In practice, there are two sub-variants. Either, for each component of the position that has been just calculated, i.e. for each dimension d, one randomly draws a value b_d according to the noise distribution, and the component is multiplied by $(1+b_d)$.

$$\forall d, b_d = N(0,\sigma), x_d \leftarrow (1+b_d)x_d$$

Alternatively, the noise is applied only according to the direction of vector x, i.e. the same random value b is used for all the components. In what follows, we will use this second sub-variant, the first often giving, by experiment, too much dispersion. Hence the equations defining this distribution:

Distribution 5

$$x \leftarrow c_2 alea(H_p) + c_3 alea(H_g)$$
$$\begin{cases} b = N(0,\sigma) \\ \forall d, x_d \leftarrow (1+b)x_d \end{cases}$$

Gaussian pivots

Another manner of obtaining a distribution the support of which is no longer limited to a hypersphere is to use from the outset non-uniform distributions with infinite support, such as Gaussians. Each hypersphere is then replaced by a Gaussian "equivalent", having the same center and a selected standard deviation so that, for example, 98% of the distribution is in the initial hypersphere (normalized standard deviation = 2). Let us call G_p and G_g the resulting isotropic Gaussian distributions, respectively centered on the positions p and g. The condensed formalization of this distribution is then simply:

Distribution 6

$$x \leftarrow c_2 alea(G_p) + c_3 alea(G_g)$$

Such a method, rather like the preceding one, is very effective in solving certain difficult problems (in both cases, one thus obtains a null rate of failure for the Ackley function). On the benchmark set, the result is more mitigated: with pivots with noise the average rate of failure is 37%, and it is 44% with Gaussian pivots. However, as we will see below, a good strategy is to combine these two methods.

One can vary *ad infinitum* the type of centrally symmetric distribution used, but, as yet, there are no rules (even empirical ones) allowing us to choose *a priori* the distribution adequate to the only problem that it appears necessary to solve. Let us note in addition that central symmetry is not necessarily a good idea in itself, because in general it does not reflect the structure of the function the minimum of which is sought. An interesting compromise to try to mitigate this problem is the use of judiciously centered and oriented ellipsoids.

8.3.6. *Adjusted ellipsoids*

In this method, one replaces each of the two D-rectangles of the traditional method (distribution 1) by an ellipsoid not depending on the coordinate system. Let us give the algorithm building these ellipsoids:

– definition of the center: $q = x + c_{max}(p-x)/2$;

– construction of the sphere of center q and $\rho = \|q - x\|$;

– calculation of volume V of the cube of diagonal 2ρ;

– deformation of the sphere, perpendicular to the vector $p - x$, in order to obtain an ellipsoid of volume V' less than V. The ratio V'/V can be a parameter or, better, V' is randomly selected in the interval $[0, V]$. It is this last method that was adopted in the examples treated below. Then we obtain a support of distribution denoted E_p;

– in the same way, obtain the support of distribution for g, E_g.

The condensed equations defining the distribution are then:

Distribution 7

$$\begin{cases} v \leftarrow c_1 v + c_2 alea(E_p) + c_3 alea(E_g) \\ x \leftarrow x + v \end{cases}$$

Figure 8.3 shows the result obtained in dimension 2, with $V' = V$. This method has the theoretical advantage of giving a distribution that no longer depends on the coordinate system. Like that of pivots, it can easily be adapted for isotropic distributions others than the sphere (e.g. Gaussian). Volume is then calculated by

Distributions of Proximity   113

setting a threshold of probability, such as 95%. However, in practice, it does not seem to give better results, while requiring more computing time. Nevertheless, this is a provisional judgment, based only on restricted benchmark sets. At the time of writing, no real published application has used this method.

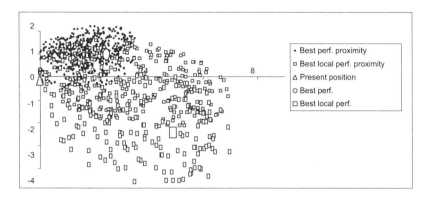

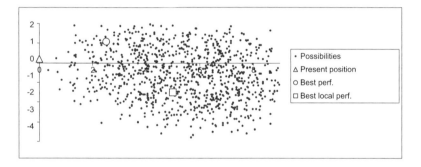

Figure 8.3. *Distribution of possibilities by combination of oriented ellipsoids. The result is independent of the coordinate system but, in practice, the method does not seem to be more effective than those already seen, while being greedier in computing times*

8.4. Some comparisons of results

To make it possible to continue the comparison with OEP 0, only the distributions are modified. The other parameters remain unchanged ($N = M = 20$, $K = 3$, random graph of information $\varphi = 2.07$).

Table 8.1 shows the very contrasting results that one obtains with the first two alternatives: the method of ellipsoidal positive sectors and that of pivots. Hence, the idea of combining them in an astute way, the method of pivots being called to the rescue during an iteration, only if the other did not improve during the preceding iteration. On the benchmark set, the improvement in performance is significant, and we will reconsider this idea of judicious modification of strategy in the chapter on the adaptive PSO.

Name	Ellipsoidal positive sectors	Pivots	Sectors if improvement, pivots if not
Tripod	53%	41%	34%
Alpine 10D	0%	81%	52%
Parabola 30D	0%	58%	0%
Griewank 30D	59%	14%	21%
Rosenbrock 30D	100% (30.9)	100% (52)	100% (38)
Ackley 30D	60%	0%	2%
Average of the rates of failure	42%	49%	34%

Table 8.1. *Results with two distributions of possibilities (ellipsoidal positive sectors and pivots) and their combination. The method of pivots presents a profile of effectiveness according to problems which supplements rather well that of the method of ellipsoidal positive sectors. Their judicious combination gives an intermediate performance for each function and the total improvement is appreciable*

We can also examine the results for two of the other distributions presented, independent Gaussians and oriented ellipsoids (see Table 8.2). The profiles of effectiveness are then, on the contrary, rather similar (except for the Alpine function). Thus the intermediate profile obtained by combination of the two distributions cannot be better on the whole than the initial profiles. The table presents only one of the two possible combinations (Gaussian if improvement, ellipsoids if not), but the other is even less interesting.

Name	Independent Gaussians	Oriented ellipsoids	Gaussians if improvement, ellipsoids if not
Tripod	41%	33%	36%
Alpine 10D	1%	81%	15%
Parabola 30D	0%	0%	0%
Griewank 30D	55%	71%	48%
Rosenbrock 30D	100% (32.3)	100% (24.7)	100% (27)
Ackley 30D	76%	100%	92%
Average of the rates of failure	45%	64%	49%

Table 8.2. *Results with two distributions of possibilities (independent Gaussians and oriented ellipsoids) and their combination. Here the profiles of effectiveness are too similar. As the combination of the two types of distribution still gives intermediate performances between two which are close enough for all the functions except one, the final result is also intermediary and, therefore, uninteresting*

Among all the methods we have looked at, the best combination is that of alternating pivots with noise and Gaussian pivots, as we can see in Table 8.3. This confirms, if it were necessary, that a statement of the equations of motion clarifying velocity is not in itself necessary. Velocity is only an intuitive intermediate variable, but it can perfectly well be replaced by another more abstract concept: the random choice of the next position according to a probability distribution judiciously modified after each iteration.

At the risk of repetition (but the point is so significant that it is worth emphasizing), all the stochastic algorithms can in the last analysis be described in terms of such random choices, whatever the underlying metaphors and the level of sophistication of the rules of operation.

It is also clear that each distribution is better adapted to some types of problems than others. More generally, if we consider all the control parameters at the user's disposal, we can ask, for each problem, which are the best possible performances if the number of attempts to find the good parameters is not limited.

Name	Pivots with noise	Gaussian pivots	Pivots with noise if improvement, Gaussian pivots if not
Tripod	20%	51%	40%
Alpine 10D	0%	85%	2%
Parabola 30D	0%	8%	0%
Griewank 30D	100%	18%	25%
Rosenbrock 30D	100% (25.6)	100% (41)	100% (25.5)
Ackley 30D	0%	0%	0%
Average of the rates of failure	37%	44%	29%

Table 8.3. *Results with two distributions of possibilities (disturbed pivots and Gaussian pivots). The good performance of the method of pivots with noise by itself can already be seen, but it is further improved by combination with the method of Gaussian pivots, primarily because degradation is very low for Alpine and improvement very clear for Griewank*

The object of the next chapter is to drive the parametric PSO into a corner, while trying to understand in passing why one set of parameters is more suitable for a given problem than another.

8.5. For "amatheurs"

8.5.1. *Squaring of a hypersphere*

We have already seen, in Chapter 1, the formulas giving the volume of a sphere in D dimensions, according to whether D is even or odd. Let us consider, for example, the first case. If the radius is ρ, volume $V_S(D,\rho)$ is given by:

$$V_S(D,\rho) = \frac{\pi^{D/2}}{(D/2)!}\rho^D$$

The volume of a cube of edge a in D dimensions is $V_C(D,a) = a^D$. By equalizing these two volumes, one finds the relation:

$$\rho = a\frac{(D/2)!^{1/D}}{\sqrt{\pi}}$$

If D odd, one would find in the same way, $\rho = a \dfrac{D!^{1/D} \pi^{1/2D}}{2\sqrt{\pi}}$.

The coefficient $v(D) = \rho/a$ is used to calculate the radius for the "spherical" proximities. Table 8.4 gives the values corresponding to dimensions of the benchmark set.

D	$v(D)$
2	0.56
10	0.91
30	1.43

Table 8.4. *Squaring of a D-sphere. For a D-sphere of radius ρ and a D-cube of edge a to have the same volume, the ratio ρ/A must have the value v(D)*

8.5.2. From sphere to ellipsoid

Any point m of the sphere of center $q = c_{max}(p-x)$ (resp. $q = c_{max}(g-x)$) and radius $\rho = \|q - x\|$ can be written $m = x + \lambda(q-x) + v$, where v is the vector normal to $q-x$. By carrying out the scalar product by $q-x$, one deduces from it immediately $\lambda = (m-x).(q-x)/\|q-x\|^2$ and, therefore, vector v. To build an ellipsoid of which one of the axes is 2ρ and volume V' is given, it is enough to consider the set of points, $m' = x + \lambda(q-x) + \omega v$, with:

$$\omega = \left(\dfrac{V'}{V_S(D, \rho)} \right)^{\frac{1}{D-1}}$$

8.5.3. Random volume for an adjusted ellipsoid

In the traditional method with rectangular distributions, the D-rectangle of diagonal $\|q-x\|$ has a variable volume V_v according to the coordinate system chosen, which goes from 0 to $V = \left(\|q-x\|/\sqrt{D}\right)^D$. The law of probability followed by V_v is not uniform.

The rectangular distribution is replaced by a distribution according to an ellipsoid of principal diameter $\|q-x\|$ and volume V'. The idea is to choose V'

randomly according to the same law as V_v. In practice, it is carried out by an algorithm according to the following stages:

– choice of a point *m* randomly (uniformly) on the sphere of center O (origin of the coordinates) and of diameter $\|q - x\|$ (see below for uniform distribution in a D-sphere);

– calculation of volume. $V' = \prod_{d=1}^{D} |m_d|$.

8.5.4. *Uniform distribution in a D-sphere*

The first idea that comes to mind when writing a program that returns a position resulting from a uniform distribution in a D-sphere is to start from a program that does it for the envelope D-cube, by making it buckle until the point obtained is indeed in the sphere.

But this method is acceptable only for lower values of *D*, because the ratio of volume of the sphere to that of the cube tends quickly towards zero as *D* increases. The probability of randomly picking a point in the cube that it is also in the sphere thus becomes very low: the program will take a very long time to complete.

So a direct method is preferable. The simplest rests on a well-known fact from astronomy: a vector that points randomly towards a position on the night sky according to a uniform distribution has components that follow the same normal law. This gives us a method for points that are on the surface of the sphere, i.e. in fact, for the choice of a uniform random direction. It is then enough also to define the radius randomly, according to the law $alea(0,1)^{1/D}$, to guarantee the uniformity in the volume of the sphere.

If one wishes, on the contrary, a non-uniform (but still isotropic) distribution, it is enough to change the law of distribution of the radius. For example, for a normal distribution (and, in this case, naturally, there is no longer a "sphere" inside which the points would be), the law to be taken is $rand\_normal(0,\sigma)^{1/D}$

The C program of section 8.6 carries out these various operations, as well as other non-uniform distributions restricted to the sphere.

8.6. C program of isotropic distribution

```
struct vector alea_sphere(int D, double radius, double unif)
/ * randomly Provides a point in a D-sphere
or according to an isotropic normal distribution
Maurice Clerc 2003-07-11

Center 0
```

```
  unif = 1 = > uniform distribution
  unif > 0 but # 1 = > distribution nonuniform
  unif < 0 = > Gaussian, with standard deviation = abs(unif)
  */

  int        j;
  double     l;
  double     pw;

  double     r;
  double     sigma;
  struct     vector x;

  x.taille = D;
  pw = 1/(double)D;

  // Stage 1. Random direction
  //It is a theorem...
  l= 0;
  for (j = 0;j < D;j++)
  x.v[j] = alea_normal(0,1); l= 1+ x.v[j]*x.v[j];
  l= sqrt(l);
  / Stage 2. Random radius
  if (unif > 0)
  r = alea(0,1); r = pow(r, pw*unif);
  else
  sigma = -unif; r = fabs(alea_normal(0, sigma)); r = pow(r, pw);

  for (j = 0;j < D;j++) x.v[j] = rayon*r*x.v[j]/l;

  return x;
```

8.7. Summary

The equations of motion of a particle contain random terms. By considering all the values they can take and their probabilities, one defines the distribution of the next possible positions. Two great families of alternatives are considered: those using independent distributions for each dimension, as in traditional PSO, and those not related on the coordinate system but only to the relative positions of the particles, like the method of pivots.

The judicious use of one or other alternative according to whether there was or not improvement during an iteration can improve the performances appreciably.

Chapter 9

Optimal Parameter Settings

9.1. Defense of manual parameter setting

One often contrasts adaptive optimization (which, ideally, only requires the user to define the problem) with parametric optimization (which, in addition, requires the method of resolution to be specified, if only by giving certain numerical coefficients). However, the border between these two types of methods is vague. Thus, for example, the alternation of several distributions of proximities used in the preceding chapter can be seen as a kind of adaptation, if it is not made randomly.

In addition, when a problem is repetitive, with only some numerical variations that change neither its difficulty nor its nature, it will be worthwhile to seek a set of effective parameters, even if it means carrying out many tests. Conversely, when the problem is to be solved only a small number of times or when it really would be prohibitive to seek to refine parameters, an adaptive method should be considered.

In short, the two steps are complementary and this is why it is interesting to see up to what point the parametric PSO can be effective, case by case. Moreover, that will give us a basis of comparison or, more precisely, a "guiding utopia": the goal, generally inaccessible, for an adaptive PSO will be to be as effective on any given problem as a parametric PSO ideally configured for that problem.

9.2. Better parameter settings for the benchmark set

9.2.1. *Search space*

All the parameters we have seen can be gathered in four sets:
 – the graph of information, which gives the size of explorer-swarm N, the size of memory-swarm M, and the links between the various particles,
  – possible distributions of proximity,
  – strategies of evolution of the graph of information,
  – strategies of choice of the distributions.

Here we temporarily deny ourselves every real adaptation during the process, i.e. a parameter will be either constant or modified absolutely randomly without taking into account the information collected. In particular, we thus give up the strategies already seen consisting of making a particular choice of topology and proximity according to whether there were improvements or not.

Even so, the possibilities are too numerous. For example, for the topology of the graph of information, the number of configurations is equal to $\left(2^M-1\right)^N \left(2^N-1\right)^M 2^{M(M-1)}$. If $M = N = 20$, it is about 10^{355}. Obviously testing all of them is out of the question! In fact – and this will be justified *a posteriori* by the good results obtained – we will restrict ourselves to the topologies defined by only two parameters: the number of informants per particle K and the manner of choosing these informants. More drastic still, we will consider only two types of choice of informant: circular fixed topology or random choice with each iteration.

Again to simplify, the three coefficients of the general equation of motion, c_1, c_2, and c_3, will be defined only *via* the coefficient φ, which we saw in Chapter 6 for the establishment of the performance maps. Moreover, precisely, these maps will enable us to limit the range of plausible values, besides that for the size N of the explorer-swarm.

Finally, the choice of distributions will be limited to those we have already examined. The list (with abbreviations) is as follows:
 1 (rect.): = rectangles,
 2 (ell. pos. sect): = ellipsoidal positive sectors,
 3 (ind. gauss.): = independent Gaussians,
 4 (piv.): = pivots,
 5 (piv. n.):= pivots with noise,
 6 (piv. G.): = Gaussian pivots,
 7 (ell. adj.): = adjusted ellipsoids.

We will not even test the various combinations randomly: once again, they are too numerous. Each test will be carried out with only one type of distribution.

Table 9.1 then recapitulates the acceptable parameters and their values, defining a search space. It will be a question of finding, for each problem of the benchmark set, the position in this space that provides the best result, i.e. the set of parameters that gives the lowest rate of failure or, failing this, if the rate of failure is 100%, the low value of the function.

Parameter	Range
N, size of the explorer-swarm	integer, 5 to 100
M, size of the memory-swarm	integer, 5 to 100
K, number of informants per particle	integer, 2 with N
φ	real number, in $]2\ 2,5]$
topology	circular or random
Distribution	7 possible cases

Table 9.1. *Space parameters. Here acceptable values are severely limited, constraints justified* a posteriori *by the quality of the results obtained*

9.2.2. *To optimize the optimizer*

We are now facing a second-level problem of optimization. Let us consider a function f to be minimized by our algorithm of parametric PSO. In our examples, the stop criterion is a given number T of evaluations of f. The stages are as follows:

(a) choose a set of parameters;
(b) carry out the algorithm for T evaluations;
(c) examine the result, to decide if it can be improved. In so, return to (a).

It is indeed a process aiming at "optimizing the optimizer", at least for the function f. The problem can be formulated as follows:

– search space = space of the parameters;

– function to be minimized = function that, at any point of the search space, returns the performance obtained after the attempt at minimization of f.

In theory, it is thus enough to use an algorithm that can call itself, but there are two pitfalls. First, this algorithm should already be parameterized. A parameter setting with average empirical values will do. But, in addition and especially, the evaluation of each point of the search space requires T evaluations of the function f.

In our examples, T is worth at most 40,000. The search space for the parameters is of dimension 6. By experiment, we can infer that we probably have to evaluate a few thousand points of this space to find the best solution. Let us say, modestly, 2,000. Moreover, the algorithm being stochastic, it should be launched typically 100 times to estimate its performances statistically. Finally, obtaining the (probable) best set of parameters will have required 40,000 ×2,000 ×100 = 8 billion evaluations of the function f.

Name	N	M	φ	K	Topology	Distribution of the possible positions	Rate of failure (average Number of eval.)
Tripod	53	12	2.3	3	random	2 (ell. pos. sect)	0% (2,603)
	80	19	2.3	3	random	7 (ell. gold.)	0% (4,111)
Alpine 10D *	6	8		4	random	5 (piv. n.)	0% (194)
Parabola 30D	6	4		10	random	5 (piv. n.)	0% (88)
Griewank 30D	96	96	2.12	3	random	2 (ell. pos. sect)	2%
Rosenbrock 30D	58	29	2.3	3	random	3 (ind. gauss.)	100% min. 0.034 avg. 19.93
Ackley 30D *	20	20		3	random	5 (piv. n.)	0% (2,394)

Table 9.2. *Best parameters (without adaptation). The rates of failure are estimated after 100 evaluations. If they are null, the average number of evaluations has a significance and is also indicated. Since the rate of failure for Rosenbrock is 100%, the average and best failure rates are given instead. For distribution 5 (pivots with noise) the parameter φ is not used. The asterisk indicates a parameter setting discovered or imposed empirically and not by an automatic process*

It is possible, but nevertheless a little long and, above all, not always necessary in this case, thanks to the performance maps established previously. In practice, the results indicated in Table 8.1 were found manually for the functions indicated by an asterisk. Even for the others, automatic optimization was limited, then refined by manual local research. In all cases, we tried to favor the solutions with $N = M$, in order to approach the traditional PSO, which does not distinguish explorer-swarm and memory-swarm.

9.2.3. *Analysis of results*

Such a table is more informative than appears at first sight, in particular from the perspective of designing a future robust adaptive algorithm. We shall comment on it column by column, starting with the last.

9.2.3.1. *Rate of failure*

Even for problems considered difficult, it is possible to obtain excellent results. Of course, possible does not mean easy or economic. As we have seen, the search of the optimal parameters can be very expensive. But that shows that the guiding principles of PSO are good. Then it is for us to use them as best as we can, thanks to sufficiently astute alternatives, for example by combining several types of topologies and distributions during the process, as we have already started to do.

9.2.3.2. *Distribution*

The most effective distributions are distributed equitably between two classes: one-dimensional independent ones that depend on each dimension (Gaussian and ellipsoidal positive sectors) and multidimensional (pivots with noise).

To obtain a robust algorithm, it is thus a parameter on which we will undoubtedly have to rely, by alternating two distributions, one of each class.

9.2.3.3. *Topology and the number of informants*

By reading the table in the negative, we note that the fixed topology (circular) does not appear: it is always bettered by the random one varying with each iteration. Complementary tests with other fixed topologies, not detailed here, confirm this conclusion. We find a very general principle: in the absence of information, it is better to choose at random.

Of course, it is likely that for an adaptive algorithm that takes into account the information collected during the process the random choice is no longer the best. However, the lesson to draw from it is that to preserve a fixed topology is certainly not a good idea.

9.2.3.4. *Informants K*

We note without surprise that it is better that each particle has few informants as soon as the problem comprises several local minima. As we have already seen, that makes it possible to avoid premature convergences.

On the contrary, as the example of the Parabola function shows, an entirely connected swarm of particles is more effective if there are no local minima. Nevertheless, the choice $K = 3$ remains completely acceptable. Consequently, it is most relevant if there is no information *a priori* on the form of the landscape generated by the function to minimize.

Let us recall that when the topology of the information links is randomly selected, K is in fact a mean value for the number of informants. A memory drawing at random K explorers to inform may happen to choose the same one several times (see Chapter 7) and a given particle may be informed by more than K others.

9.2.3.5. *Coefficient* φ

We know that this parameter is used to calculate the confidence coefficients of the "traditional" alternatives, in which the components of the next movement are calculated independently for each dimension. However, for the distributions with pivot, it is useless, which is a point in their favor.

The pure and simple later suppression of this parameter is thus quite tempting. However, as we have just seen, not using it sometimes results in not finding the best solution. Always from the perspective of a future nonparametric algorithm, it will be advisable to examine carefully whether this occasional loss of performance is significant or not.

9.2.3.6. *Informants N and memories M*

As we have said, the case $N = M$ was deliberately privileged. It is thus probable that other values lead to the same result. Moreover, for example, for the Tripod function, it does not seem possible to obtain a zero rate of failure in any other way than by having approximately three to four times more explorers than memories. If the behavior of the particles is examined accurately, that seems related to the fact that there are three minima, of which only one is global. This empirical remark seems to be confirmed by the case of the Rosenbrock function. But it is useful only if there is *a priori* knowledge of the number of minima of the studied function.

As a result, it seems tempting, for a function with only one minimum, like Parabola, to try to work with only one memory. That does not work: at least three of them are required so that mechanism PSO can function correctly. The difference is extremely clear. The result is not reported in the table, but with only one memory, the rate of failure is always 100%, whereas one can easily go down to 2% with three.

Another remark relates to the existence of a relation between the choice of the type of distribution and the number of particles. When the best performance is obtained thanks to a distribution with pivot, fewer particles are required than if it is thanks to a distribution with independent dimensions. By caricaturing a little, we are in the presence of two steps which can each be as effective as the other, but are based on rather different principles: crude force, which moves many particles without being concerned with possible relations between their coordinates; and reasoned strategy, which tries on the contrary to benefit from it.

The results we have seen up to now really do not make it possible to give preference to one or the other method, but the very idea of a permanent adaptation tilts the balance in favor of the second, because it implies using all the information one has as best as one can.

9.3. Towards adaptation

On our benchmark set, we have now established results that are most probably the best possible ones if we force the algorithm of PSO to work in a relatively stupid way, i.e. by refusing any training in the course of its research.

Will a more intelligent alternative be able to do better? Perhaps, but it is not exactly our objective. What interests us is the fact that we have been able to define a standard by the yardstick of which other algorithms could be evaluated, in particular adaptive algorithms, in a sense that will soon be specified. And also, at the same time, we have been able in passing to note some ideas that ought to help us design such algorithms.

It is time to return to and develop the small amount of adaptation we introduced into the two preceding chapters. But that will be done according to a step which, at first sight, sets aside all methods not satisfying certain demanding criteria.

9.4. For "amatheurs": number of graphs of information

We have an explorer-swarm of N particles and a memory-swarm of M particles. The possible links are of three types:
 – of an explorer towards a memory,
 – of a memory towards an explorer,
 – of a memory towards a memory.

The number of possible links of N particles towards M different is NM. Each link, to establish a graph of information, can be selected or not. That gives us 2^{NM} possible cases. In the same way, by considering the links of M particles, we still have 2^{NM} possible cases. Finally, the number of links of M particles towards themselves is $M(M-1)$, which still gives $2^{M(M-1)}$ possible cases. The total number of configurations is thus the product of these three numbers, that is to say $2^{NM}2^{NM}2^{M(M-1)} = 2^{2NM+M^2-M}$.

In practice, however, we have imposed constraints (see Chapter 7):
- each explorer has a link towards at least 1 memory,
- each memory has a link towards at least 1 explorer.

Under these conditions, the first two numbers are reduced to $\left(2^M-1\right)^N$ and $\left(2^N-1\right)^M$. Indeed, for each particle, it is necessary to eliminate the case "no link towards the others".

The total number of configurations is reduced to:

$$\left(2^M-1\right)^N \left(2^N-1\right)^M 2^{M(M-1)}$$

But the reduction is very small and the result remains enormous. For the average case $N = M = 20$, one finds a number about 10^{355}.

9.5. Summary

One considers here only one algorithm of PSO without adaptation, i.e. which does not modify its behavior according to information collected during the search process. Very many tests then make it possible to find the parameters that give the best result for each function of the benchmark set.

The excellent quality of these results shows that the guiding principles of PSO are effective. However, it is not realistic to think that the user will always have the possibility of lengthily seeking an adequate parameter setting for his problem. This is why the optimal parameter settings here discovered are analysed in order to infer their indices as for the rules of behavior which should follow a robust and practical adaptive algorithm.

Chapter 10

Adaptations

10.1. Demanding criteria

The terms "adaptation", with "adaptive algorithm", cover so many different realities that it is advisable to specify in what very restrictive meaning they are taken here.

10.1.1. *Criterion 1*

First, and this has been expressed previously in one form or another, an adaptive algorithm must treat at least part of the information it obtains by exploring the search space and consequently modify its behavior. An immediate corollary is that such an algorithm is necessarily iterative.

10.1.2. *Criterion 2*

In addition, we are only interested here in algorithms that make life easier for the user, i.e., in practice, those that decrease the number of parameters whose values one has to choose.

This criterion is much more demanding than the previous one, because, if it is easy to invent rules of adaptation comprising the additional parameters dependent on the user, it is much less easy to relieve one of the empirical choice of a parameter thanks to an automatic process he does not have to bother about.

10.2. Rough sketches

Attempts to give a little more flexibility to the mechanisms of PSO began just after its official birth [EBE 96]. A rapid glance at the principal ones is not only of historical interest. In fact, it is only on the basis of inspiration from these attempts that it is possible today to present a version that respects our two criteria, as we will see in the following chapter.

None of these alternatives is completely satisfactory because, at best, they remove only some of the parameters and, at worst, they add some. However, a meticulous examination of them makes it possible to note that the underlying ideas can sometimes be retranscribed in nonparametric forms and thus be usable for the step chosen here.

10.2.1. *Weighting with temporal decrease*

Once more, let us point out the basic equations of the historical PSO:

$$\begin{cases} v_d \leftarrow c_1 v_d + c_{\max} alea(0,1)(p_d - x_d) + c_{\max} alea(0,1)(g_d - x_d) \\ x_d \leftarrow x_d + v_d \end{cases}$$

The coefficient c_1, which can be interpreted as the confidence that the particle grants to its own movement, has up to now been regarded as constant. It is thus rather natural to try to vary it. Let us note immediately that a simple random choice would not answer either of the two criteria seen above. On the one hand, this method would not take into account the information collected and, on the other hand, defining the probability distribution for random draw would require defining at least one new parameter.

A method that has been much used is one that consists of making this coefficient decrease over the course of time, each iteration representing a time increment [EBE 96, ISM 99, SHI 98B, VAN 99]. Typically, the law of decrease gives a value tending asymptotically towards zero. The idea is that when the iteration count increases, then the algorithm is probably converging (at least one hopes so) and, therefore, it is better to make the particles progress more and more slowly in order not to miss the optimum.

In certain applications this intuition appears exact, but compared to our requirements, we see immediately where the shoe pinches: the definition of the law of decrease requires at least one parameter (often two, in fact). Moreover, to tell the truth, even criterion 1 is not frankly respected. An evolution of parameters

Adaptations 131

depending only on the iteration count can be seen only as an extremely indirect and dubious manner of processing the data obtained during these same iterations.

Indeed, this method rests on a self-fulfilling prediction: convergence will improve with the iteration count. That is inevitably true since making the coefficient c_1 decrease amounts on the whole to making all the velocities decrease. There will therefore be a convergence towards a quasi-stationary state. However, nothing guarantees that one of the positions obtained will be the minimum sought. And, in fact, it is necessary for each problem to seek empirically a definition of the function of decrease that will make it possible to find a solution without taking too much time but also without premature convergence.

10.2.2. *Selection and replacement*

PSO is much more recent than the genetic algorithms and it was thus natural to seek to take advantage of at least some of the principles of the latter, since they proved reliable in a number of applications. The principles of mutation and crossover have their analogues in PSO (velocity and combination of information). But it is not the case for selection, i.e. the elimination of individuals considered insufficiently effective. It is even completely contrary to the "philosophy" of PSO, which we saw at the very beginning and which rests on cooperation and not, precisely, on competition. Nevertheless, dogmatism is not a proper philosophy in research, and if a PSO with selection appears interesting one should not hesitate to use it.

Historically, the first attempt goes back to 1998 [ANG 98]. Obviously, this step respects our first criterion, since an action is undertaken which takes into account the situation obtained after each iteration. In fact, the selection consisted in eliminating 50% of individuals that had obtained no such good results and replacing them by individuals generated by traditional crossover between those remaining, or by mutations. Let us note, therefore, that this method always requires the size (constant) of the swarm to be defined as a preliminary.

The second criterion is almost satisfied, or at least it would have been if the percentage of individuals to be eliminated could have been ignored by the user. Unfortunately, the tests showed that the performances could be better overall than those of the traditional PSO only if the value of this percentage were adjusted for each problem. Ultimately it was thus an additional parameter.

However, that made it possible to show that selection could indeed sometimes improve PSO. Therefore the method below again takes this principle, as well as others, but with a significant difference: the comparisons of performance are done only locally (in a sense which we will specify immediately), which makes it possible to adjust them much more finely and, especially, the size of the swarm is no longer constant.

10.2.3. *Parametric adaptations*

A more sophisticated method of selection was then implemented, with good results [ZHA 03a]. To explain it, let us return to the primitive terminology, in which each particle has a memory and some neighbors, the memory containing the best performance carried out. The equations of motion are those using the coefficient of constriction χ [CLE 02], i.e. the confidence coefficients are calculated according to only one parameter φ:

$$\begin{cases} c_1 = \chi = \dfrac{1}{\varphi - 1 + \sqrt{\varphi^2 - 2\varphi}} \\ c_{max} = \varphi c_1 \end{cases}$$

The comparisons of performance are made only locally, i.e., for each particle tested, one considers only its neighborhood (which means all of its neighbors). The idea is that if at least one of the particles of the neighborhood (which, as we recall, includes the particle itself) "sufficiently" improved its performance, then one can remove the worst particle of the aforesaid neighborhood. Now, however, even if the best particle did not sufficiently improve its performance, one generates a new particle (completely at random, in fact).

Thus, the size of the swarm being variable, one can deal with all the problems while always starting with the same small number of particles (at least 2, so that the adaptations can get underway).

The threshold of improvement Δ defining "sufficiently" is itself modified with each removal or generation of particles, according to both its preceding value and the current size of the swarm. Its first value is calculated simply after the initialization of the swarm, by the formula $\Delta = 1 - f_{min}/f_{max}$, where f_{min} and f_{max} are respectively the smallest and the greatest values of the function to be minimized found by the swarm.

The size of the neighborhood is also modified by a similar step, formalizing the intuitive rule that if a particle improves its performances, it does not need to continue to get informed by many neighbors and conversely.

Lastly, the parameter φ is itself adjusted after each iteration. When there was improvement, it is increased, which thus decreases the confidence coefficients and restricted volume explorable by the particle during the next displacement, and conversely.

The disadvantage, again, is that whenever we say formulas we necessarily mean parameters. Let us make the assessment. The traditional PSO, the starting point of this method, requires four parameters:
– size of the swarm;
– the number of neighbors per particle;
– two confidence coefficients.

Now, we have:
– a formula for the variable size of the swarm (a parameter);
– a formula for the variable size of the neighborhood (a parameter);
– a formula for the variation of the coefficient φ (two parameters).

Thus, there is no improvement in the total number of parameters depending on the user. However, as we will see, it is possible to take up these ideas by replacing the formulas with rules without qualitative rather than quantitative parameters.

10.2.4. *Nonparametric adaptations*

We saw, in the preceding chapters, two methods that are already adaptive, since they rest on the criterion "there was improvement after the iteration". Let us briefly point them out:
  – rule 1: if there has been no improvement, modify the topology of the information links at random;
  – rule 2: if there has been improvement, use the type of distributions of proximity X, if not use Y.

Let us note that they strictly respect our two criteria. That is obvious for the first. For the second, it is enough to note that the decision whether or not there has been improvement does not require the use of an additional parameter. It is enough to compare the best result obtained after the iteration with that known before this iteration.

To be completely honest, the number of parameters will not really fall and the term "nonparametric" will be justified only if distributions X and Y are not to be defined by the user. We should therefore find a pair (X, Y) sufficiently robust to give good results whatever the function to minimize. Once again, let us list the distributions we have studied:

- "with independent dimensions" (one-dimensional) class:

    1 (rect.): = rectangles;

    2 (ell. pos. sect.): = ellipsoidal positive sectors ;

    3 (ind. gauss): = independent Gaussians;

    3' (loc. ind. gauss.): = local by independent Gaussians.

- "multidimensional" class:

    4 (piv.): = pivots;

    5 (piv. n.): = pivots with noise;

    6 (piv. G.): = Gaussian pivots;

    7 (ell. adj.): = adjusted ellipsoidal.

We already know that good candidates are such that X belongs to the class of one-dimensional distributions and Y, on the contrary, to that of multidimensional distributions. However, the distributions of the first class still require the data of a parameter. Nevertheless, the ideal would thus be to find a pair whose two elements are second class.

We have thus *a priori* $4^3 + 3^4 = 155$ combinations to study. Let us note that intuition is a bad adviser here. A plausible *a priori* rule might be that Y, to activate when there no was improvement, has a support of volume greater than that of X, to extend exploration. For example, the pair (4,5) satisfies this condition, but not its reverse (5,4). But, in fact, with the pair (5,4), one obtains an average rate of failure of 39%, against only 28% with the pair (4,5). The latter is therefore better.

The reason is that the ratchet effect plays a role and it seems that the empirical rule is rather this one: a good particle, which in any case remembers its best performance, can afford to rove more than another that is not so good, which must, on the contrary, move more prudently.

To facilitate the comparisons, the values of the other parameters are those already used in the preceding chapters: $N = M = 20$, $K = 3$, $\varphi = 2.07$. The topology of the information links is still randomly selected, but, in agreement with rule 1, it is not necessarily modified any more with each iteration, but only if there is no improvement. The best three combinations of distributions for rule 2 are then indicated in Table 10.1.

Name	Rule 1 Rule 2 (5,4)	Rule 1 Rule 2 (3,5)	Rule 1 Rule 2 (2,5)
Tripod	45%	31%	29%
Alpine 10D	5%	0%	0%
Parabola 30D	0%	0%	0%
Griewank 30D	20%	96%	100%
Rosenbrock 30D	100% 25.68	100% 24.31	100% 25.29
Ackley 30D	0%	0%	0%
Average of the rates of failure	28.3%	37.8%	38.2%

Table 10.1. *Adaptations according to rules 1 and 2. Three best combinations of distributions for rule 2 and the benchmark set. The values indicated are the percentages of failure noted over 100 tests. For Rosenbrock the average of the best values obtained during each test has been added*

We note that distribution 5 (disturbed pivots) is present each time, but it is difficult to draw any other information from this table. In addition, we saw in Chapter 9 that in certain cases the performances can be appreciably improved by making the number of memories different from that of explorers. However, at present, the adaptive alternatives are founded on the traditional PSO with only one type of particle. Obviously, they did not seek simultaneously to modulate a memory-swarm and an explorer-swarm.

This is however equally true for the rather complete case that we will look at in the following chapter, which presents thus the possibility for obvious improvement.

10.3. For "amateurs"

10.3.1. *Formulas of temporal decrease*

The formulas used by various authors are not always clarified in their articles, where they often indicate simply something like "the coefficient is decreasing from 1 to 0.4 over 10,000 iterations". However, reading the source codes of the programs used makes it possible to find them. They are primarily of three types: linear, nonlinear with threshold, and asymptotic.

By noting t the current moment (the iteration), T a given time, one has the following possible expressions:

– Linear:

$$\begin{cases} t < T \Rightarrow w(t) = 1 - \dfrac{t}{T}(1 - w_{min}) \\ t \geq T \Rightarrow w(t) = w_{min} \end{cases}$$

– Nonlinear with threshold (example of quadratic formula):

$$\begin{cases} t < T \Rightarrow w(t) = \dfrac{1 - w_{min}}{T^2}(T - t)^2 + w_{min} \\ t \geq T \Rightarrow w(t) = w_{min} \end{cases}$$

– Asymptotic (exponential example):

$$w(t) = (1 - w_{min})e^{-\lambda t} + w_{min}$$

In this last case, one can generally easily choose 0 as minimal value, by adjusting differently the parameter λ. The formula then becomes simply:

$$w(t) = e^{-\lambda t}$$

10.3.2. *Parametric adaptations*

The presentation below comes primarily from [ZHA 03a]. The improvement of performance of a particle P_i is given by:

$$\delta(P_i) = \dfrac{f(P_i(t_0)) - f(P_i(t))}{f(P_i(t_0))}$$

where t_0 is the moment of birth of the particle, t the current moment and $f(P_i(t))$ the value of the function to be minimized at the point of the search space where the particle is located at the moment t.

The initial threshold of improvement is given by $\Delta = 1 - f_{min}/f_{max}$, where the values f_{min} and f_{max} are respectively the smallest and greatest value of the function to be minimized found after initialization of the swarm randomly in the search space. It is then modified by the following formulas, where N is the current size of the swarm:

- $\Delta = \Delta(2-e^{-N})$ when a particle has been just eliminated;
- $\Delta = \Delta/(2-e^{-N})$ when a particle has been just generated.

In addition, the parameter φ_i associated with the particle P_i in the equation of motion is also modified, in two different ways according to whether the particle improved its position or not:

$$\begin{cases} m_i = \delta(P_i) - \Delta \\ m_i \geq 0 \Rightarrow \delta\varphi = (\varphi_{max} - \varphi_i)m_i \\ m_i < 0 \Rightarrow \begin{cases} \lambda = (\varphi_{max} - \varphi_i)/(\varphi_i - \varphi_{min}) \\ \delta\varphi = (\varphi_i - \varphi_{min})\left((1-m_i)^{-\lambda} - 1\right) \end{cases} \\ \varphi_i := \varphi_i + \delta\varphi \end{cases}$$

The intermediate variable m_i evaluates how much the improvement is greater or less than the current threshold. Two cases are possible:

10.3.2.1. *Case 1* ($m_i \geq 0$)

The particle really improved its position or, at least, did not deteriorate it. Thus, it is not necessary for it to continue to explore a broad field. It is then possible to increase φ_i, i.e. to decrease slightly the constriction coefficient χ, and, therefore, strive to decrease the velocity. This is why the formula gives $\delta\varphi$ positive and this all the more so as the improvement is large.

10.3.2.2. *Case 2* ($m_i < 0$)

It is the opposite. The particle did not improve its position and, therefore, its velocity must be increased a little, to explore a larger field. Then $\delta\varphi$ is negative.

Lastly, the size of the neighborhood is increased or decreased according to the formulas below, granted that the neighborhood is of the circular type:

$$\begin{cases} \delta(P_i) \geq \Delta \Rightarrow \delta|hi| := \delta|hi| - \dfrac{\delta|h_i|-1}{N-1} \\ \delta(P_i) < \Delta \Rightarrow \delta|hi| := \delta|h_i| + \dfrac{N-\delta|h_i|}{N-1} \end{cases}$$

$$\delta|h_i| \geq 1 \Rightarrow \begin{cases} h_i := h_i + 1 \\ \delta|h_i| := 0 \end{cases} \text{ and } \delta|h_i| \leq -1 \Rightarrow \begin{cases} h_i := h_i - 1 \\ \delta|hi| := 0 \end{cases}$$

If the particle improved its position, it is not necessary for it to continue to question as many neighbors as before. Conversely, if it did not improve its position, it is undoubtedly a good idea to seek more information. Let us note that since the size of the neighborhood is an integer, the modifications must accumulate in the variable $\delta|h_i|$ until it exceeds 1 or –1 before having a significant incidence.

10.4. Summary

The ultimate objective is to build an iterative algorithm of optimization that modifies its behavior according to its progressive discovery of the problem to be solved, without initial parameter setting by the user.

A rapid glance at some attempts in this direction, defining adaptive alternatives of PSO, makes it possible to detect interesting ideas that will enable us to progress largely towards this goal. In particular, the concepts of variable size of swarm, variable size of neighborhoods, and alternate use of several distributions of proximity will later be applied to a nonparametric qualitative formalization.

Chapter 11

TRIBES or Cooperation of Tribes

11.1. Towards an ultimate program

In the beginning was the one. Such could be the starting point of a process of completely autonomous PSO, insofar as it must be capable of finding a solution by having only one particle initially, but it is up to it to add or remove some advisedly. Up to now, even for the adaptive versions examined, you must not only describe the problem to solve, but also to indicate *the manner* of doing it, with instructions of the type "Begin with 20 particles", "Use a circular neighborhood" or "Weigh the velocity by a coefficient decreasing in the course of time according to the following law ...".

As we saw on several occasions, the description of the problem consists of delimiting the search space (in the simple cases by specifying for each dimension the interval of the acceptable values); indicating how to evaluate at each point of this space the function to be minimized; and, finally, specifying the maximum error permitted. Also, but by way of precaution, it is advisable to provide a safeguard, either a maximum number of evaluations, or a maximum computing time. This obviously remains necessary: the program will guess neither your problem, nor your requirement of precision! But that should also be sufficient. In other words, the method must incorporate rules defining how, at every moment, the structure of the swarm must be modified and also how a given particle must behave, all according to the information gradually collected during the process itself.

Naturally, these rules are still indirect ways of giving operating instructions to the program. The essential difference is due to the fact that you can be completely unaware of them if they are sufficiently robust and general to satisfy all your practical needs. It would be easy to hard code a rule like "Always use 20 particles", but the experiment shows that with certain types of problems, the results are extremely bad, even if they are very good with others: such a rule is not robust.

Now, precisely, what we want – speaking from the point of view of an engineer – are results which, while not always excellent, are, at least, never disastrous; the more so as a strategy of Stop/Restart can in any case improve their quality. What one gains in ease of use should logically be sometimes lost in effectiveness. It is indeed quite usual, for a given problem, that a program having to find its own parameters all alone, and this during just one execution, sometimes has poorer results than another whose parameters were lengthily polished using many tests. Thus, if one wants to make honest comparisons, for example in a number of evaluations of the function to be minimized before finding a solution, it would precisely be necessary to include these tests themselves.

The best method to prove that such a program is possible is to present one of them. We will thus describe the TRIBES program and show that it responds rather well to our definition of an easily usable black box that delivers satisfactory performances, even if, of course, improvements are possible, in particular concerning the problems with non-null granularity and, probably, by using two swarms instead of only one, for the memories and for the explorers.

Indeed, here, the swarm practically corresponds to the original definition of PSO: it is single and each particle has its own memory. The description given below comprises structural strategies of adaptation, controlling the modifications of the size of this swarm and the information links between the particles, and strategies of displacement, indicating how a given particle must change position.

We will assume initially that the search space is provided with a distance. This assumption makes it possible to define a strategy of effective displacement, founded on hyperspherical probability distributions. We will see then how, while preserving the strategies of adaptation, it is possible to define other strategies of displacement, using for example one-dimensional Gaussian probability distributions, to deal with more general problems, in particular partially combinatorial. By "combinatorial", we understand here *simple* combinatorial. As already stated, other problems, of the "traveling salesman" type, can also be treated effectively thanks to PSO, but only thanks to hybrid strategies, which are not studied in this book.

11.2. Description of TRIBES

11.2.1. *Tribes*

Let us recall that an informant of particle A is a particle B whose best memorized position can be "read" by A. This definition clearly implies that A is an informant for itself.

If each particle of the swarm is seen as the vertex of a graph, one can represent the information link by an arc of B towards A. The opposite arc, of A towards B, can exist, and does exist in the majority of versions of PSO, including this one, but it is not obligatory. In addition, as we saw in the presentation of neighborhoods and except for a particular topology, all the particles do not point towards A. We can thus define subsets (symmetrical cliques in the graph theoretical sense) such that, in each one of them, any particle points to (informs) all the others. We will call them here *tribes*, the metaphor being that of groups of individuals of variable size moving in an unknown environment, in search of a "good" site. This structuring will so to speak mechanically induce a process similar to niching in the genetic algorithms and with the same aim: simultaneously to explore several promising areas, generally around local minima.

11.2.2. *The tribal relationships*

Even if each tribe manages to find a local minimum, a group decision is necessary to determine which is the global minimum: the tribes must communicate between them. Consequently the network of information between tribes must be connected. In practice, it means that there is an information path from any particle A towards any particle B, like "A informs A1, which informs A2, ... which informs B".

Let us summarize the overall structure: within each tribe, a dense network; and, between tribes, a network simply ensuring connexity. We are typically in a graph of relations of the type "small world", which, as we have seen, has every chance of being an effective compromise between diffusion and exploitation of information [WAT 03]. But this structure must be generated and modified automatically, by means of creation, evolution, and removal of tribes.

11.2.3. *Quality of a particle*

We know that each particle has a current position and a "better performance", which is memorized. It is thus initially on this level of detail that one can say if there is progress or not. A particle will be known as *good* if it has just improved its best performance, *neutral* if not. Let us note that this definition is qualitative, one does not measure the improvement, one is satisfied with examining whether it is strictly positive (real improvement) or null (no improvement). By definition, the best performance of a particle cannot worsen, this is why one does not in the absolute define a "bad" particle. However, within a tribe, one can determine the particle whose performance is not so good. It will be called *the worst* (relative to its tribe). In the same way, one can determine *the best* particle.

Moreover, compared to the traditional PSO, the memory of the particle is improved slightly, so that it remembers its last two variations of performance, thus outlining a history of its displacements. From this, one can define a third status: a particle will be known as *excellent* if these two variations are improvements. This will be useful for us to choose the adapted strategy of displacement.

11.2.4. *Quality of a tribe*

However, what interests us here is the total performance of a tribe. We will thus define two statuses, *good* and *bad*, and will postulate a very simple fuzzy rule: "The larger the number of good particles in the tribe, the better the tribe itself and conversely".

In practice, the status of a tribe is evaluated in the following way. One considers its size T (its number of particles) and its number of good particles B (at most equal to T). A number p is generated at random between 0 and T, according to a uniform distribution. If B is less than or equal to p, the tribe is known as bad; if not, it is known as good. Rules of evolution will be associated with these statuses, tending to support the creation of new tribes and, therefore, the exploration of the search space.

11.2.5. *Evolution of the tribes*

11.2.5.1. Removal of a particle

The goal is to find the optimum, if possible with less expense, i.e. by carrying out the least possible number of evaluations of the function. Consequently, as soon as the opportunity arises to remove a particle practically without risk, it should be taken. Let us note that it is better to preserve a particle wrongly (in the worst case, one will slightly increase the number of evaluations beyond what is strictly necessary) than to eliminate one from them wrongly (with the risk of missing the solution completely). This is why only a good tribe will be able to eliminate one of its particles and only the worst of them. In the case of a monoparticle tribe, elimination will be made only if one of informants has a better performance. Indeed, one at least wants to be sure to store information of better quality than that which is going to be eliminated.

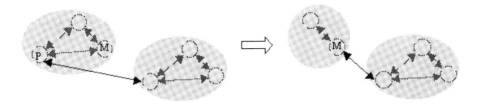

Figure 11.1. *Removal of a particle from a multiparticle tribe. The particle P is the worst of its tribe and the tribe was declared "good". In this case P is removed and the redistribution of its external links (here only one symmetrical link) is done on M, the best particle of the tribe. The information links that each particle has with itself were not represented, because they do not play any role here*

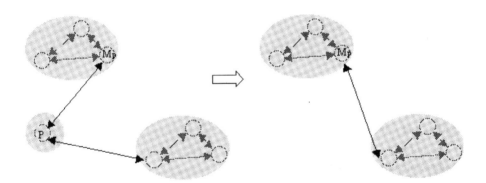

Figure 11.2. *Removal of a monoparticle tribe. The tribe was declared "good" and thus the single particle P, which is necessarily the worst of the tribe, even if it is at the same time "good", should be removed. But it will be removed only if its best external informant M_P is better than it. The assumption is indeed that the information carried by P is then less valuable than that carried by M_P*

In addition, the elimination of a particle implies a redistribution of its information links, up and down. In the general case, this carrying forward takes place on the best particle of the tribe (see Figure 11.1). In the case of a monoparticle tribe, since the removal of the particle leads to the removal of the whole tribe, they are placed on the best informant of the particle to be removed (see Figure 11.2).

11.2.5.2. *Generation of a particle*

Conversely, a bad tribe is obviously in need of information. It will therefore generate at least 1 new particle, while keeping contact with it. In fact, in the version used here, two particles are generated, one which could be anywhere in the search space and the other in a much more restricted field. Let us call them a *free* particle and a *confined* particle.

More precisely, all the bad tribes will each generate a pair of such particles and these new particles will form a new tribe. The term "to keep contact" means here the establishment of a symmetrical link between the generated particle and the generating tribe, represented, for example, by its best element.

11.2.5.2.1. Free particle

It is generated randomly, according to a uniform distribution, itself chosen randomly among three:

– in the whole of the search space (supposed here to be a D-parallelepiped),
– on a side of the search space,
– on a vertex of the search space.

The idea is not so much to count on the chance to find directly a promising area, but to be sure that the future course of the new particle has more probability of crossing such a zone.

11.2.5.2.2. Confined particle

Let us call x the best particle of the generating tribe and $\hat{x}$ its best memorized position. Let g be the best informant of x and $\hat{g}$ the best position that this informant has memorized. Then the new particle will be generated randomly uniformly in the D-sphere of center $\hat{g}$ and radius $\|\hat{g} - \hat{x}\|$.

Here, the idea is almost the opposite. It is, on the contrary, a question of intensifying research in an area that seems already interesting.

11.2.5.2.3. Frequency of the adaptations

It is not necessary, or desirable, to carry out these structural adaptations to each iteration, because there is a requirement to allow time for information to be propagated between the particles. Again there are several plausible rules possible. In theory, after each adaptation, one should calculate the diameter of the graph of the relations. For that, it would be necessary to consider all the pairs of particles in which each belongs to different tribes and to find the shortest path of information connecting them, in terms of a number of arcs. The longest of these shorter ways would give us an estimate of the iteration count necessary to be sure that information possessed by a particle can be transmitted, more or less directly and to be more or less deformed, to all the others. Nevertheless, this calculation is a little long and one can be satisfied to use the total number of links with information. If, after a structural adaptation, this number is L, then the next one will take place in $L/2$ iterations.

11.2.5.2.4. Evolution of the swarm

What kind of operation is induced by these rules? At the beginning, there is only one particle, representing a single tribe. After the first iteration, if its situation does not improve, which is extremely probable (and even certain, with the strategies of displacement examined below, because the particle does not move at all with the first time increment), another particle will be generated, forming a second tribe.

At the next iteration, if neither of the two particles improves its situation, the two tribes will simultaneously generate two particles each: a new tribe of four particles will be created and so on (noting that the more the number of links increases, the more significant the iteration number between two adaptations). Thus, as long as things go wrong, increasingly large tribes are generated, increasing the exploratory capacity of the swarm, but more and more rarely. Between two adaptations, the swarm has more and more chances of finding a solution.

However, conversely, as soon as an outline of a solution is found, each tribe will gradually eliminate its worst particles, possibly until it disappears completely. In an ideal situation, when convergence is confirmed, all the tribes, except possibly the last created, are reduced to one particle. Overall, the swarm tends to grow, more and more slowly, in an asymptotic way (see examples below). It is not really made to decrease, except temporarily in certain simple cases, when the tribes are for the most part good.

11.2.6. *Strategies of displacement*

Intuitively, it seems judicious for a particle to adopt a strategy of displacement depending on its recent past. In accordance with the empirical rule stated in the preceding chapter, we will arrange this in such a way that the better a particle behaves, the more it can afford an exploration of greater scope, with however a special strategy for the very best particles, which we can compare to a kind of local search.

Indeed, according to the problems, it is more interesting to use proximities calculated independently for each dimension (like the D-rectangles) or, on the contrary, globally in the space (like the D-spheres). For the greatest possible ease of use, it is thus necessary to enable the algorithm to call upon a certain class of methods if necessary, according to what it tells us about the problem in the course of research. Choosing the other strategies remains to be seen.

There are three possibilities of variation of performance of a particle: deterioration, maintaining the status quo, or improvement, which we will symbolize by the signs –, =, and +. Since the history of a particle includes two versions of its performance, TRIBES thus distinguishes nine cases, which are located by the status of the particle. For example, an improvement followed by maintaining the status quo will be denoted (+ =). However, we will be satisfied here with three, to take advantage of the pairs of distributions that we have identified as being interesting, and adding the local strategy that we have just described above. That will be sufficient to explain the principle of operation of the algorithm. Table 11.1 then indicates the strategies used according to statuses, brought together in three classes.

Gathered statuses	Strategy of displacement
(– –) (= –) (+ –) (– =) (= =)	4 (pivot)
(+ =) (– +)	5 (disturbed pivot)
(= +) (+ +)	3' (local by independent Gaussians)

Table 11.1. *Regroupings of statuses and corresponding strategies of displacement for a simplified use of TRIBES. The status of a particle is purely qualitative. It simply notes, for each of the two preceding movements, if the position of the particle improved, deteriorated or maintained the status quo*

Let us note, in addition, that the confinement of the particle in the search space is carried out in the same manner as in traditional PSO, except that there is no velocity to modify. If a component of the position tends to go beyond the acceptable values, it is simply brought back to that which is closest. This point will be shown in detail in Chapter 12, because it does not relate only to the overflows of interval.

11.2.7. *Best informant*

The TRIBES program can function on search spaces without a metric. In this case, obviously, the distributions of possibles must be chosen from those with independent dimensions, such as D-rectangles or ellipsoidal positive sectors. But, especially, two positions can then be compared only as in traditional PSO, i.e. only according to respective values of the function f to be minimized in these two points. So the best informant of a particle x is simply the one having memorized the best position.

Nevertheless, when the space has a metric, it would be a shame not to benefit from it, not only by the use of distributions like those of the pivots, but also by the calculation of pseudo-gradients, which is often more effective for comparing two positions. This is why the user of TRIBES can choose between two options, depending on whether the search space is metrical or non-metrical.

Let x be the particle of which one seeks the best informant. Let us note $\hat{y}$ the best position memorized by informant y, $\hat{z}$ that memorized by informant z, and $z \succ_x y$ the fact that z is better informant than y for x. The formulae of computation corresponding to the most general case and to one that is a little particular about metric spaces are indicated below.

11.2.7.1. *Direct comparison, general case*

$$z \succ_x y \Leftrightarrow f(\hat{z}) < f(\hat{y})$$

It will be noted that here the formula does not use particle x at all: informant z is better than y in the absolute, i.e. seen from any other particle.

11.2.7.2. *Comparison by pseudo-gradients, metric spaces*

$$z \succ_x y \Leftrightarrow \frac{f(\hat{x}) - f(\hat{z})}{\|\hat{x} - \hat{z}\|} > \frac{f(\hat{x}) - f(\hat{y})}{\|\hat{x} - \hat{y}\|}$$

The goal of this technique is to give preference to close informants. That makes it possible for the particle not to give up a local search too quickly under the pretext that "the grass seems greener elsewhere". The regroupings in subswarms are thus supported, as in the technique of the niching of the genetic algorithms. This was presented in [VEE 03] in a slightly different form, under the name of *Fitness-Distance-Ratio based Particle Swarm Optimization* (*FDR-PSO*).

NOTE – The generation of a confined particle also calls upon the concept of best informant. But in this particular case it is always the more constraining direct comparison that is used.

11.3. Results of the benchmark set

We now have to hand all the elements to code the program and make it function. In addition, a source is available on the Internet in C language (see the Chapter entitled "Further Information"). The results presented in Table 11.2 were obtained with TRIBES 6.2. Let us try to analyze them.

First, it is clear that the use of the pseudo-gradients, when it is possible, as it is here, is advantageous. It very slightly degrades the performance in one case (Griewank), while improving it considerably in another (Tripod).

Then, the application of the empirical rule of choice of the strategies that we were able to clarify in the preceding chapter is now less necessary. To use the simple pivot for bad particles and the disturbed pivot for good ones or vice versa amounts almost to the same thing. The difference remains in favor of the first technique, but in a less marked way.

The reason is that the conditions have changed. In particular, the information links are no longer established randomly. As a result, the choice of the best strategy of next displacement for each status of the particle concerned would probably have to be re-studied. Nevertheless complementary tests not detailed here already make it possible to affirm one thing: to use just one strategy is less effective than to combine several of them. For example, on our benchmark set, always choosing the strategy of the simple pivot (4) gives an average rate of failure of 28% and, above all, always choosing that of the disturbed pivot (5) gives a rate of 50%, with 100% failure for Tripod and Griewank.

Finally, what can we say about the intrinsic quality of these results? They are excellent, in fact better than those reported for algorithms already considered as very good (genetics, differential evolution, SOMA [ZEL 04], etc). That will be confirmed on more realistic examples, in Chapter 13.

Function	Strategies (4, 5, 3') *without* pseudo-gradients	Strategies (4, 5, 3') with pseudo-gradients
Tripod	57%	2%
Alpine 10D	0%, 1,310	0%, 1,139
Parabola 30D	0%, 651	0%, 533
Griewank 30D	46%	49%
Rosenbrock 30D	100% (26.04)	100% (26.5)
Ackley 30D	0% 7,045	0%, 3,382
Average of the rates of failure	34%	25%

Table 11.2. *Results of the benchmark set with TRIBES. Since the search spaces all have metrics, the choice of best informant of a particle can be realized by the method of pseudo-gradients (column 3). The gain in effectiveness is very clear for the Tripod function and even for Ackley, largely compensating for the slight degradation of performance on some other functions (Griewank and Rosenbrock)*

11.4. Summary

It is possible to design algorithms of PSO in the form of a "black box", the user having only to define the search space, the function to be minimized, the desired precision and, as a precaution, a maximum number of evaluations.

The TRIBES program, whose sources are available on the Internet, is an example of the realization of such an algorithm. It functions by cooperation of tribes of particles. In each tribe, the information links form a strongly connected graph. Between tribes, the links are looser, but the graph as a whole always remains connected. The strategies of structural modification implemented automatically are related to the addition or suppression of particles and their information links. The strategies of displacement of a particle are founded on several hyperspheric or Gaussian probability distributions, whether disturbed or not, the choice taking account of the recent history of this particle.

From the simple fact that it makes it possible to avoid the tiresome search for "good" parameters, in particular the size of the swarm, TRIBES already appears better than the traditional PSO, the more so as the results obtained are often as good, or even better.

Chapter 12

On the Constraints

12.1. Some preliminary reflections

In order to be able to tackle a broad range of problems, we must now examine how, in PSO, those whose description calls for what are usually called constraints on the variables are treated. We will pass very quickly over well-known techniques, such as weighted integration of constraints and the function to be minimized in a new function, to explore in a little more detail those that are less well known and especially those that were originally developed for PSO and can in turn be used by other optimization algorithms. But first, it will be useful to specify a little what this term "constraints" covers.

In fact, a problem of optimization is always "under constraints", because the search space must necessarily be limited. And, in the final analysis, a constraint is always a confinement. The most traditional ones, as we have already seen, are confinements of interval (the coordinates of the position must remain within a certain interval of values). But many others are useful, such as "the components of the solution must be integers" or "the components of the solution must be all different", in particular for combinatorial problems. Like all those more traditional constraints, they require that certain relations between the coordinates of a position be respected, the best-known case being that of linear relations. Incidentally, moreover, and as already pointed out in Chapter 1, PSO is not an adequate tool in purely linear optimization, because there are much more effective specific methods.

To define constraints is always to specify more or less explicitly the set of acceptable values or, more generally, because it is not necessarily numbers that are treated, the set of acceptable *a priori* positions among which one will seek the best.

Thus, there is no difference in nature between, on the one hand, a function to minimize and, on the other hand, constraints to be respected.

That is particularly obvious when the minimal value to reach is known, say zero, because then the description of the problem starts with something like "to find a position x such $f(x) = 0$", which can equally well be read as "to respect the constraint $f(x) = 0$". More generally, when a lower limit m of the minimum is known (and, in practice, this is always the case), one can still replace the formulation "to minimize f" with "respecting the constraint $f(x) = m$", even if it is known perfectly well that it is not possible. The important thing is that while trying to follow this directive, the algorithm finally gives us the desired solution.

The possibility of regarding any problem of optimization as being entirely and exclusively a set of constraints to be respected is not merely of academic interest. It indeed justifies the simple and comfortable method described later, which consists of carrying out a multicriterion search systematically.

12.2. Representation of the constraints

A constraint is classically represented by an equation or an inequation relating to a numerical function of position x. Thus, the general writing of a constraint will take one of the two following forms:

(1) $g(x) = 0$

(2) $g(x) < 0$

And what of the constraints of the type $g(x) \leq 0$? In fact, they are attached to case 1, noticing that one has equivalence $g(x) \leq 0 \Leftrightarrow g(x) + |g(x)| = 0$. Obviously we are speaking here about theoretical representations, because, in practice, others can be simpler to understand or handle in a data-processing program. Hence two constraints:

$$\begin{cases} 1 - x_1 + |1 - x_1| \leq 0 \\ x_1 - 2 + |x_1 - 2| \leq 0 \end{cases}$$

relating to the first coordinate of x, correspond to the interval confinement. $x_1 \in [1, 2]$.

Let us note besides that a constraint of type 2 can often be easily made slightly more flexible by permitting zero value. Indeed, except for some mathematically monstrous functions, there are two possible cases. If the function g is continuous, any negative value as near to zero as one wants is acceptable. To accept the zero value formally does not in itself change anything in the result that will be obtained by a data-processing program. If the function is discrete, there is a negative maximum acceptable value g_{max} and it is then enough to rewrite the constraint in the form $g(x) - g_{max} \leq 0$.

Let us note in passing that this means all the constraints can then be reduced to type 1. For certain methods of taking into account the constraints, this can be useful.

12.3. Imperative constraints and indicative constraints

However, for real problems, it is interesting to distinguish between *imperative* constraints (sometimes known as "hard") and *indicative* (or "soft") constraints. As their names indicate, the former must be absolutely respected, whereas the latter need be only partially respected. Still it is necessary to specify what the latter term means.

For that, let us define a non-negative numerical quantity, *a measurement of dissatisfaction s(x)*, which is lower as the constraint is closer to being satisfied for position x. Here, for example, are two simple formulas, corresponding to the two types of constraints (to avoid any confusion, we will write them by replacing the sign = by $\cong$ and the sign < by $\tilde{<}$):

$s = |g(x)|$, for indicative constraints of the type $g(x) \cong 0$

$$s' = \frac{g'(x) + |g'(x)|}{2} + \lambda$$, for indicative constraints of the type $g'(x) \tilde{<} 0$

The parameter λ, positive, is to be defined by the user. It indicates which "penalty" one intends to apply to a position for which the function g' would be just null instead of being negative. As already stated, it is rare that one cannot replace a constraint of strict negativity, especially if it is indicative, by a constraint of the "negative or null" type. In this case, the parameter λ is quite simply null.

More generally, the formulae above can be weighted according to whether the user gives more or less importance to the respect of a particular constraint.

12.4. Interval confinement

It is mentioned here as a reminder, because in fact we have been using it since the beginning and it is explained in detail in Chapter 3. Let us recall just the principle, since the same idea will be used for other confinements.

When the value of a coordinate of a particle lies outside the interval of acceptable values, it means, by definition, that the aforementioned particle leaves the search space. The objective is thus to bring it back inside this space.

The general method consists of trying to find the point in this space that is closest to the point theoretically reached by the particle and moving it there, also modifying velocity if the equations of motion are used (it is not the case, *inter alia*, with the method of pivots). As we have seen, that gives, for example, for each dimension d, the following formalization:

$$x_d \notin [x_{\min}, x_{\max}] \Rightarrow \begin{cases} v_d \leftarrow 0 \\ x_d < x_{\min} \Rightarrow x_d \leftarrow x_{\min} \\ x_d > x_{\max} \Rightarrow x_d \leftarrow x_{\max} \end{cases}$$

This means that if the search space is only defined by an ensemble of intervals of values, it is enough to replace the faulty coordinates by the extremity nearest to the interval of their acceptable values and to cancel the corresponding component of velocity. Since the particle must move in a D-rectangle, it is certain that this technique gives the nearest acceptable position.

If there are other constraints, and the search space is of more complicated form, one generally continues to apply this technique because of its simplicity. The new position is then certainly acceptable in comparison with the interval constraint, but one cannot more absolutely guarantee that it is so for the other constraints nor, *a fortiori*, that it is closest to the faulty position. One relies then on the iterative aspect of the algorithm to reach, gradually, a position that respects all the constraints simultaneously.

12.5. Discrete variable

The acceptable values form a finite list. Being given a value of variable (a coordinate of a position in the search space), we wish to replace it by the list value to which it is closest. In the direct method, this replacement is rough and immediate, in the indirect method it is progressive and is made in the very course of iterative search process.

12.5.1. *Direct method*

There are two main cases: the list can be ordered or it cannot be (no order relation). We will neglect here the intermediate cases where a partial order can be defined but not a total order.

12.5.1.1. *List not ordered (and not orderable)*

This case corresponds to qualitative variables, for example, of the colors. To determine whether a value is faulty or not, i.e. whether or not it is on the list, there is no method more effective than the exhaustive course.

Moreover, it is not possible to determine the nearest acceptable value because this has no meaning, as a small apagogy shows immediately. Indeed, if it had one, the reason is that there would be a concept of distance that would make it possible to order the list. However, to be exact, we have assumed that the list cannot be ordered. That is why the faulty value can only be replaced by an acceptable value, chosen at random and not, moreover, inevitably according to a uniform distribution.

12.5.1.2. *Ordered list*

Here several more effective algorithms can be used. The simplest consists of traversing the list by ascending values and stopping as soon as the found value exceeds or equals the one that is tested. Then at the same time the closest value is easily obtained: it is the one that is found or the one that is found after.

This algorithm is sufficient for short lists. Nevertheless, it should not be forgotten that it is meant to be repeated a great number of times. It may thus be necessary to call upon the theoretically most effective algorithm, by dichotomy, although it is a little more difficult to program. The source code in C is given for this at the end of the chapter.

12.5.2. *Indirect method*

Let $\{a_1,...,a_j,...a_J\}$ be the list of possible values for the variable (the coordinate) considered, x_d. One writes the constraint "must belong to the list" in the following form:

$$g(x) = \prod_{j=1}^{J} |x_d - a_j| = 0$$

The simplest thing to do is to treat this constraint by the multicriterion method, as we shall see later. The result is not absolutely guaranteed in the sense that the algorithm is satisfied with minimizing $g(x)$ jointly with the function objective and other possible constraints, but the advantage is that the process of convergence is no longer disturbed by the abrupt jumps of values (and therefore of position) imposed by the direct method.

12.6. Granularity confinement

This type of confinement relates to the particular case of a discrete variable from which the acceptable values result from a minimal value by addition of an increment δ, repeated a finite number of times. A common case is that of an integral variable in an interval, but there are others too, for example in industrial production.

As before, the faulty value is brought back to the nearest acceptable value, but that can be programmed by the use of a simple formula rather than by the survey of a list:

$$x_d \leftarrow x_{\min} + \delta E\left(\frac{x_d - x_{\min}}{\delta} + \frac{1}{2}\right)$$

where $E(u)$ represents the integer part of the number u.

12.7. "All different" confinement

Let us consider a position $x = (x_1,...x_d,..x_D)$. The objective here is to find the nearest position from which all the components x_d are different. Naturally that has interest only if they are discrete, for if they are continuous, it is enough to modify them in an infinitesimal way.

A typical example is that of a combinatorial problem from which the various possibilities are coded by integer values. For example, a circuit of N cities for the traveling salesman problem is classically coded by a list of integers between 1 and N. Certain specific versions of PSO [CLE 04] have equations of motion that directly carry out permutations of the integers of 1 to N or work in a constructive way by avoiding passing twice by the same city [SEC 01a]. In this case, confinement "all different" does not have much to recommend it.

However, other versions need it because the movements can lead to unacceptable positions [ONW 04a]. The criterion of distance to find the nearest acceptable position is then the minimum number of coordinates to be modified. For example, if the found position is (20, 1, 30, 5, 8, 1, 10, 20, 9, 10), at least three modifications are needed. An acceptable position at this "distance" 3 is then (20, 1, 30, 5, 8, 2, 10, 19, 9, 11). There are others, but the algorithm used in the work referred to provides only one of them (source code included in that of TRIBES). One could plan to modify it to give one of them at random among those possible.

12.8. Confinement by dichotomy

We saw specific algorithms of confinement for three scenarios: when the constraint is of the "interval of value" type, of the "non-null granularity" type or more generally discrete, and, finally, of the type "coordinates all different". The principle of these algorithms is always the same: to bring the particle back into the search space and if possible to the point in the space nearest to the faulty position.

Generally, it is certainly better to use a specific algorithm of confinement, but the types of constraints being infinite in number, we must also have at least a "default" confinement technique that functions in nearly all scenarios. Now let us study a simple version of such an algorithm, founded on the principle of successive dichotomies and which requires only a few assumptions on the nature of the search space.

To launch this algorithm, which is iterative, it is necessary to have at least an acceptable position. Very generally, it is approximately the preceding position of the particle. Let us call it x_{adm}. Let x be the current position, and let us note $x_0, x_1,...x_k...$ the successive positions that we will build and test. Calculation is done according to following processes:

1) $x_0 = x$;

2) as long as x_k is not admissible, make $x_{k+1} = \dfrac{x_k + x_{adm}}{2}$ then $k = k+1$.

It is possible to define constraints represented by such strange functions that this process never manages to find an acceptable position (e.g. the famous continuous curve of Peano, entirely filling a square). But for real problems, it is quite suitable.

However, it presents two disadvantages. On the one hand, it can increase the computing time appreciably if the test of respect of the constraints is a little long. On the other hand, it generally does not give the acceptable position nearest to the initial position or even necessarily a position close to the border of the search space defined by the constraints (see Figure 12.1).

Nevertheless, it is possible to reiterate the process itself. If x_k is the found acceptable position, it is enough to lay down:

$$\begin{cases} x_0 = x_{k-1} \\ x_{adm} = x_k \end{cases}$$

and to start again loop 2.

For discrete problems, we will certainly end up finding a position close to the border of the search space, and that will result in the fact that two successive positions will be identical. For continuous problems, unfortunately, it will be necessary to give a stop criterion, for example a threshold of distance (absolute or relative) between the two last positions, below which it is not necessary to go.

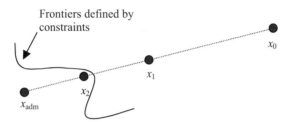

Figure 12.1. *Confinement by dichotomy. The position x_0 is not acceptable, position x_{adm} (generally the preceding position of the particle) is. The constraints define the border of the search space. By taking, in an iterative way, the median point between an acceptable position and one that is not, one can find an acceptable position x_2 nearer to this border*

Nevertheless, in all the cases, there is still no guarantee that the acceptable position selected will be that nearest to the initial faulty position. Let us note that this can sometimes be an advantage, in particular if the choice of the best neighbor uses a pseudo-gradient. If the particle left the search space in a certain direction, it is probably because this was promising. To take the opposite direction to return to the search space is not necessarily a bad idea.

12.9. Multicriterion treatment

Let us consider a problem of optimization of a function f formalized as follows:
– to minimize f, function of the vectorial variable x,
– under the constraints:

$$\begin{cases} g_1(x) \leq 0 \\ ... \\ g_i(x) \leq 0 \\ ... \\ g_I(x) \leq 0 \end{cases}$$

In practice, the constraints are classified in two groups: those that are rather easily directly manageable during iterations by mechanisms like those seen above (typically interval constraints) and others. It is then these other constraints, say, to simplify the notations, those of row 1 to m, which will be the object, with f, of a multicriterion optimization. Let us lay down:

$$h_0 = f \quad h_1 = g_1 + |g_1| \quad \ldots, \quad h_m = g_m + |g_m|$$

The multicriterion method consists of considering that all these constraints are indicative and solving a problem of simultaneous minimization:

to minimize $F = (h_0, h_1, \ldots, h_m)$

For this statement to have a meaning, we must define how to compare two vectorial quantities such as $F(x)$ and $F(y)$, in order to be able to decide whether or not position x is better than position y. This comparison rests on the traditional concept of dominance [PAR 1896]. Let us quickly remind ourselves about this in context.

The vectorial quantity $F(x) = (h_0(x), h_1(x), \ldots, h_m(x))$ is said to dominate $F(y) = (h_0(y), h_1(y), \ldots, h_m(y))$ if, for any index i, the value $h_i(x)$ is less than or equal to the value $h_i(y)$ and if the inequality is strict for at least an index j.

In this case, we will say that position x is better than position y. With this definition, two positions can be non-comparable. It is enough for this that the inequality is true for certain indices i and not for others.

Thus, a multicriterion algorithm of optimization will in general provide several noncomparable solutions according to the relation of dominance, whose set is called the Pareto front or trade-off surface.

To stick to PSO, we will be able to use specific alternatives [COE 02, HU 02b, PARS 02] or simply a program like TRIBES, by launching it several times with the option of comparison by dominance.

Once a certain list of solutions is obtained, from our perspective of treatment of constraints, two additional stages are necessary. First, it is necessary to select the solutions whose components other than the first are null (but for the precision desired), because it is those for which the constraints are respected. And, then, among those, it is necessary to seek the one whose first component is minimal, since it corresponds to the value of f.

EXAMPLE – The function to be minimized is defined by:

$$f(x) = (x_1 - 1)^2 + (x_2 - 1)^2$$

interval constraints $\begin{cases} x_1 \in [0,2] \\ x_2 \in [0,2] \end{cases}$

another constraint $g(x) = x_1^2 + x_2^2 - 1 \leq 0$

Figure 12.2 represents the function f and its intersection with the cylinder. $g(x) = 0$. The analytical resolution is easy and the solution is the point $x = \left(\dfrac{1}{\sqrt{2}}, \dfrac{1}{\sqrt{2}} \right)$, which gives a minimal value. $f(x) \cong 0.17157$.

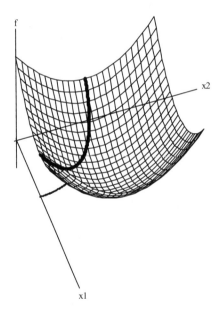

Figure 12.2. *Problem under constraint other than that of interval. The minimum to be found is the lowest point of the curve in thick line*

The interval constraints will be taken into account directly by the mechanism described above. The last constraint is written $h_1(x) = g(x) + |g(x)| = 0$. We then have to carry out a multicriterion optimization on $F(x) = (f, h_1)$. By launching the TRIBES program three times (with 1,000 evaluations for each execution), we obtain Table 12.1.

x	F(x)
(0.731 0.683)	(0.1732 0.0000)
(0.085 0.524)	(0.7785 0.8099)
(0.708 0.706)	(0.1716 0.0000)

Table 12.1. *Taking into account a constraint by multicriterion optimization. Three non-dominated solutions. The second solution does not respect the constraint (second element of F(x) not null). Among those that remain, the last is the best (lower value for the first component of F(x), i.e. f(x))*

Thus, the selection phase eliminates the second solution, which does not respect the constraint (second element of $F(X)$ not null). Then, the phase of comparison on the first element gives us the third solution as being the best.

12.10. Treatment by penalties

The multicriterion method is to be set against the traditional one, consisting of carrying out a combination of the constraints to build only one new function to be minimized. There again all the directly untreated constraints in the algorithm (and supposed standard $g(x) \leq 0$) are regarded as indicative constraints and gradually taken into account, but it is for the user to define weighting parameters. In the spirit of the step that led us to define an adaptive algorithm without parameters, the preceding method is preferable, but nevertheless let us recall the principle of one of the many methods by penalties, because we will apply it later on for comparison [STO 99]. One thus keeps only the interval constraints and possibly those bearing on the discrete character of certain variables. The others are integrated in a new function to minimize, defined in the following way:

$$\begin{cases} g_i(x) \leq 0 \Rightarrow c_i(x) = 1 \\ g_i(x) > 0 \Rightarrow c_i(x) = 1 + s_i g_i(x) \text{ with } s_i \geq 1 \\ F(x) = (f(x) + a) \prod_{i=1}^{m} c_i(x)^{b_i} \text{ with } b_i \geq 1 \end{cases}$$

The user must define $2m + 1$ parameters, which is far from being a trivial task if one wants to make sure that the global minimum of F is reached at the same point of the search space as that of f.

12.11. C source code. Dichotomic search in a list

```
/ * Dichotomic search in an ordered list (ascending order)
Input:     any x value
Output:    the rank in the list of the nearest value

Note: the program is deliberately not optimized
to be easier to understand
*/

# include < math.h >
# include < stdio.h >
# include < stdlib.h >

static double list[10] = 1, 3, 7, 20, 21, 22, 25, 28,31,32;
int        N = 10;

void main()

int       i, i_min, i_max, rang;
double x;

x = 7.3; //Value to test

i_min = 0; i_max = N-1;
test:
if (i_max = = i_min + 1) goto compares;
if (x = = list[i_min]) rang = i_min;goto FIN;
if (x = = list[i_max]) rang = i_max;goto FIN;
i = (int)(0.5*(double)(i_min + i_max));
if (x < list[i]) i_max = i; goto test;
if (x > list[i]) i_min = i; goto test;
rang = I; goto FIN;
compare:
if (x-list[i_min] < list[i_max]-x) rang = i_min; else rang = i_max;
FIN:
printf("rank%i, value%f", rang + 1, list[rang]);
```

12.12. For "amatheurs"

Any volume is a cube, or how to cope with constraints by homeomorphism

Let us consider a problem of continuous or semi-continuous optimization having only interval constraints:

$$\text{to minimize } f(x), \text{ with } x_d \in \left[x_{d,\min}, x_{d,\max} \right], \forall d \in \{1,...,D\}$$

It can be reformulated "to minimize $\phi(y)$, with $y \in [0,1]^D$" by the simple bijective continuous transformation (homeomorphism) $y_d = \dfrac{x_d - x_{d,\min}}{x_{d,\max} - x_{d,\min}}$, and by defining ϕ by $\phi(y) = f(x)$.

Thus, the search space, which was initially a D-parallelepiped, is now a D-cube.

This can be generalized. There is a strange theorem stipulating that the "number" of points in $[0,1]$ is the same as in any other finite interval (of course that is not true for discrete values). More generally, it is possible to put in continuous bijection the unit D-cube with any bounded subset H of $\mathbf{R}^D$, provided that the topology of H is that of a cube (no "holes"). However, in practice, any search space defined by constraints either is of this type or can be seen like a finite union of sets of this type.

It is thus theoretically possible to replace it by one or several D-cubes and for each one to define ϕ as above. The problem of optimization to be solved thus no longer has anything but interval constraints. The only tricky point is that "theoretically" can sometimes mean "impossible in practice"! However, even if properly mathematical work upstream is difficult, it can be worthwhile.

Let us treat two small examples by this method.

The first is that which we saw in the multicriterion section of treatment of the constraints.

EXAMPLE 1 – Quarter of disc = square:

to minimize $f(x) = (x_1 - 1)^2 + (x_2 - 1)^2$

under the constraints $\begin{cases} x_1 \in [0,2] \\ x_2 \in [0,2] \end{cases}$ and $g(x) = x_1^2 + x_2^2 - 1 \leq 0$

The search space H defined by these constraints is the quarter of a positive disc of radius 1 and center $(0,0)$. Let us call $C(2)$ the unitary 2-cube, i.e. the square of side 1. A possible homeomorphism (there is an infinite number of them) is given by:

$$\begin{cases} (x_1, x_2) \in H \xrightarrow{\mu} (y_1, y_2) \in C(2) \\ y_1 = \sqrt{x_1^2 + x_2^2} \\ y_2 = \frac{2}{\pi} \text{atan}\left(\frac{x_2}{x_1}\right) \end{cases}$$

The function ϕ is then defined by:

$$\forall (y_1, y_2) \in C(2), \phi(y_1, y_2) = f\left(y_1 \cos\left(\frac{\pi}{2} y_2\right), y_1 \sin\left(\frac{\pi}{2} y_2\right)\right)$$

and the equivalent problem becomes:

$$\text{to minimize } \phi(y_1, y_2), \text{ under the constraints } \begin{cases} y_1 \in [0,1] \\ y_2 \in [0,1] \end{cases}$$

Once the position of the minimum (y_1^*, y_2^*) is found in $C(2)$, the corresponding position in the original reference frame is calculated by applying the transformation:

μ^{-1}, that is to say $\left(y_1^* \cos\left(\dfrac{\pi}{2} y_2^*\right), y_1^* \sin\left(\dfrac{\pi}{2} y_2^*\right)\right)$

If we use same TRIBES program as above, we now find the nearest solution within 10^{-4} in five times fewer evaluations (approximately 200).

EXAMPLE 2 – Triangle = square:

$$\text{to minimize } f(x_1, x_2), \text{ under the constraints } \begin{cases} x_1 \geq 0 \\ x_2 \geq 0 \\ x_1 + x_2 \leq 1 \end{cases}$$

The search space H is then the triangle $\{(0,0),(1,0),(0,1)\}$. A possible homeomorphism is:

$$\begin{cases} (x_1, x_2) \in H \xrightarrow{\mu} (y_1, y_2) \in C(2) \\ y_1 = x_1 + x_2 \\ y_2 = \dfrac{x_2}{x_1 + x_2} \end{cases}$$

The function ϕ is defined by:

$$\forall (y_1, y_2) \in C(2), \phi(y_1, y_2) = f(y_1(1 - y_2), y_1 y_2)$$

Again, the equivalent problem becomes:

$$\text{to minimize } \phi(y_1, y_2), \text{ under the constraints } \begin{cases} y_1 \in [0,1] \\ y_2 \in [0,1] \end{cases}$$

NOTE – As you have probably seen, one can transform example 1 into example 2 by the changes of variable $z_1 = x_1^2$ and $z_2 = x_2^2$. It is not rare that one can, thus, in real problems, be brought back, in the first stage, to linear constraints. The search space then becomes a polyhedron, always decomposable in D-triangles (true triangle for D = 2, tetrahedron for D = 3, etc.). For each of them the bijective mapping with the unit cube is rather easy. The problem of optimization boils down to several subproblems having only interval constraints.

12.13. Summary

A problem of optimization always amounts to finding a position that satisfies a certain number of constraints. In an iterative algorithm like PSO, some of these constraints can be taken into account entirely with each displacement of a particle, or simply respected in an increasingly strict progressive way during iterations.

The first technique is preferred for interval constraints or the "all the different coordinates" type, whereas, for example, the treatment of discrete variables is related to the choice one or the other technique, each one having its advantages and its disadvantages.

Three progressive techniques are of very general use: by dichotomy, by penalties, and multicriterion optimization. The latter is the simplest to implement and remains well in the spirit of a method of optimization without parameters to be defined by the user.

A considerable gain in effectiveness can be obtained when a preliminary mathematical transformation puts the search space in bijective mapping with one or several D-cubes.

Chapter 13

Problems and Applications

13.1. Ecological niche

At this stage, and perhaps for quite some time, the parabola functions, Ackley, Griewank and others may have started to seem quite tedious. It is high time we considered some examples that are a little more interesting. It is a question nevertheless here of just illustrating the field of competence, the "ecological niche", of PSO and of evaluating its level of effectiveness.

We have already spoken about it a little, but let us specify here the types of optimization problems that the current versions of PSO can tackle effectively:

 – continuous, discrete, or mixed search space. For certain combinatorial problems, it is nevertheless preferable to use a specific or hybrid version;

 – function with several local minima. Naturally, PSO can treat functions with only one minimum, as we have seen and re-examined with the inevitable Parabola function, but sometimes a little less well than other algorithms, such as gradient descent. Let us note, nevertheless, that PSO becomes interesting again if the function, even if unimodal, is not continuous (and, *a fortiori*, not differentiable).

For these two characteristics, it is advisable to add the fact that convergence being often fast, dynamic optimization in quasi real time is also a favorite field in PSO; for example, for the uninterrupted training of neural networks. It was one of the first real applications, and remains a very active field of research, with sometimes considerable savings of time compared to other methods (backpropagation, genetic algorithms) [CON 02, GUD 03, ISM 99, SET 03, TAN 02, VAN 01, ZHA 01].

As we have seen, this velocity of convergence can also be used profitably for multiobjective problems, even without calling upon specific versions of PSO, such as those developed by some researchers [COE 02, HU 02B, PARS 02].

13.2. Typology and choice of problems

The problems of optimization can *roughly speaking* be grouped in four classes, according to what the function f to minimize represents and the way in which it is calculated. To simplify, let us consider only one function, but the typology remains valid for multicriterion optimization.

Type 1

f represents exactly the problem to be solved. It is calculable in an analytical or algorithmic way. It is typical of the test functions that are used as a benchmark. The description of the problem is generally simple and concise (formula or relatively short source code).

Type 2

f models a real process in an analytical way. It is hoped that the optimization of f will enable that of the process, but there is now an uncertainty, as a model never completely represents reality. Working out the problem can take rather a long time. Approximations are made; there are often complex constraints on the acceptable solutions.

Type 2'

Like 2, but f is no longer analytical. Its calculation is carried out by a simulation of a real process. In principle, it is the same thing as the preceding case, but the computing time of a position is greater. Comprehension of the problem can only be achieved by using simulation, the description of which can be rather long.

Type 3

f is estimated by really launching a physical process. The time necessary for an evaluation can then be extremely long, likely to take hours. The description of the problem can also be very long and needs a good comprehension of the process concerned.

PSO has already treated successfully all these types of problems, but since the goal of this book is to present the method itself rather than its applications, we will examine below only examples of types 1 and 2.

13.3. Canonical representation of a problem of optimization

In a problem of optimization, it is necessary to know *what* one optimizes. It is not necessarily obvious. Or, more precisely, it is not always simple to formalize a problem, even when one can express it in current language. We will not enter into debates that try to define what is meant by expressions like "optimizing the timetables in a college" or "optimizing a position of work in a factory", because so many non-quantifiable factors come into play.

Thus let us suppose from the start that the function f to optimize is known or, more precisely, calculable and, moreover, numerical. But calculable where? For which positions? The simple fact of putting these questions highlights that it is necessary first to detail the imperative constraints, because they delimit the search space; then to give the function to be optimized, which must be defined everywhere in this search space; and finally, possibly, the indicative constraints. Finally, our general representation of a problem of optimization will comprise three sets:

– the list of the imperative constraints, defining the search space,

– the function to be minimized on this space, (in the broad sense, as we have seen, it can be non-explicit and appraisable only *via* one simulation or even a real process),

– the list of the indicative constraints, with their measurements of dissatisfaction.

Once a problem is well-posed, we will obviously be interested in its resolution by PSO. But here we are interested only in the native PSO, i.e. the methods such as those we have already seen, parametric or not, and which have the following characteristics in common: they work on real numbers (possibly with granularity, therefore being able to be in fact integers) and they assume that, at least for each dimension, the concept of distance between two coordinates has a meaning. We will turn to the canonical PSO, thanks to which specific versions can be worked out, only in the second part of this work.

Let us now begin to look at problems that have been specially selected so that the native PSO cannot solve them in a satisfactory way.

13.4. Knapsack

We seek 10 different integers between 1 and 100 whose sum makes 100. The search space is *a priori* $\mathbf{R}^{10}$ but we add the constraints of granularity equal to 1 and all different coordinates. Thus, after each movement, each particle is readjusted on an acceptable position $(x_1,...,x_{10})$. The value of this position is simply given by the function:

$$f(x) = \left|100 - \sum_{d=1}^{10} x_d\right|$$

If we run a program like TRIBES 20 times on this problem, there must be between 43 and 277 evaluations to find 20 solutions, including 18 different ones. For this combinatorial problem the tool could seem acceptable, but that is only because of the relatively significant density of the solutions in the set of all possible combinations. It thus has good chances of finding some by chance. Again, we are in a situation where the numerical values of the coordinates have a meaning and are not a simple arbitrary coding.

Some examples of results:

$(3,1,12,21,2,8,6,30,13,4)$ in 80 evaluations

$(2,5,55,3,7,1,4,6,8,9)$ in 144 evaluations

13.5. Magic squares

We seek here magic squares $n \times n$, filled with different integers all between 1 and 100, with the rule that the sums in rows must be equal and that the sums in columns must be equal. To calculate the function to be minimized, it is thus enough to consider on the one hand all the differences in sums for each pair of lines and on the other hand all those for each pair of columns. By adding the squares of these differences, we build a function for which it is necessary to find a value zero. It is not necessary to specify that the sum of the lines must be equal to that of the columns, because that is necessarily true.

As before the values of the coordinates have a meaning as well as the numerical operations made on them. But the density of solutions is much lower. For 3×3 squares the problem is of dimension 9 and that functions perfectly. But as soon as we reach 5×5 squares, the performances are degraded seriously. With 50,000 evaluations per execution, we again find no more than 12 solutions after 20 executions.

Some examples of solutions are given below:

$\begin{bmatrix} 89 & 46 & 22 \\ 62 & 55 & 40 \\ 6 & 56 & 95 \end{bmatrix}$ in 823 evaluations

$$\begin{bmatrix} 15 & 85 & 81 & 47 & 46 \\ 50 & 72 & 42 & 30 & 80 \\ 44 & 87 & 79 & 24 & 40 \\ 83 & 8 & 33 & 95 & 55 \\ 82 & 22 & 39 & 78 & 53 \end{bmatrix}$$ in 2,455 evaluations

The next two types of problem, in which the integers used are in fact only arbitrary codes, are even more beyond the possibilities of the native PSO.

13.6. Quadratic assignment

This kind of problem is more interesting in practice, because of its rather general application. Let us point out a possible formulation. One considers a graph with D nodes and whose arcs are valued (here the values are often called flows). The nodes are to be positioned on D sites for which one knows the pair distances. For a given disposition, for each pair of nodes, the flow to be made to pass must thus be at the distance separating these nodes. The quantity considered is then the product of the flow by this distance and the function to minimize the sum of these D^2 quantities. See for example [DRE 03] for a more complete presentation of this problem and some methods of resolution.

It is common to represent the sites by numbers 1 to D and also the nodes of the graph by numbers 1 to D. A position in the search space is then given as a permutation of the integers of 1 to D, with the convention that the dth number represents that of the site of the node coded by the integer d.

Contrary to the preceding examples, all these numbers are purely conventional. However, the native PSO (non-specific) will handle them like numbers, since the equations of motion imply additions, subtractions, and multiplications by scalars. To distinguish clearly the difference between the two ranges and to multiply it by a coefficient means almost nothing with regard to the problem to be solved or, at least, not really what is implicitly envisaged in PSO. It is therefore not surprising that the results are now disastrous; for the traditional problem named SCR12, no solution is found even after 10^6 evaluations (to reassure you immediately, fewer than 1,500 will be needed by adding a local search).

Lastly, to conclude this small list of problems located outside the field of competence of the native PSO, let us quote the prototype of combinatorial problems, the famous traveling salesman. We do expect results to be quite as bad, since it is formally equivalent to the previous problem, and from this point of view it would not even be necessary to try to treat it, but it will be useful for us as an example in the second part to show how a specific PSO can be developed.

13.7. Traveling salesman

Everybody is aware of this problem, consisting of finding the shortest Hamiltonian circuit (not twice the same node) in a graph whose arcs are valuated by lengths. There also it is common to indicate the nodes of the graph by integers, but it is still only an arbitrary coding and the algebraic operations of the equations of motion of the native PSO do not have great significance.

However, the matter should be nuanced. It was already true in the preceding example, but easier to explain here. Let us consider two positions coded by two permutations of the integers of 1 to D, that is to say $x = (x_1, ..., x_d, ..., x_D)$ and $y = (y_1, ..., y_d, ..., y_D)$, and ask ourselves what can be meant by, for example, hyperspheric proximity of x of radius $\rho = \|x - y\|$, by using the Euclidean norm systematically.

On the one hand, we do see that there is no question of speaking about distance, if only because the same position can be coded in D different ways (by cyclic permutations). However, on the other hand, despite everything, the positions z that observe the condition $\|x - z\| \leq \rho$ are, in a certain way, very "close" to x even if their set can hardly be defined like a sphere. Indeed, let us call ρ' the greatest integer less than or equal to ρ. Then z cannot have any more ρ' coordinates that are different from those of x of the same rank. Similar reasoning holds for other types of proximity distributions.

This explains why, even if it is a little like the preceding case, a rather simple problem such as the one with 17 nodes, referred to as BR17, cannot be solved with a search effort of 10^6 evaluations, but this could be reduced to less than 5,000 by the simple addition of local search. More generally, the exploratory capacity of PSO remains interesting for combinatorial problems, but it cannot be used for more than the approximate detection of promising fields in the search space. It is then necessary to pass it on to another algorithm for accurate localization of a solution.

On the other hand, if we place ourselves now in the heart of the field of competence of the traditional PSO, i.e. roughly the continuous and mixed continuous-discrete (non-combinatorial) problems, it is remarkably effective. We have already seen it applied to traditional test functions; let us show it now in some slightly more interesting examples.

13.8. Hybrid JM

This small three-dimensional problem of type 1 was proposed by Bernard Jeannet and Frederic Messina [JEA 03]. The imperative constraints defining the search space for dimension 3 are:

$$\begin{cases} x_1 \in \{1,2,3,4,5,6\} \\ x_2 \in [-15,25] \\ x_3 \in [3,10] \end{cases}$$

and the function to be minimized is given in analytical form:

$$f(x_1, x_2, x_3) = 20 a_1(x_1) x_2^2 + 2 a_2(x_1) x_2 x_3$$

The variable x_1 is in fact only an index used to return values starting from two lists a_1 = (0.5 0.3 0.8 0.1 0.9 0.12) and a_2 = (–0.5 0.6 0.1 1.5 –1 0.8). A minimum of –112.5 is obtained for x_1 = 4, x_2 = –7.5, and x_3 = 10.

The method suggested by the authors (from arithmetic of intervals and inclusion functions) gives the solution after 3,271 evaluations. This method being deterministic, the result is absolutely certain, which is obviously never the case with PSO. For an honest comparison, we must therefore impose a very high success rate, for example, 99.99%. As Figure 13.1 shows clearly, a program such as TRIBES is definitely more effective. Even if an accuracy of 10^{-6} is required on the result, fewer than 1,500 evaluations are required on average to reach this success rate.

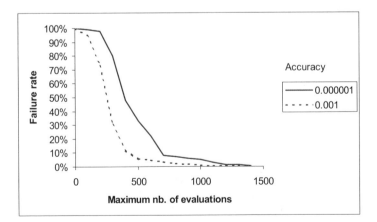

Figure 13.1. *Hybrid problem 3D. One dimension is continuous, the other two are discrete. The desired precision is either 10^{-3} or 10^{-6}. For each maximum number of evaluations per execution run, one estimates the rate of failure by carrying out 500 executions with TRIBES without re-initialization of the pseudo-random number generator*

13.9. Training of a neural network

Historically, the first applications of PSO consisted of accelerating the evaluation of the transfer functions in neural networks. This phase is often called training, when the network self-modifies according to data provided gradually, to entries and to the expected results. It is called training because the evaluations are imposed by a third party, in fact, precisely, by PSO.

In these applications, PSO has very largely surpassed the traditional method of the time, backpropagation. But improved alternatives already existed. More recent comparative work has in fact shown that if PSO remains the best general algorithm (better, for example, than the evolutionary algorithms [CHI 98]), several specific methods are generally more effective (Rprop, in particular [RIE 94]), but not always and sometimes only a little.

Let us examine that on some traditional examples. In those that follow, the networks have three layers (Input with E nodes, Hidden with C nodes, and Output with S nodes). All the Entry arcs towards Hidden exist, just as all the arcs of Hidden towards Exit. The total number of arcs is thus $A = EC + CS$. Let us index by i the nodes of the Entry layer, by j those of the Hidden layer, and by k those of the Exit layer. If E given e_i are presented in entry, then each node j carries out a weighted combination of these entries and generates an activation equal to:

$$f_j = \frac{1}{1+e^{-\alpha_j - \sum_{i=1}^{E} e_i w_{i,j}}}$$

In the same way, each node k produces an exit equal to:

$$g_k = \frac{1}{1+e^{-\beta_j - \sum_{j=1}^{C} f_j w_{j,k}}}$$

The exact formulas are in the source code of TRIBES, thanks to the kindness of Rui Mendes [MEN 02]. The significant point is that on the whole there are $D = A + E + C$ variables to find: weights $w_{i,j}$ and $w_{j,k}$, as well as the shifts α_j and β_k. Thus, the dimension of the search space is D. From now on, all these variables are supposed to be the components of a real D-vector X.

To educate the network, one has P sets of values of entry, with, for each play p, the desired values of exit $\left(g_{1,p}^*, ..., g_{k,p}^*, ..., g_{S,p}^*\right)$. The function to be minimized is calculated classically on the ensemble of the benchmark sets, as the average quadratic distance between all the found outputs and those desired:

$$f(x) = \frac{1}{\sqrt{PS}} \sqrt{\sum_{p=1}^{P}\sum_{k=1}^{S}\left(g_{k,p} - g_{k,p}^{*}\right)^{2}}$$

The examples are treated with TRIBES, with the help of a small modification allowing a more relevant comparison with the results published for other methods: the initialization of a position is always done in $[-1\ 1]^D$ and the interval constraints are not activated. For the same reason, the averages are calculated only on over 30 executions of the program. It turns out that the variance of the results is rather small, about 0.04. In practice, that means that the found average values have more than 99% chance of being right to within less than 0.02 (confidence interval of width 0.04).

13.9.1. *Exclusive OR*

These are the rudiments of neural networks. Two nodes in input, two in hidden layer and one at output. The inputs are binary and there are four possible cases. The aim of the game is to find at exit the truth table of the logical exclusive OR.

The dimension of the search space is 9. PSO (TRIBES) finds a solution with $f(x) < 0.00005$ on average after 2,040 evaluations. On this simple problem, it seems that it is the best result published.

13.9.2. *Diabetes among Pima Indians*

The neural network must be calibrated to give a diagnosis of diabetes according to seven numeric variables (such as the number of childbirths). The benchmark set comprises 200 cases. The decision is theoretically binary and the network thus has seven entries and an exit. The transition course comprises seven nodes. The dimension of the problem is thus 64.

Let us note that the exit is nevertheless given in the form of a real number between 0 and 1. We can see this number as indicating the confidence to be granted to the diagnosis. For example, a value of 0.5 corresponds to a null confidence.

In this example, the average value of the error $f(x)$ after 40,000 evaluations is 0.26. We will see that the specific algorithms do better.

13.9.3. Servomechanism

The detail of this problem can be found in [QUI 93]. In short, it is a question of optimizing a neural network having to predict the reaction time of a servomechanism dependent on four parameters: two electronic gains and two mechanical configurations. The network thus has four entries and an exit. The intermediate layer comprises four nodes and the dimension of the problem is thus 28.

The benchmark set comprises 167 cases. With treatment by TRIBES, the average value of the error $f(x)$ after 40,000 evaluations is 0.60. There still, the specific algorithms do better, as we will now see in a small summary table.

13.9.4. Comparisons

Except for the last line, the results of Table 13.1 come from [MEN 02]. The first four methods are parametric. The selected parameters are standard values, known to give good results. For the parametric PSO, the authors chose a version with classical constriction, without distinction between explorers and memories. The only originality is the topology of the network of information, called *Pyramid*. It can be seen as a stacking of tetrahedrons whose summits are the particles and the edges the information links. The particles thus do not have all the same number of links (between three and six).

The specific method Rprop is unquestionably the overall best, pursued closely by the parametric PSO. The non-parametric adaptive PSO, represented by TRIBES, attains a very honorable third position, preceding the genetic algorithm. Curiously enough, backpropagation, long considered as the panacea, is largely outdistanced, primarily because of its very bad score on the simplest problem (exclusive OR).

	exclusive OR	Pima Indians	Servomechanism	Average
Backpropag.	0.48	0.18	0.57	0.41
Genetic Algo.	0.17	0.26	0.54	0.32
Rprop	0.06	**0.18**	**0.45**	**0.23**
Param. PSO	0.00	0.27	0.48	0.25
TRIBES	**0.00**	0.26	0.60	0.29

Table 13.1. *Training of a neural network. Comparisons of five methods applied to three problems. The specific algorithm Rprop is as a whole appreciably better, but PSO, parametric or adaptive, is well-placed*

13.10. Pressure vessel

This realistic problem of type 2 has been dealt with by many methods, hence its interest. The goal is to design a container of compressed air consisting of a cylindrical body and two segments of a sphere. It must withstand an internal pressure P_{max} and offer a volume V. To achieve this, one uses sheets, the thicknesses of which are necessarily multiples of a certain value δ.

The variables concerned are as follows:
- x_1, the thickness of sheet of the cylindrical part,
- x_2, the thickness of sheet of the segments of a sphere,
- x_3, the internal radius of the cylinder and segments of a sphere,
- x_4, the length of the cylindrical part.

The pressure P_{max} is 3,000 and volume V is 750. The numerical values are purposely given without units, because it obviously does not influence the research solution. In the original definition of the problem, the pressure was in psi (pounds per square inch) and volume in ft^3 (cubic feet). The increment δ thickness of sheet is 0.0625. The constraints defining the search space are explained in [SAN 90]. It is enough for us to list them:

$$g_1(x) = 0.0193x_3 - x_1 \leq 0$$

$$g_2(x) = 0.00954x_3 - x_2 \leq 0$$

$$g_3(x) = 750 \times 1728 - \pi x_3^2 \left(x_4 - \frac{4}{3}x_3 \right) \leq 0$$

$$g_4(x) = x_1 - \delta E\left(\frac{x_1}{\delta} \right) = 0$$

$$g_5(x) = x_2 - \delta E\left(\frac{x_2}{\delta} \right) = 0$$

$$x_1 \in [1.1 \ \ 12.5]$$
$$x_2 \in [0.6 \ \ 12.5]$$
$$x_3 \in \,]0 \ \ 240]$$
$$x_4 \in \,]0 \ \ 240]$$

Let us note immediately that constraints 4 and 5 indicate simply the discrete character of the variables x_1 and x_2 according to the increment δ and that the following ones are interval constraints put in condensed form. The size to be minimized is the cost price of manufacture, which incorporates that of materials, their working, and their assembly (welding). It is modeled by the formula:

$$f(x) = 0.6224 x_1 x_3 x_4 + 1.7781 x_2 x_3^2 + 3.1611 x_1^2 x_4 + 19.84 x_1^2 x_3$$

The analytical solution is:

$$\begin{cases} x_1 = 1.125 \\ x_2 = 0.625 \\ x_3 = \dfrac{x_1}{0.0193} \cong 58.2901554 \\ x_4 = \dfrac{750 \times 1728 - (4/3)\pi x_3^3}{\pi x_3^2} \cong 43.6926562 \end{cases}$$

which gives the value of 7,197.72893 for the function.

This problem was dealt with by 10 methods (differential evolution, Lagrange multipliers, genetic algorithms, MARS [LIT 98], SOMA [ZEL 04], etc.). The very best result published in mid-2004 was that of SOMA, that is to say a minimal value reached of 7,197.729 after 100 tests of 51,918 evaluations each. This "round" number does not arise from the preliminary fine adjustment of seven parameters (a choice of strategy and six numerical parameters). The number of attempts to find this adjustment is not indicated by the author.

Moreover, to take into account constraints 1 to 3, the problem was initially transformed according to the method of the penalties, which we have seen to give a new function F to be minimized, which is equal to f in an item X only when all the following constraints are satisfied:

$$\begin{cases} s_1 = 10^{10}, s_2 = s_3 = 1 \\ g_i(x) \leq 0 \Rightarrow c_i(x) = 1 \\ g_i(x) > 0 \Rightarrow c_i(x) = 1 + s_i g_i(x) \\ F(x) = f(x) \prod_{i=1}^{3} c_i(x)^2 \end{cases}$$

Again, it is not specified how the weighting coefficients were established, but it is easy to imagine that it required several tests.

We will thus solve this problem with TRIBES under the same conditions – a number of executions (100) and a maximum number of evaluations per execution (51,818) – and will compare them with those of SOMA. In fact, this problem is often dealt with in two forms: exactly as described below; and, as a continuous problem (one relaxes the constraint of discretization δ of the thicknesses of the sheets).

13.10.1. *Continuous relaxed form*

The analytical solution is different only because the lower limits for x_1 and x_2 are now acceptable values:

$$\begin{cases} x_1 = 1.1 \\ x_2 = 0.6 \\ x_3 = \dfrac{x_1}{0.0193} \cong 56.9948187 \\ x_4 = \dfrac{750 \times 1728 - (4/3)\pi x_3^3}{\pi x_3^2} \cong 51.0012517 \end{cases}$$

which gives the minimal value of 7,019.03109 for the function. Table 13.2 summarizes the results obtained by comparing them with those of SOMA. For the precise definition of the many parameters of this method, you can refer to the work of Ivan Zelinka referred to above.

First, note that PSO, or at least the adaptive algorithm TRIBES, is slightly more effective without having parameters to define. Second, and perhaps most interesting, with an adaptive version of PSO it is not even necessary to seek a system of penalties to take into account the constraints: the multicriterion method gives an excellent result, only slightly less good than the previous one. From the point of view of an engineer, it is an unquestionable advantage.

Method ⇒	SOMA, penalties	TRIBES, penalties	TRIBES, multicriterion
Max. no. of evalutions per execution	51,818	51,818	51,818
No. of executions	100	100	100
Parameters ⇒ Result ⇓	AlltoOne PathLength = 3 Step = 0.11 PopSize = 20 PRT = 0.1 Migration = 100 MinDiv = negative		
x_1	1.10015	1.1	1.1
x_2	0.600001	0.6	0.6
x_3	57.0024	56.99482	56.99447
x_4	50.9591	51.00125	51.00138
$F(x)$ or $f(x)$	7,019.032	7,019.031	7,019.033

Table 13.2. *Pressure vessel, continuous relaxed problem. Best results of 100 executions of 51,818 evaluations each, for comparison with SOMA method. The adaptive PSO, implemented here by TRIBES algorithm, is slightly more effective while not requiring a parameter setting. Directly taking into account the constraints by the multicriterion method gives a result very close to the optimum*

13.10.2. *Complete discrete form*

If we return to the complete problem, i.e. with discrete values for the variables x_1 and x_2, we arrive at similar conclusions, as Table 13.3 indicates, although for SOMA it is necessary to modify a parameter (PRT, which is a level of perturbation). Here also TRIBES is equally effective, the more so as it finds the true optimum instead of the local optimum detected by SOMA. This global optimum can also be obtained by SOMA, but at the price of a different strategy (called AllToAll) and of more than 200,000 evaluations per execution. Indeed, the variation of value of the function between the two solutions is detectable only beyond the fourth decimal.

Method ⇒	SOMA, penalties	TRIBES, penalties	TRIBES, multicriterion
Max. no. of evaluations per execution	51,818	51,818	51,818
No. of executions	100	100	100
Parameters ⇒ Result ⇓	AlltoOne PathLength = 3 Step = 0.11 PopSize = 20 PRT = 0.5 Migration = 100 MinDiv = negative		
x_1	1.125	1.125	1.125
x_2	0.625	0.625	0.625
x_3	55.8592	58.2901	58.2901
x_4	57.7315	43.6926	43.6927
$F(x)$ or $f(x)$	7,197.729	7,197.729	7,197.729

Table 13.3. *Pressure vessel, complete discrete problem. SOMA requires a modification of parameter PRT, whereas TRIBES remains just as effective and even finds the really optimal solution, whether it be with the method of penalties or, in a much more practical way, with the multicriterion method*

Out of curiosity, we can look at what a non-adaptive PSO program, such as we detailed in the first chapters, gives. This time, we should define parameters. Let us take the standard values already used many times: $N = 20$ (size of the explorer-swarm), $M = 20$ (size of the swarm report), $K = 3$ (number of information links by memory), $\varphi = 2.07$ (for the calculation of the confidence coefficients), and definition of the information links at random before each iteration. We point out, nevertheless, that these values are the fruit of many tests on various problems. Then we easily obtain a result of the same quality in only 15,000 evaluations. Obviously as a consequence, we can ask whether this number of evaluations would also be sufficient for TRIBES. As Table 13.4 shows, it is not completely the case, although the solutions obtained are nevertheless of very good quality. It is the price to pay for not having parameters to define.

Method ⇒	Parametric PSO, penalties	TRIBES, penalties	TRIBES, multicriterion
Maximum no. of evaluations per execution	15,000	15,000	15,000
No. of executions	100	100	100
Parameters ⇒	$N = 20$ $M = 20$ $K = 3$ $\varphi = 2.07$		
Result ⇓	links redefined randomly with each iteration		
x_1	1.125	1.125	1.125
x_2	0.625	0.625	0.625
x_3	58.2901	58.2891	58.2867
x_4	43.6926	43.6987	43.7115
$F(x)$ or $f(x)$	7,197.729	7,197.806	7,197.938

Table 13.4. *Pressure vessel, with parametric PSO. Fewer than 15,000 evaluations are needed to obtain the best-known solution, provided, of course, a good set of parameters has been defined. With an adaptive version and the same constraint on the number of evaluations, the result is slightly less good*

13.11. Compression spring

This problem is in the same vein as the previous one and was dealt with by the same methods. The goal is to produce a cylindrical compression spring having certain mechanical characteristics by using the least possible metal. The variables concerned are as follows: x_1, the number of coils; x_2, the external diameter of the spring; x_3, the diameter of the wire forming the spring.

The constraints defining the search space are also explained in [SAN 90]. They are a little more complicated and are expressed using intermediate variables:

$F_{max} = 1000$

$F_p = 300$

$C_f = 1 + 0.75 \dfrac{x_3}{x_2 - x_3} + 0.615 \dfrac{x_3}{x_2}$

$K = 11.5 \times 10^6 \dfrac{x_3^4}{8 x_1 x_2^3}$

$\sigma_p = \dfrac{F_p}{K}$

$l_f = \dfrac{F_{max}}{K} + 1.05(x_1 + 2) x_3$

The constraints themselves are indicated below. Those of intervals and discrete values are directly presented in a condensed form:

$g_1(x) = \dfrac{8 C_f F_{max}}{\pi} \dfrac{x_2}{x_3^3} - 189000 \leq 0$

$g_2(x) = l_f - 14 \leq 0$

$g_3(x) = \sigma_p - 6 \leq 0$

$g_4(x) = \sigma_p - \dfrac{F_p}{K} \leq 0$

$g_5(x) = 1.25 - \dfrac{F_{max} - F_p}{K} \leq 0$

$x_1 \in \{1\ 2\ ...\ 70\}$

$x_2 \in [0.6\ 3]$

$x_3 \in \{0.207\ 0.225\ 0.244\ 0.263\ 0.283\ 0.307\ 0.331\ 0.362\ 0.394\ 0.4375\ 0.5\}$

The volume of metal to be minimized is given by:

$$f(x) = \dfrac{\pi^2}{4} x_2 x_3^2 (x_1 + 2)$$

In mid-2004, this problem was dealt with using 22 methods, including simulated annealing, cellular automats, and several alternatives of genetic and evolutionary algorithms. The complete list is in [LAM 04], which details the one that gives the best result: differential evolution. The constraints are taken into account there by the use of penalties. Various formulations seem to give equivalent results and we will use the following one:

$$\begin{cases} s_1 = s_2 = s_3 = 1 \\ s_4 = s_5 = 10^{10} \\ g_i(x) \leq 0 \Rightarrow c_i(x) = 1 \\ g_i(x) > 0 \Rightarrow c_i(x) = 1 + s_i g_i(x) \\ F(x) = f(x) \prod_{i=1}^{5} c_i^3 \end{cases}$$

Here again, it is not specified how, or after how many tests, the various coefficients could be given. Let us note that differential evolution definitely uses fewer parameters than SOMA: a constant size of population NP, a probability of crossing CR, and a constant coefficient F, which plays something of the same role as the random confidence coefficients of the traditional PSO. For this problem, the optimal values retained by Jouni Lampinen and Rainer Storn are $NP = 50$, and $F = 0.9$, and number of evaluations = 12,500.

Table 13.5 indicates the best result among 100 executions for differential evolution and TRIBES. The latter used the same function $F(x)$, incorporating the constraints as for differential evolution, and the multicriterion method, which makes it possible to take the constraints as they appear, without having to define weighting coefficients. As we can see, the results are still very good there, the more so as, in fact, if we stick to the method by penalties, the optimum is obtained to within 10^{-6} in fewer than 8,000 evaluations. For the multicriterion method, one needs rather more evaluations (13,000), because with 12,500 we just find a local optimum, extremely close in value.

Method ⇒	Differential evolution, penalties	TRIBES, penalties	TRIBES, multicriterion
Max. no. of evalutions per execution	12,500	12,500	12,500 *13,000*
No. of executions	100	100	100
Parameters ⇒ Result ⇓	$NP = 50$ $CR = 0.9$ $F = 0.9$		
x_1	9	9	5 *9*
x_2	1.2230410	1.22304097	1.658318 *1.228618*
x_3	0.283	0.283	0.307 *0.283*
or $f(x)$	2.65856	2.658559	2.699494 *2.670683*

Table 13.5. *Compression spring. The adaptive PSO is at least as effective as the best earlier known method, differential evolution. The number of evaluations (12,500) was retained for comparison but actually the optimum is reached to within 10^{-6} in fewer than 8,000 if one uses the same aggregation of constraints by penalties as in the resolution by differential evolution. However, one needs a few more evaluations (13,000) to find the solution by the multicriterion method*

13.12. Moving Peaks

In this academic example, it is a question of testing the capacity of an optimization algorithm not only to find an optimum, but also not to lose too much sight of it if the function to be optimized changes in the course of the process. The benchmark set of "Moving Peaks", with its mathematical explanation and the source code in C, is on the site http://www.aifb.uni-karlsruhe.de/~jbr/MovPeaks/. In two dimensions, with ten peaks, one obtains, at a given moment, something like what is represented in Figure 13.1.

A certain number of parameters make it possible to create various problems. Let us take the following values, which correspond to a scenario treated by several authors, in particular the originator of the benchmark set, Jürgen Branke [BRA 03]:

– search space $[0\ 100]^5$;
– 50 peaks of conical form;
– displacement in a random direction all 5,000 evaluations, on a distance from 1;

– height of each initially random peak between 30 and 70 (for the positive parts) then varying with more than 7;

– width of each initially random peak between 1 and 12 (for the positive parts) then varying with more than 1;

– 50 executions of 500,000 evaluations, to calculate average values.

This problem is rather difficult, because even if the peaks move slowly, their height can vary rather a large amount. The maximum can thus be moved abruptly.

It is now necessary to define a measurement of the performance, the maximum value of the peaks being assumed to be known after initialization and each displacement. A first mode of calculation consists in setting the distance between the current value and the maximum so that it is known immediately before each change. This has the advantage of being coherent with the usual calculation of performance for the static problems: if the peaks do not move at all, one finds the same result, i.e. the best value obtained during the execution. Let us call this value *error of follow-up*. However, the author of the benchmark set proceeds differently. He defines a meter in which, with each evaluation, he accumulates the best-known performance and, at the end of the execution, he divides this total by the number of evaluations. The number obtained is obviously greater than the preceding. Let us call it *continuous error of follow-up*.

With the genetic algorithm used by J. Branke, the continuous error of follow-up average on 50 executions of 500,000 evaluations is 4.6, as is indicated on its site. We will see in the second part of this work that there is a PSO more or less specific to this kind of dynamic optimization. For example, the multi-swarm parametric algorithm designed by Tim Blackwell functions very well, but with the proviso of taking the number of swarms equal to the number of peaks. On the same problem, the continuous error of follow-up average is only 2.6 [BLA 04]. This is due to the velocity of convergence of PSO in itself.

To the extent, moreover, that even with a non-specific PSO like TRIBES, one already obtains good results (average error of follow-up 3.31, average error of continuous follow-up 4.18). It is enough, after each change, to re-initialize the swarm, keeping the best particle if the new value of the function for the position it occupies proves to be still largest. Figure 13.2 shows us a typical execution, for which the variation to the maximum was calculated after each evaluation. It decreases initially very quickly, then much more slowly, but succeeds in remaining always rather close to the true maximum, even just after a change.

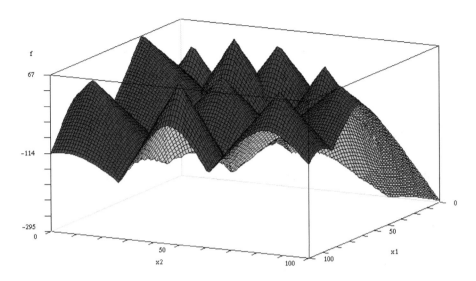

Figure 13.2. *Snapshots of ten mobile peaks on a search space for two dimensions. In this particular case, the maximum is on a border, a situation that the majority of stochastic optimization algorithms do not unduly appreciate*

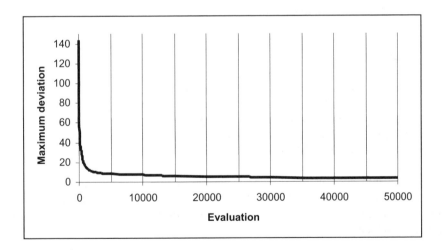

Figure 13.3. *Follow-up of the variation to the maximum for a problem of dimension 5 with 50 mobile peaks. The peaks move all the 5,000 evaluations (moments represented by vertical bars). Here only the first 50,000 evaluations are shown*

13.13. For "amatheurs": the magic of squares

A square $n \times n$ is represented by a position in a space with n^2 dimensions, $x = (x_1, ..., x_d, ..., x_{n^2})$. One can represent it as the list of the elements of the square read line by line. For the sums of the rows, the function to be minimized is then:

$$f_1(x) = \sum_{i=1}^{n-1} \sum_{j=i+1}^{n} \left(\sum_{d=1}^{n} \left(x_{n(i-1)+d} - x_{n(j-1)+d} \right) \right)^2$$

If it equals zero (which is what we are looking for), it indicates that for each pair of rows, the sums of the elements of each are equal.

In the same way, for those in the columns:

$$f_2(x) = \sum_{i=1}^{n-1} \sum_{j=i+1}^{n} \left(\sum_{d=1}^{n} \left(x_{i+n(d-1)} - x_{j+n(d-1)} \right) \right)^2$$

The total quantity to minimize is then $f_1(x) + f_2(x)$. Let us suppose now that one found a solution, namely, L the common sum of the lines and C that of the columns. The total sum of the elements of the square is then worth nL, but also nC. Hence $L = C$. That is why there is absolutely no need to add this constraint explicitly in the function to be minimized.

13.14. Summary

Several examples make it possible to better determine the field of competence of PSO, in particular for an adaptive version such as TRIBES. The difficult combinatorial problems do not really form part of it (except special versions not studied here). However, the method is very effective for nonlinear problems with continuous or discrete variables.

Taking into account the constraints by the multicriterion technique makes it possible to consider them just as they are, without having to carry out an integration weighted within a new minimizing function. Moreover, with an adaptive version, no parameter setting is necessary.

Chapter 14

Conclusion

14.1. End of the beginning

The few examples of the preceding chapter bring to a close this first part, which has hopefully fulfilled its purpose: to place at your disposal all the elements to effectively treat a great number of optimization problems. A great number but obviously not all and it is very possible that none of the PSO described so far corresponds to your expectation.

Nevertheless, what we have just seen is far from covering all the aspects of this method and is likely to give you only a restricted idea of its possibilities. Before deciding that it is not the tool that is appropriate to you, you should thus glance through the second part, which will give you *inter alia* an outline of various extensions of the field of competence of PSO, such as dynamic optimization or combinatorial optimization. Besides, even this list is not exhaustive and regular research on the Internet of the latest innovations on the matter may be profitable.

Furthermore, on the basis of the principles and techniques studied here, you can develop your own alternative. Let us take advantage of this remark to say some words on an interesting tendency, which could be described as syncretism.

14.2. Mono, poly, meta

Initially let us note that PSO is clearly heuristics, "a method of resolution of problems, not founded on a formal model and which necessarily does not lead to a solution". Nevertheless, the term is too general and the need for establishing distinctions was felt. Therefore, its use is reserved more and more for the specific algorithms of only one type of problem. For example, the Lin-Kernighan method for the resolution of the traveling salesman problem is called LKH (*Lin-Kernighan Heuristic*). It is very effective, but it can do only that. It is, so to speak, monoheuristic.

Conversely, stochastic methods, such as differential evolution [LAM 04], SOMA [ZEL 04], ant colonies [DOR 04], Tabou search [GLO 97], etc., appear usable for many types of problems, even if their fields of competence do not overlap exactly. They are general purpose heuristics, or polyheuristic. They are also called metaheuristic [DRE 03], though this term can lead to confusion (see below). PSO forms part of it. For a given problem, if there is no specific algorithm, one of these methods is probably a good choice.

In addition, second-level methods have appeared, i.e. algorithms whose function is to control the choice and the execution of definite algorithms. Sometimes they are referred to as hybrid methods, but, etymologically, it is they that should be called metaheuristic, even metapolyheuristic! In the same way, indeed, as a metarule is a rule of handling of rules, a metalanguage a language of description of language, etc., we deal here with heuristics handling (the poly) heuristics.

As regards PSO and continuous optimization, one of the most promising hybrids is perhaps DEPSO [ZHA 03b], combining PSO and differential evolution. The latter is indeed definitely more effective than PSO on certain problems (often of low dimensionality) but also definitely less effective on others. Hence, obviously, the idea of associating them judiciously ... by avoiding accumulating their respective defects!

14.3. The beginning of the end?

Thus is born the syncretic tendency that we have evoked, even if, for the moment, studied synergies relate only to pairs of methods: genetic algorithm and Tabou search [ZDA 02], genetic algorithm and ant colony [WHI 98], genetic algorithm and simulated annealing [KRA 04], simulated annealing and gradient [OVE 03], etc.

This is at the same time good and bad news. Good, in the sense that the question of knowing if one method is better than another, already rarely relevant because it is too general and will have little to recommend it in face of an approach that amalgamates them. Bad, if you like, because it will become increasingly difficult to progress in the field of optimization without studying several possible methods, their complementarities, and their interactions in depth.

But, really, it is rather a stimulating research program. We do feel that all these general purpose heuristics already have many similarities and are probably only partial transcriptions, according to various points of view, of a more general algorithm. This last is perhaps inaccessible to us, but trying to approach it is already an aim in itself.

PART II
Outlines

Chapter 15

On Parallelism

15.1. The short-sighted swarm

First beautiful days. At the end of April, or perhaps the beginning of May. The densely populated hive swarms. This multitude of honey bees, drunk and stuffed with food, hums and circles before gathering around the old queen who has just alighted on a branch. Only the scouts explore the neighborhoods, in search of a new home. They return, set out again, compare, until a decision is made. Then, just like that, the whole swarm flies away towards the chosen haven, as if each bee followed a single scout.

But this is not the case. Each one sees only its closest neighbors. Each one, except the very first one, is at the same time guide and guided. When the head bee changes direction, information is propagated from the front to the rear, from one to many, but not instantaneously, and the swarm is spread out by following a curve, before closing up. The transmission of information is done locally in parallel and globally in sequence. By the biological metaphor which underlies it, the original PSO functions in the same way, but is it the most effective?

15.2. A parallel model

Let us remind ourselves of the sequential operating mode we have always used so far. The particles are numbered from 1 to N. Particle 1 questions its informing memories, moves according to received information, and possibly updates the memory which is associated with it, if it finds a better position than that memorized (we suppose here that the number of memories is at most equal to that of

196   Particle Swarm Optimization

informants). Then particle 2 does the same, with the difference that one of its informants is perhaps precisely the memory that has been just modified. It can sometimes take advantage of this new information. In the same way for the following particles, with an increasing probability that a modified memory is used to guide a displacement.

The parallel mode, on the contrary, is nothing like that at all. All the particles use the same state of the memory-swarm and the possible order (simulated in parallel) in which their displacements are calculated is of no importance. This method can seem more elegant, but let us immediately look at a comparison of the results on our benchmark set.

15.3. A counter-intuitive result

To make this comparison, let us proceed as described in the chapter on optimum parameter setting, but by making the program function in simulated parallel mode. A first interesting point is that the optimal parameter settings obtained are the same ones. There is nothing very surprising about that. But the second point is more unexpected.

Table 15.1 shows us that, in fact, the parallel mode is a little less effective than the sequential mode. The difference is not very large, but statistical calculation shows that it is significant (let us recall that there are 100 executions for each problem).

Of course, and particularly for problems in which each evaluation is very long (simulation of a process or even execution of a real process), the time saving thanks to parallelism can nevertheless be considerable. But we must be aware that it is likely to be paid by a larger number of evaluations.

Thus, if T_{seq} is the total number of evaluations necessary in sequential mode and T_{parall} that in parallel mode, and if the criterion is the duration of the search for a solution, the mode is more interesting as long as one has $T_{parall} < NT_{seq}$, where N is the number of explorers.

As N is about a few 10s and the ratio T_{parall}/T_{seq} never seems to exceed 10, in practice it is apparently always the case.

	Sequential PSO	**Parallel PSO**
Tripod	0% (2,603)	0% (4,322)
Alpine 10D	0% (194)	0% (194)
Parabola 30D	0% (88)	0% (374)
Griewank 30	2%	8%
Rosenbrock 30D	100% min. 0.034 avg. 19.93	100% min. 0.763 avg. 25.79
Ackley 30D	0% (2,394)	0% (2,424)

Table 15.1. *Sequential PSO vs parallel PSO. The results of the sequential PSO are taken from Chapter 9. For the parallel PSO, the optimal parameters were also sought, finally finding the same ones. The performances are slightly lower, in terms of the number of evaluations, rates of failure or found values*

15.4. Qualitative explanation

Let us consider a swarm of N explorers and M memories. Each explorer is informed by K memories chosen randomly with each iteration and possibly updates only one memory, if there is improvement. To simplify the reasoning, these sizes are supposed to be constant. Let us examine more closely what occurs during an iteration, i.e. of a time increment, in parallel mode on the one hand and sequential mode on the other hand.

Let us call "information" for explorer a pair $(x, f(x))$ formed from a position and the value of this position. Under parallel operation, each explorer profits from K pieces of information whose quality is fixed at the end of the preceding iteration. This is taken into account to calculate its displacement, after which it possibly modifies its associated memory.

Under sequential operation, the first explorer benefits in the same way from K information whose quality is fixed at the end of the preceding iteration. It uses this information to move and will improve a memory m_1 with a certain non-null probability p_1. The second explorer questions K reports among M. The probability that m_1 is amongst them is q_2, non-null. Thus, this explorer has a probability equal to $p_1 q_2$ to benefit from information of better quality than in the parallel case. The same holds good for the following explorers, with an increasing probability of questioning a memory that was improved by at least one of the previous explorers.

It is thus comprehensible that the sequential mode is slightly more effective than the parallel mode, in terms of number of evaluations to reach the solution. The variation of effectiveness becomes smaller as M is large and K is small. However, we saw that it is in general desirable, for difficult problems, to adopt a low value for K. In particular, for all the test functions the optimum parameter setting is obtained with $K = 3$ or $K = 4$, except for the function Parabola ($K = 10$). For the latter, we notice that, even if the rate of failure is null with the two methods, the relative difference of the number of evaluations is indeed the highest of all.

15.5. For "amatheurs": probability of questioning an improved memory

The first explorer improved a memory m_1 with a probability p_1. The second explorer questions K memories chosen randomly among M, with putting back. The probability that the first drawn is not m_1 is $(M-1)/M$, the same for the second ... K^{th}. The probability that m_1 is not drawn at all is $((M-1)/M)^K$ and the probability that it is drawn is its complement with 1, that is to say:

$$q_2 = 1 - \left(\frac{M-1}{M}\right)^K$$

Finally, the probability that the second explorer questions a memory improved by the first is the conjunction of the two independent events: "to choose m_1" *and* "was improved". It is therefore equal to the product $p_1 q_2$.

For the following particles, the calculation becomes complicated if M is less than N. Thus let us suppose simply that there are as many explorers as memories and that, more precisely, each explorer informs a different memory m_i with the probability p_i (as is the case in traditional PSO). Then, in a way similar to what we have just seen, at the time of calculating the displacement of explorer j the probability of the event "of choosing at least one m_i with $i \leq j-1$ and m_i was improved" is greater than or equal to:

$$\min_{i \leq j-1}(p_i)\left(1 - \left(\frac{M-j+1}{M}\right)^K\right) = \min_{i \leq j-1}(p_i) q$$

It is hardly possible to estimate $\min_{i \leq j-1}(p_i)$ in advance, but the evolution of the probability q can easily be represented. As we see in Figure 15.1, it increases logically with the row j of the explorer. But it also increases with K, whereas the real effectiveness tends rather to decrease when K increases, except in certain simple problems. The reason is that the increase in K must in fact often also induce a reduction in the probabilities p_i. However, it justifies the fact that the variation of efficiency between sequential mode and parallel mode becomes smaller as *K* is itself small. There is enough matter here for an entire study.

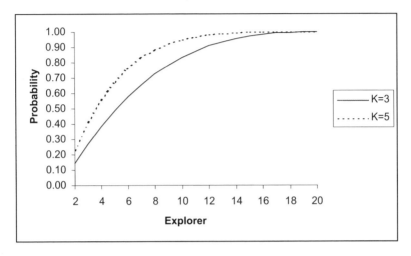

Figure 15.1. *Sequential mode. Probability of explorer questioning a memory possibly modified by a previous explorer during the current iteration. There are here 20 explorers who can update 20 memories. Each explorer questions randomly K memories drawn with putting back*

15.6. Summary

With each iteration, displacements of the particles can be calculated either in parallel or in sequence. The parallel mode is *a priori* desirable when the evaluation of a position is long and difficult, because the evaluations of the positions of each particle can be carried out simultaneously. But, in general, it rather requires more evaluations to reach the solution than the sequential mode.

In practice, however, the variation remains always sufficiently small so that the parallel mode is to be preferred if the essential criterion is the total duration necessary for obtaining a solution.

Chapter 16

Combinatorial Problems

16.1. Difficulty of chaos

Combinatorial problems are regarded as difficult, at least as soon as their size becomes somewhat substantial. But where does this difficulty come from and why is it considered to be larger than that of continuous problems of the same size? To answer this question, let us consider the archetypal traveling salesman problem. To simplify the reasoning, let us suppose that there is only one solution. With a graph with N nodes numbered 1 to N, to find the solution thus amounts to finding a precise permutation of an integer N among $N!$ possibles. The probability of reaching that point by chance, which we defined as being a measurement of the difficulty, is thus $1/N!$.

Now, let us consider a continuous problem whose search space is $[1, N]^N$ and in which we wish to minimize a numerical function f "accurate to within ε". Let us suppose, which is almost always the case, that the function is Lipschitzian, i.e. with limited variations. More precisely, there is a value L such that if two points x_1 and x_2 are separated by less than ε', then the variation of the function between these two points is less than $\varepsilon' L$:

$$\|x_1 - x_2\| < \varepsilon' \Rightarrow |f(x_1) - f(x_2)| < \varepsilon' L$$

Thus, to seek a solution "accurate to within ε" it is enough for us to examine "cells" of diameter about ε/L. Their total number is approximately:

$$\left(\frac{N-1}{\varepsilon/L}\right)^N$$

To compare this number with the number of permutations above, we must give values to ε, ε', and L. Since, in fact, we are interested only in the integer positions, let us posit $\varepsilon' = 1$. In addition, in practice, one can always consider that the lengths of the arcs are integers. Then the search for the shortest circuit can be done "to near 1^-" where 1^- represents any positive value less than 1. Thus let us posit $\varepsilon = 1$.

Let us now take as example a circular graph of which all the arcs are 1 long. According to a traditional method, the non-existent arcs are replaced by arcs of sufficiently great length that they cannot belong to a solution, for example, $N + 1$. The difference in value L between two positions is thus at least equal to $N + 1$. Thus the number of "cells" is about $((N+1)(N-1))^N$, a value much larger than $N!$ It follows from this that, from a theoretical point of view, the problem seen in its continuous form is much more difficult than in its combinatorial form.

The reason is that, when a combinatorial problem is difficult to solve by an iterative optimization algorithm, it is not because it is combinatorial but actually because the function of evaluation is very chaotic. In a more or less explicit way such an algorithm always supposes that the closer two positions are, the closer their evaluations are too. For a problem like the traveling salesman, that is easily false: a simple transposition of two cities in the circuit, i.e. the shortest possible displacement in the search space, can change the evaluation (the length of the cycle) from its minimum to its maximum.

16.2. Like a crystal

What is a combinatorial problem in any case? There is certainly a consensus on the fact that the search space must be finite (and thus discrete), but beyond this it is not obvious what would constitute a unanimous definition. A rather general description would be as follows.

We have a finite number of "sites" and a finite number of "objects", each site being able to contain at most one object. A position in the search space is then an assignment of copies of objects on sites and we suppose that for any pair of positions it is possible to say either that one is better than the other or that they are equivalent. Let us note that to impose all the different objects, such as the cities in the case of the traveling salesman, would be too restrictive and that is why it is more judicious to speak about a copy of the object than of the object itself. For example, the problem of coloring a graph is classically regarded as combinatorial, but several nodes can have the same color, insofar as no arc connects them.

But, as a result there is no difference in nature between a combinatorial problem and a finite discrete problem. Indeed, to solve a finite discrete problem of dimension D amounts to considering that we have D sites to which we assign values chosen in a finite set. This set can be viewed in the same way as that of the objects of the description of a combinatorial problem.

Better still, in practice, any bounded continuous problem is dealt with like a finite discrete problem. Indeed, in almost all cases calculations are made on a numerical (as opposed to analogue) computer and, therefore, with a limited and known precision. If, for example, the smallest representable number is 10^{-300}, then by multiplying all the facts of the case by 10^{300}, we obtain an equivalent problem handling only integers. The only difference, but it is significant, is the desired level of precision. If for the continuous problem it is 10^{-5}, there is an enormous number of acceptable solutions in the equivalent discrete problem, about 10^{295}. Or, conversely, if the problem is presented initially as discrete, very often having only one acceptable solution, that amounts to dealing with continuous problem with a very high requirement of precision, about 10^{-300} in our example.

The search space, which is necessarily discrete with a numerical computer, can be seen as similar to a crystal. To consider the problem as continuous consists in examining this crystal at least with a magnifying glass. To consider it as combinatorial is to work with an electron microscope.

16.3. Confinement method

We can thus treat a combinatorial problem exactly like a continuous problem, using two confinements that we have seen in the chapter on constraints: discrete variable and possibly "all different". In practice, after each theoretically continuous displacement, the particle is readjusted on the nearest integer position then, if the problem requires it, on the nearest having all its coordinates different.

For problems of very small size, we saw that this method is sufficient. It has the advantage of making it possible to use almost any version of PSO, since the requirement of two confinements either is already included or can easily be added. It is possible to improve the results appreciably by adding a local search algorithm implemented for each particle after each displacement. To stick to traveling salesman, a simple greedy algorithm already makes the number of evaluations necessary decrease several orders of magnitude.

For example, on the example with 17 nodes BR17 of library TSPLIB (http://www.ing.unlp.edu.ar/cetad/mos/TSPBIB_home.html), a strategy of the type "to test all the transpositions of two nodes and to start again as long as there is improvement" makes it possible to find a solution in fewer than 5,000 evaluations, which is already definitely more acceptable than failing after a million evaluations in "native" PSO! But for problems of more consequence, it is better to call upon a version of PSO taking directly into account the combinatorial aspects in the equations of displacement. The principal idea is then, for each type of combinatorial problem, to manage to define a true distance in the search space, because we know that a noticeable improvement can result from it regarding two significant aspects of the algorithm: the definition of a proximity distribution and the search for the best informant of a particle.

Moreover, this does not exempt us from conceiving hybrid strategies with complementary local search. In mid-2004 the development of such methods was still embryonic with regard to PSO, but several projects were in hand. The common base is the description of the algorithm in a way that is as independent as possible of the nature of the objects involved: numbers (real or discrete), quantitative or qualitative sizes, structure of the search space, nature of optimization. This fundamental representation can be made in a very condensed way, as we will see now.

16.4. Canonical PSO

To be able to implement PSO, the conditions below are necessary and sufficient:

– a search space, set of positions $H = \{x\}$. Each position is defined by a list of D components;

– an application f defined on H and in values in a set C $H \xrightarrow{f} C = \{c\}$. Each element of C itself is defined by D' components;

– a relation of order on C or, more generally, semi-order, so that for each pair of elements $\{c, c'\}$ it is always possible to say that c is "better" than c' or that c' is better than c or, finally, that c and c' are equivalent. Note that this definition includes both the traditional optimization for which c and c' are numbers and the multicriterion optimization where c and c' are compared according to a relation of dominance.

The definition of a distance on H is not obligatory, but makes it possible to use more effective techniques, such as the pseudo-gradient in the search for the best particle information source about another and the search to give a direction to the multidimensional proximity distributions, such as the D-spheres.

Combinatorial Problems 205

In general, H is real space $\mathbf{R}^D$ and f a numerical function (C is the set of the real numbers provided with its usual relation of order). But H can be a finite set of statuses and f a discrete function. By referring to the equations of motion of the traditional PSO, the important thing is to be able to define the following objects and mathematical operations:

– *position* of a particle
– *velocity* of a particle
– subtraction $(position, position) \xrightarrow{-} velocity$
– external multiplication $(number\_real, velocity) \xrightarrow{\cdot} velocity$
– addition $(velocity, velocity) \xrightarrow{\oplus} velocity$
– displacement $(position, velocity) \xrightarrow{+} position$

As an application of this canonical representation, let us look at how these objects and operators can be defined for the treatment of a combinatorial problem: the indefatigable traveling salesman. The goal is obviously not to try to equal the effectiveness of very specific algorithms such LKH [HEL 98], but simply to illustrate the following assertion: "if you do not have a specific algorithm for your problem, try PSO, it will do". Besides, versions of discrete and combinatorial PSO have already been defined and used successfully [KEN 97, MOH 01, ONW 04B, SAL 01, SCH 02, SEC 01A, YOS 01].

PSO for traveling salesman

Positions

Let $G = \{N_G, A_G\}$ be the valuated graph in which we seek a Hamiltonian circuit of minimal length. N_G is the set of the nodes and A_G the set of the arcs. The nodes are numbered from 1 to N and will be denoted n_i or, if there is no possibility of confusion, we will just represent them by their numbers $i, i \in \{1, ..., N\}$. Each arc is in fact identified with the triplet $(i, j, l_{i,j}), i \in N_G, j \in N_G, l_{i,j} \in \mathbf{R}^+$, which can be read as follows: "the arc of origin i, end j, and length $l_{i,j}$". Since we seek circuits, we can consider, to simplify the notations, sequences of $N+1$ nodes, all different, except that the last is equal to the first (and which can easily be always equal to 1). Let us call N-cycle such a sequence and define it as being a position. Thus the search space is the finite set of the N-cycles.

Function to be minimized

Let us consider a position such as:

$$x = (n_1, n_2, \ldots, n_N, n_{N+1}), n_i \in A_G, n_1 = n_{N+1}$$

It is acceptable only if all the arcs (n_i, n_{i+1}) exist. To standardize the operations, it is traditional to replace the non-existent arcs by virtual arcs of which the length l_{sup} is sufficiently large that no minimum cycle can contain one of them. For example, if $l_{\min}$ and $l_{\max}$ are respectively the smallest and the biggest length of the existing arcs, we can define l_{sup} as follows:

$$\begin{cases} l_{\max} = MAX(w_{i,j}) \\ l_{\min} = MIN(w_{i,j}) \\ l_{\text{sup}} > l_{\max} + (N-1)(l_{\max} - l_{\min}) \end{cases}$$

Thus, in this manner, each arc, real or virtual, has a length. The function to be minimized is defined on the set of the N-cycles and, for each one, is worth simply its length:

$$f(x) = \sum_{i=1}^{N} l_{n_i, n_{i+1}}$$

Velocity

The term "velocity" results from the history of PSO, but it is simply a question of defining an operator which, applied to a position, gives another position. It is thus a permutation of $N - 1$ elements, which can always be broken up into a list of transpositions; in other words, $\|v\|$ the length of this list. Thus, a velocity is represented by a list of pairs of nodes to exchange:

$$v = ((i_k, j_k)), i_k \in N_G, j_k \in N_G, k = 1, \ldots, \|v\|$$

or, in digest form $v = ((i_k, j_k))$, which can be read "to exchange nodes (i_1, j_1), then nodes (i_2, j_2), etc."

Two different lists, and v_2, applied to the same position, are perfectly well able to give the same result (the same new position). Two such velocities will be known as equivalent and we will note that $v_1 \cong v_2$. For example, we have $((1,3),(2,5)) \cong ((2,5),(1,3))$. In this example, two velocities are not only equivalent but also opposite (see below). The use of such velocities is connected with displacement on a sphere: you can reach the same point while following two opposite directions.

Lastly, to admit all the necessary operations, null velocity, denoted $\emptyset$, should be defined: it will be simply the empty list.

Let us point out a traditional theorem of algebra that will be useful for us later in the definition of metric. Not only can any permutation be carried out by a succession of transpositions, but there is a necessary and sufficient minimum number of such transpositions. With the vocabulary used here, in other words, if one considers all the equivalent velocities at a given velocity v, then there is at least one of minimal size. Let us call such a velocity a *representative* of v.

Opposed to a velocity

It is defined by:

$$\neg v = \left(\left(i_{\|v\|-k+1}, j_{\|v\|-k+1}\right)\right)$$

This formula simply means "to carry out the same transpositions as for v, but in reverse order". We immediately have $\neg\neg v = v$ (and also $v \oplus \neg v \cong \emptyset$, according to the definition of the addition of two velocities, which we will see a little later).

Displacement (position plus velocity)

Let x be a position and v a velocity. The new position $x' = x + v$ is obtained by applying the first transposition of v to x, then the second with the result obtained, etc.

EXAMPLE –

$$\begin{cases} x = (1,2,3,4,5,1) \\ v = ((1,2),(2,3)) \end{cases}$$

By applying v to x, we successively obtain (with each stage, if necessary, the components of the N-cycle are shifted in order always to have node 1 in first):

$(2,1,3,4,5,2) = (1,3,4,5,2,1)$
$(1,2,4,5,3,1)$

Subtraction (position minus position)

For two positions x_1 and x_2, the difference $x_2 - x_1$ is defined as the velocity v obtained by a given method, such as by applying v to x_1 one finds x_2. The condition "obtained by a given method" (in practice an algorithm) is necessary because, as we have seen, two velocities can be different but equivalent, even if they have the same size (the same number of transpositions). In particular, the method must be coherent, in the sense that the subtraction of two identical positions must give null velocity and the difference in two positions in a direction must give the opposite of the difference in the other direction:

$$x_1 = x_2 \Rightarrow v = x_2 - x_1 = \emptyset$$
$$x_2 - x_1 = \neg(x_1 - x_2)$$

Addition (velocity plus velocity)

Let us consider two velocities v_1 and v_2. To calculate their sum $v_1 \oplus v_2$, we build the list of transpositions that initially contains those of v_1 then those of v_2. In practice, to avoid ill-considered lengthening of such lists, it is also necessary to operate a contraction in order to obtain an equivalent velocity of smaller size.

Let us note that we do have the triangular inequality $\|v_1 \oplus v_2\| \leq \|v_1\| + \|v_2\|$ but no commutativity. In general $v_1 \oplus v_2$ is different from $v_2 \oplus v_1$.

Multiplication (coefficient by velocity)

Let v be a velocity to be multiplied by a real coefficient c. We must consider several cases, according to the value of c. There is a small theoretical (but non-practical) difficulty: to multiply two equivalent velocities by the same coefficient will give two still equivalent velocities only if this coefficient is an integer.

Case $c = 0$

Let us posit simply $cv = \emptyset$.

Case $0 < c \leq 1$

We are satisfied with "to truncate" v. Let $m = \|cv\|$ be the integer part of $c\|v\|$. The new velocity is defined by taking only the m first transpositions of v:

$$c.v = ((i_k, j_k)), k = 1,...,\|cv\|.$$

Case $c > 1$

We can then write c as a sum of an integer k and a real c' less than 1. It is then enough to proceed in three steps: to add v to itself k times, to multiply v by c', and finally to add two velocities obtained. This can be summarized by the following formulae:

$$c = k + c', k \in \mathbf{N}^*, c' \in [0\ 1[$$
$$c.v = \underbrace{v \oplus v \oplus ... \oplus v}_{k \text{ times}} \oplus c'.v$$

Once again, it is desirable to replace the result by an equivalent velocity of smaller size. In any case, this can be done progressively with the addition of v to itself k times.

Case $c < 0$

It is enough to write $c.v = (-c)\neg v$ and we are reduced to the combination of two operations seen above, the opposite of a velocity and multiplication by a positive coefficient.

Distance between two positions

We saw that it can be interesting to use a pseudo-gradient to define the best informant of a particle but that for that the search space must be provided with metrics. It is the case here, since it is enough to define the distance between two positions as the size of a representative of a velocity making it pass from one to the other. As we have seen, this size is unique.

If x_1 and x_2 are two positions, the distance between them is defined by:

$$d(x_1, x_2) = \|x_2 - x_1\|$$

and it is easy to check the axioms of metrics. If x_3 is a third unspecified position, we have:

$$\|x_2 - x_1\| = \|x_1 - x_2\|$$
$$\|x_2 - x_1\| = 0 \Leftrightarrow x_1 = x_2$$
$$\|x_2 - x_1\| \le \|x_2 - x_3\| + \|x_3 - x_1\|$$

Implementation

Once all these definitions are established (and programmed!), we can use the system of equations of motion of an unspecified version of PSO. For example, the traditional PSO will be rewritten as follows:

$$\begin{cases} v_d \leftarrow c_1.v_d \oplus c_2.(p_d - x_d) \oplus c_3.(p_g - x_d) \\ x_d \leftarrow x_d + v_d \end{cases}$$

Each operation concerned has a meaning very different from the usual one, but the spirit of the process is exactly the same. As it was stated earlier, various complementary techniques can of course be used jointly (local search, stop/restart, local leveling, etc). For more details, see for example [CLE 04, ONW 04a, SEC 01b]. However, this field is evolving so rapidly that any article published will very soon be only of historical interest. It is thus preferable to carry out search on the Internet or, at least, to consult *Particle Swarm Central* [PSC].

16.5. Summary

By reducing to the bare minimum the conditions necessary for a PSO, one defines a very general canonical algorithm using only some algebraic operators. Hence, it is possible to build a specific PSO (for example, for combinatorial problems) by specifying the operation of these operators for the type of problem considered. An example is given for the traveling salesman problem. In this case, the principal difficulty is to give a meaning to the operation of multiplication of a list of transpositions by a numerical coefficient.

Chapter 17

Dynamics of a Swarm

17.1. Motivations and tools

At the time of writing (in 2005), there was still no satisfactory theoretical analysis of PSO. The reason is that the problem is not simple, because of the interactions between particles. It has been well-known since Poincaré that the evolution of such systems can lead to a literally indescribable chaos. It would, however, be quite interesting to have, as guides of improvement of the method, elements that are more reliable than simple overall experimentation. How can we go about this?

We have here mobile particles that influence each other, admittedly in general in a space of much higher dimension than those of the spaces defined in physics, but the tools and methods of statistical dynamics are perhaps usable, subject to two comments:

– the field implemented is more complicated than, for example, a single gravitational field, since each particle is influenced only by some others, informants, and not by all. If one wants to push the analogy further, it would thus be necessary to consider the simultaneous influence of several fields of various natures;

– the size of the swarm is generally low. The variance of statistical sizes defined on such a small population is extremely likely to be very large.

Nevertheless, studies based on such modeling are underway, but so far they have not produced results that are usable in practice.

A less ambitious step consists of considering a swarm reduced to only one particle. That can seem paradoxical, since the interactions play a crucial role, but in fact, as we saw in the chapter on the memory-swarm, talking about only one particle is a result of the historical terminology. Actually, there are always at least two particles: the explorer and the memory. Mathematical analyses are then possible and have indeed provided, as already mentioned, precise recommendations which are theoretically validated for the choice of the confidence coefficients, in particular *via* the coefficients of constriction [CLE 02, TRE 03, VAN 02].

We will not review them again here, the more so as they are rather unpleasing ("amatheurs" will be able to relish them at the end of this chapter). Instead we will study in detail a very simple example and the lesson we can already draw.

17.2. An example with the magnifying glass

Let us consider the function Parabola 1D, defined on $[-20\ 20]$ by the equation $f(x) = x^2$. We wish a particle to find the minimum (zero, obviously), with a precision equal to at least $\varepsilon = 0,001$. In other words, a particle must at least reach a position located in the interval $[-\sqrt{\varepsilon}\ \sqrt{\varepsilon}]$. The theoretical difficulty of this problem is 6.45. To simplify the analysis still more, we will use only version OEP 0.

The question that interests us is the influence of the interactions on the effectiveness of the algorithm. That is why we will consider and compare the results obtained with a swarm reduced to only one particle (in fact, as has already been said, an explorer and a memory) and a swarm of two particles (making 2 + 2).

17.2.1. *One particle*

With only one particle, the equations of motion can be written in a simplified form:

$$\begin{cases} v \leftarrow c_1 v + c_2(p - x) \\ x \leftarrow x + v \end{cases}$$

There are two primary cases: either the initial velocity is such that the first two positions frame that of the minimum, or on the contrary these two positions are on the same side. In the first case, the particle oscillates around the optimal position; in the second, it tends there directly, at the latest at the very second time increment (see Figure 17.1). Let x_2 be the position reached with the second time increment.

The significant point when the first positions are on the same side is that the memorized position p is then always equal to the current position x. There is certainly constant improvement, but each displacement is strictly equal to the preceding one multiplied by c_1. There can therefore be convergence towards the optimum only if the infinite sum of successive displacements $\left(\sum_{t=2}^{\infty} c_1^{t-1}\right)|v_2|$ is at least equal to $|x_2|$. However, in our example we have:

$$\begin{cases} c_1 = 0.7 \\ v_2 = 3.2 \\ x_2 = -20 \end{cases}$$

Under these conditions the total distance traveled by the particle even at the end of an infinite time cannot exceed approximately 10.7. It is insufficient to reach the optimum. However, if the particle oscillates around this optimum, things occur completely differently, because the last best position known is no longer necessarily the current position. Velocity will still tend towards zero but no longer in a regular way, which prevents a premature convergence.

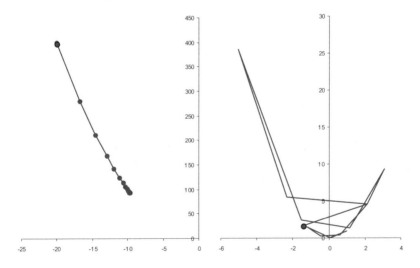

Figure 17.1. *Parabola problem, a memory and an explorer. The behavior of the system is very different according to the position and initial velocity of the explorer. On the left, the first two positions do not frame that of the minimum. The fast velocity decrease prevents the explorer reaching it. On the right, the first two positions frame that of the minimum. Here the core use leads the explorer to oscillate around the optimal position and, moreover, the velocity decreases less quickly, which allows convergence*

214 Particle Swarm Optimization

These two types of behavior are highlighted better still by the representation in the phase space in Figure 17.2. The traditional fundamental structure which appears almost systematically in the case of convergence towards the solution is that of a spiral as in the right-hand part of the Figure. As we will see, whether there is one particle or more (in the sense: explorer + memory) does not make any difference. For the algorithm to proceed successfully it is necessary, except in very particular cases, that successive positions are reached on either side of the optimal position: there must be oscillations. Mathematically, that is translated in our example by the fact that the scalar product of vectors v and $p - v$ must be negative. In this form, it is a necessary condition, which can be generalized whatever the dimension of the search space and the number of particles.

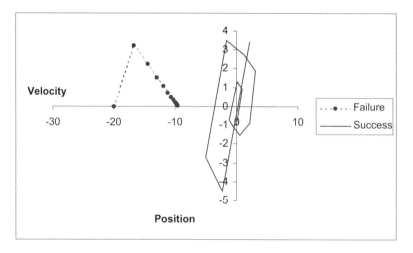

Figure 17.2. *Parabola problem, a memory and an explorer, phase space. The two cases of Figure 17.1 are taken again here, but seen in the plan (position, velocity). The converging oscillatory behavior is represented by a spiral*

17.2.2. Two particles

Let us recall that the term "particle" is taken here with its historical meaning, i.e. it embraces the double concept of explorer and memory. We thus now have two explorers and two memories. To remain formally identical to the original PSO, the information links are those represented in Figure 17.3. Each memory informs the two explorers but each explorer informs only one memory. Initializations are deliberately defined identical to the position and velocity of the single particle of the preceding example, and in both the same cases with the first two positions on the same side of the origin or on both sides.

The right-hand side of Figure 17.4 represents the course of particle 2 in this second case. It is absolutely identical to that partly on the right of Figure 17.1, because at any moment memory 2 is in better position than memory 1. Thus the existence of particle 1 does not bring anything to particle 2. However, as the comparison between the left-hand sides of the two Figure s shows, particle 1 takes advantage of the existence of particle 2. The information provided to it *via* memory 2 makes it possible for it also to enter an oscillatory process that would ensure it convergence if the iterations were prolonged beyond the success of particle 2.

Starting from a more unspecified initial configuration, we obtain the paths illustrated by Figure 17.5. Each particle takes advantage of the information provided by the other to manage to oscillate around the optimal position. Thus, on the one hand, the number of evaluations is doubled with each time increment, since there are two particles; but, on the other hand, in a simple case like this one, the probability of reaching the solution (with the precision required) is itself roughly doubled. As a result, *roughly speaking*, the effectiveness is the same: about 30 evaluations are needed to reach the solution.

But then, what is the point in using several particles? It is that the case of two particles is precisely the limit beyond which the increase in the size of the swarm will become interesting. The power of PSO lies in the fact that the probability of reaching the solution by time increment t increases more or less as $N(N-1)$, where N is the size of the swarm, whereas the number of evaluations carried out on the whole until the increment t is only proportional to N (reasoning with N constant during optimization). This is still only an empirical conclusion (which, moreover, is no longer valid for greater values of N), but it provides a beginning of an explanation for the increase in effectiveness with N. Studies in progress, in particular using statistical mechanics, are trying to validate this observation more firmly.

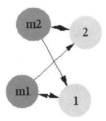

Figure 17.3. *Graph of information 2 + 2. Each explorer receives the information from the two memories, but informs only one, to conform to the diagram of the traditional PSO, where explorer and memory are merged in a single particle. That is enough for any improvement found by the explorer to be known to the other one*

216   Particle Swarm Optimization

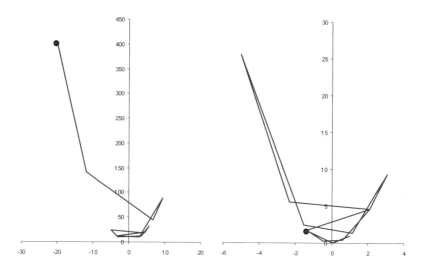

Figure 17.4. *Two explorers and two memories. The starting points are the same as in the preceding example. But now the particles work together. However, here, memory 2 is always better than memory 1: the course of explorer 2 is exactly the same as seen previously in the event of convergence (Figure on right-hand side). On the other hand, explorer 1 will benefit from the information provided by memory 2: it will end up converging if the iterations are continued (Figure on the left)*

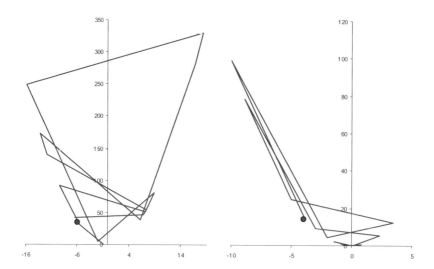

Figure 17.5. *Parabola. Two explorers and two memories. We are here in the more general case where each explorer is from time to time influenced by the memory of the other, when it becomes better than its own. Convergence, when it takes place, is not necessarily faster (here 30 iterations instead of 28), but it is more probable*

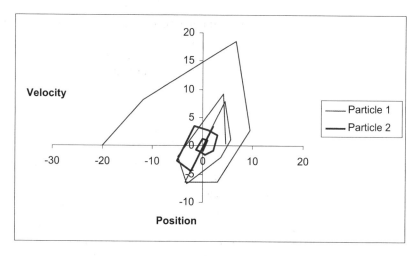

Figure 17.6. *Parabola. Two explorers and two memories. Representation of the paths in phase space. The particles help each other to enter and remain in the oscillatory process that allows convergence towards the solution*

17.3. Energies

17.3.1. *Definitions*

We have taken advantage of the preceding examples to underline the interest of the representations by trajectories in phase spaces. Another traditional method in dynamics is to consider the evolution of global variables, such as potential energy, kinetic energy, or entropy. We will be satisfied here with the first two, and particularly with kinetic energy, but, first, we must give precise definitions of them. We will accept that the search space is provided with a distance and that the function f to minimize is numerical.

For the kinetic energy of a particle, whether it is an explorer or a memory, this is very simple: it is enough to consider two successive positions x_t and x_{t+1} and calculate the size $e = \|x_t - x_{t+1}\|^2 / 2$. It is deliberate that velocity has not been called upon explicitly, because, as we saw for example with the method of pivots, this quantity is not used in all versions of PSO. Naturally, the total kinetic energy of a swarm is the sum of those of the particles that are its components.

For the potential energy, it is necessary to take into account the required precision ε for the desired solution. In addition, we can take advantage of the fact that this type of energy can be known apart from an additive constant, which avoids

218   Particle Swarm Optimization

us having to use the value of f in its minimum, in general unknown. Then the potential energy u of a position x can be defined by the formula $u = f(x)/\varepsilon$. It can be interpreted as the number of "steps" of height ε that the particle must descend to reach the minimum if its value were zero. Again, the total potential energy of a swarm is the sum of those of its components.

17.3.2. Evolutions

We already know that, approximately, velocities tend to be cancelled during the iterative process and the swarm ends up converging somewhere, even if it is not the desired solution. We can thus expect that the kinetic energy tends on average towards zero and potential energy towards a constant. But what is particularly instructive to observe using these sizes is the difference in behavior between a version of traditional PSO (N particles given at the beginning once and for all) and an adaptive version for which the size of the swarm is modified as suppressions and generations dictate.

Let us take for example the Alpine function. An execution with good parameters easily gives evolutions of energies such those of Figure 17.7. The fact that the kinetic energy tends towards zero tell us that, overall, the swarm ceases moving; therefore, that each particle converges towards a fixed position. The fact that, at the same time, the potential energy also tends towards zero means that, for all the particles, this position is indeed that of the sought minimum. Here, the number of explorers is 20, the same as the number of memories. The light fluctuations of energies, and in particular of the kinetic energy, are due only to an element of chance in the equations of motion.

With an adaptive PSO like TRIBES, each particle is at the same time explorer and memory, but their number is modified during the process, by suppressions and generations. Figure 17.8 then indicates the clear evolution of the size of the swarm as well as that of the kinetic energy. When this tends towards zero and the objective therefore is not achieved (which is not represented on the Figure, for the sake of clarity), there are appreciably more generations than suppressions, which creates a peak of energy, which we can interpret as a re-augmentation of the exploratory capacity of the swarm.

As we saw in the chapter on optimal parameters, it is certainly possible, in this example, to find a solution more quickly than with TRIBES, but it is also possible to be much less effective if the parameters are not properly selected. An adaptive version, because it re-starts exploration judiciously, is much more sound.

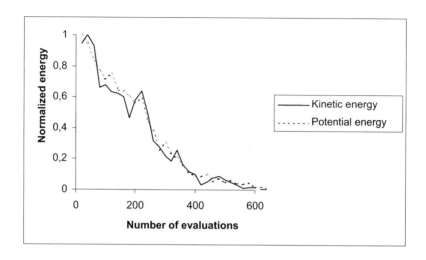

Figure 17.7. *Alpine, treated by parametric PSO. The size of the swarm is constant (20) here. The small variations of energy are only fluctuations due to the partially random character of the equations of motion*

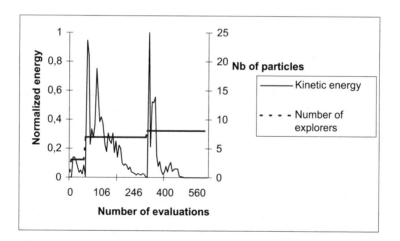

Figure 17.8. *Alpine, treated by adaptive PSO (TRIBES). During the process, particles are removed and others added. The net assessment is a constant increase in the swarm (this is not always the case) but, particularly, of the significant peaks of energy relaunching the exploration when that becomes necessary*

17.4. For experienced "amatheurs": convergence and constriction

The complete analytical study has been made only for the moment in the case of a single particle and with constant confidence coefficients (non-random). Some of its elements are given below. For more details, see [CLE 02, TRE 03, VAN 02].

17.4.1. *Criterion of convergence*

In the case of only one particle, the equations of motion can be written:

$$\begin{cases} v_{t+1} = c_1 v_t + c_2(p_t - x_t) + c_3(g_t - x_t) \\ x_{t+1} = x_t + v_{t+1} \end{cases}$$

where the indices t and $t+1$ correspond to two successive time increments. Positing:

$$\begin{cases} c = c_2 + c_3 \\ p = \dfrac{c_2 p_t + c_3 g_t}{c_2 + c_3} \end{cases}$$

we obtain the canonical system:

$$\begin{cases} v_{t+1} = c_1 v_t + c(p - x_t) \\ x_{t+1} = x_t + v_{t+1} \end{cases}$$

The idea is to look at what occurs as long as p is constant. We can then posit $y = p - x$ and, written in matrix form, the system becomes:

$$\begin{bmatrix} v_{t+1} \\ y_{t+1} \end{bmatrix} = \begin{bmatrix} c_1 & c \\ -c_1 & 1-c \end{bmatrix} \begin{bmatrix} v_t \\ y_t \end{bmatrix} = C \begin{bmatrix} v_t \\ y_t \end{bmatrix}$$

We now have a traditional dynamic system, whose behavior is entirely dependent on the eigenvalues of the matrix C. In particular, a condition of convergence is that these eigenvalues are two combined complex numbers of modulus less than 1 or two real numbers of absolute values less than 1. They are solutions of the equation:

$$\begin{vmatrix} c_1 - \lambda & c \\ -c_1 & 1-c-\lambda \end{vmatrix} = \lambda^2 + (c - c_1 - 1)\lambda + c_1 = 0$$

whose discriminant is $\Delta = (c - c_1 - 1)^2 - 4c_1$.

Let us recall that here convergence means simply that the particle tends towards a stable position (velocity tends towards zero). Nothing guarantees that this position is the sought optimum. It is only the interactions between particles that considerably increase the chances that this may be the case.

17.4.2. *Coefficients of constriction*

In traditional PSO, it can happen that the swarm "explodes" (divergence) and this is why certain authors add a constraint of maximum velocity, which makes an additional parameter. It was proven [CLE 02] that that was not necessary, with the proviso one or more coefficients of constriction are used, calculated starting from the confidence coefficients. To determine them, there are essentially two steps:

– to see to it that the eigenvalues of C are true complex numbers (negative discriminant);

– or to weight the confidence coefficients judiciously when the eigenvalues are real (positive or null discriminant).

There exists an infinite number of possibilities. Let us simply examine one of each type, which replace relatively simple formulas. The general idea is to pass by an intermediate parameter φ, according to which one expresses c and c_1, so as to respect the criterion of convergence.

Negative discriminant

A simple form corresponds to the following relations:

$$\begin{cases} c_1 = \chi(\varphi) \\ c = \chi\varphi \end{cases}$$

The matrix of the system is then:

$$C = \begin{bmatrix} \chi & \chi\varphi \\ -\chi & 1 - \chi\varphi \end{bmatrix}$$

We will seek the coefficient of constriction χ as a function of φ and as near to 1 as possible, while guaranteeing that the discriminant of the equation whose solutions are the eigenvalues of the system remains negative. The condition "negative discriminating" is written here:

$$\chi^2(1-\varphi)^2 - 2(1+\varphi) + 1 < 0$$

It is satisfied only if χ is between the two roots:

$$\chi_{min} = \frac{1+\varphi - 2\sqrt{\varphi}}{(1-\varphi)^2} \text{ and } \chi_{max} = \frac{1+\varphi + 2\sqrt{\varphi}}{(1-\varphi)^2}$$

It is easy to see that χ_{min} is always less than 1 (for φ positive). For $\varphi \leq 4$ the second root χ_{max} is greater than or equal to 1. We can thus take a coefficient of constriction equal to 1, i.e. in fact, not of constriction at all. On the other hand, for $\varphi > 4$, the coefficient nearest to 1 that we can take is χ_{max} itself. Constriction is thus summarized by the following formulas:

$$\begin{cases} c_1 = \chi(\varphi) = \begin{cases} 1 \text{ si } \varphi \leq 4 \\ \frac{1+\varphi + 2\sqrt{\varphi}}{(1-\varphi)^2} \text{ si } \varphi > 4 \end{cases} \\ c = c_1 \varphi \end{cases}$$

The common value of the modulus of the complex eigenvalues is then simply $\sqrt{c_1}$, which is at the most equal to 1: the criterion of convergence is satisfied. The curious reader will be able to find similar formulas (and even simpler ones) starting, for example, from the relations:

$$\begin{cases} c_1 = \chi(\varphi) \\ c = 1 + \chi - \chi\varphi \end{cases} \text{ or } \begin{cases} c_1 = \chi(\varphi) \\ c = 1 - \chi + \chi\varphi \end{cases}$$

Finally, the equations of motion are written:

$$\begin{cases} v_{t+1} = \chi v_t + \chi\varphi(p - x_t) \\ x_{t+1} = x_t + v_{t+1} \end{cases}$$

17.4.3. *Positive discriminant*

A canonical system even simpler than that we have seen can be written:

$$\begin{cases} v_{t+1} = v_t + \varphi(p - x_t) \\ x_{t+1} = x_t + v_{t+1} \end{cases}$$

By positing $y = p - x$, the system becomes:

$$\begin{cases} v_{t+1} = v_t + \varphi y_t \\ y_{t+1} = -v_t + (1-\varphi)y_{t+1} \end{cases}$$

Its matrix is:

$$C = \begin{bmatrix} 1 & \varphi \\ -1 & 1-\varphi \end{bmatrix}$$

A possible method of constriction consists in multiplying the whole of the matrix by a coefficient χ'. The eigenvalues are then solutions of the equation:

$$\begin{vmatrix} \chi' - \lambda & \chi'\varphi \\ -\chi' & \chi'(1-\varphi) - \lambda \end{vmatrix} = \lambda^2 + \chi'(\varphi - 2)\lambda + \chi'^2 = 0$$

We then find:

$$\lambda = \chi'\left(1 - \frac{\varphi}{2} \pm \frac{\sqrt{\varphi^2 - 4\varphi}}{2}\right)$$

These values are real only if one has $\varphi \geq 4$. So that their absolute values are at most equal to 1, it is necessary and sufficient that this is true for the the largest one, which gives us directly:

$$\chi' = \frac{2}{\varphi - 2 + \sqrt{\varphi^2 - 4\varphi}}$$

According to the way in which it was found, this coefficient is applicable to the equations of motion:

$$\begin{cases} v_{t+1} = \chi' v_t + \chi'\varphi(p - x_t) \\ x_{t+1} = x_t + v_{t+1} + (p - x_t)(1 - \chi') \end{cases}$$

whose physical interpretation is far from being obvious, owing to the fact that a corrective term is applied to displacement due only to velocity. However, it is easy to check that one always has $\chi' \leq \chi$ (see Figure 17.9). Thus, systematic use of χ' whatever the scenario (positive or negative discriminant) is mathematically acceptable. In the case of a negative discriminant, constriction is certainly a little too strong, but, in practice, the coefficient φ is taken to be very slightly greater than 4, which reduces the risk.

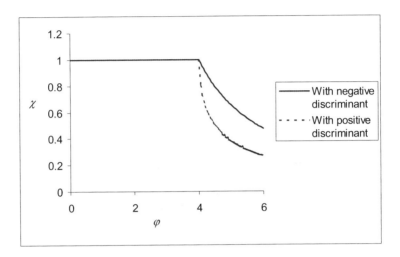

Figure 17.9. *Coefficients of constriction. The two methods indicated in the text lead to different formulas. However, the second can be used whether the discriminant of the system is positive or negative since the value obtained is in any case less than the greatest acceptable value calculated by the first. Nevertheless, it is better then to take the values of φ only slightly greater than 4, to avoid too strong a constriction and a premature convergence*

17.5. Summary

The dynamics of a swarm can be considered on the level of each particle, a privileged tool being the phase space. Convergence then results in spiral trajectories. It can also be studied globally, *via* variables such as the kinetic energy and potential energy. The examination of the evolution of the kinetic energy shows the difference in behavior between the traditional PSO and an adaptive version in which the size of the swarm varies according to the progress of the search: the peaks of energy announce the revival of exploration when convergence seems to become too slow.

In this chapter, the rather long mathematical part summarizes the calculation of certain coefficients of constriction, the use of which is of great practical importance.

Chapter 18

Techniques and Alternatives

18.1. Reprise

The major disadvantage of an almost entirely adaptive algorithm is that if the result is not satisfactory, it is difficult to cure it, since there are no parameters that the user can exploit. That is why it is interesting to develop techniques for piloting the search process. They certainly require that the user gets involved again, a little like parametric PSO, but on a more global level. It will no longer be a question of carefully defining a particular numerical value but rather of making strategic choices or, at least, choices of methods.

For example, the user can decide that there must be partial or total re-initialization of the search a certain number of times or that the generation of a new particle will have to be done according to a variable probability distribution or that it is necessary to make several swarms confined by repelling powers work simultaneously. In addition, the latter example shows that the border between what one could call complementary techniques and alternatives is not quite clear. The list is already rather long: non-specific particles with collisions [KRI 02], use of fuzzy values [SHI 01], definition of various forms of neighborhood [SUG 99, VEE 03], hybridization of PSO with other methods [KO 04, LOV 01, MIR 02a], local modification of the function to be minimized [PARS 01a], optimization of a variable function [CAR 01], "quantum" PSO [SIL 03], use of a negative entropy [XIE 02], etc.

The goal of this book is not to review them systematically, especially as some are of limited interest. We will just consider some of them, which are at both of proven effectiveness at least for certain types of problems and relatively easy to implement by some modifications of a traditional PSO program.

18.2. Stop-restart/reset

In principle, this technique is very simple and very traditional: if there is "no more hope" of finding a solution, then the process is re-initialized more or less at random. We see immediately that there are two distinct problems. On the one hand, it is necessary to define a criterion for giving up the process in progress advisedly (and especially not too early); and, on the other hand, it is necessary to choose a method of re-initialization. Such a pair "NoHope/Rehope" is, for example, defined for the parametric PSO in [CLE 99]. Let us examine it quickly, knowing that, of course, others are possible (see, for example, in the more general field of stochastic optimization [LIT 98, NIE 86]).

18.2.1. *A criterion of abandonment*

A very general criterion often used is Shannon's entropy [DAV 92], which evaluates up to what point the found positions are different. But it is especially interesting for discrete problems and, in the specific case of PSO, it is possible to be more precise. The first idea is to estimate regularly the volume that the swarm is still likely to explore, by taking into account the dispersion of the swarm and the velocities of the particles. Let us note that such a calculation is especially interesting in non-adaptive PSO or, at least, if there are no particles generated during the search process. Indeed, such generations can be viewed as partial re-initialization occurring from time to time. As a result, the need for a total re-initialization is definitely rarer.

We noted in the outline on the dynamics of the swarms that the kinetic energy is then *roughly speaking* decreasing. Indeed the equations of motion imply that, on average, the norm of the velocity vector of a particle is multiplied by a coefficient less than 1 with each time increment. So even in an infinite time, the particle could travel only a finite distance, called *maximum flight*. Thus, even by taking the extreme case where all the particles would move away from the same point in a straight line, the total explorable space is still finite. In practice, it is estimated by taking as central point the center of gravity of the swarm. The criterion considered is the ratio of volumes of still explorable space and the total search space. Intuitively, it is advisable to stop wasting time when this ratio becomes too small. Again, it is necessary to define what that means.

The second idea is then to use the sampling of the search space provided by the current swarm to calculate pseudo-gradients that give us information on the local form of the function to be minimized and to consider that this form remains valid in still explorable space. Of course, this requires that the search space be provided with a metric and this is all the more necessary as the swarm is concentrated, i.e. that the process is already quite advanced. Subject to these reservations, a minimum threshold that must not be exceeded for the ratio discussed above can in general be estimated according to the acceptable error given initially by the user. When the ratio falls below this threshold, the process is stopped, the best found solution is in general preserved and a re-initialization is carried out. The simplest approach is to do this completely randomly, exactly like the very first initialization, but it is also possible to take advantage of the pseudo-gradients already calculated to move all the particles en bloc.

18.2.2. *Guided re-initialization*

The initial swarm taken into account is that of the best positions found by the particles. The very best of them is taken as the central point. The principle is then to dilate the swarm relative to this central point. For each particle (except the best), the pseudo-gradient relative to this central point is calculated and then the particle is moved: the smaller the pseudo-gradient, the farther from this center. The disadvantage, nevertheless, is that a parameter of the initial dilatation should be defined slightly greater than 1 (typically 1.1). After each re-initialization, this coefficient must be increased, for example by multiplying the current value by the initial value. Indeed, if it is necessary to re-initialize, the reason is that the solution has not been found and it is thus necessary to dilate the swarm a little more to increase the explorable portion of space.

18.3. Multi-swarm

It can sometimes be interesting to use several swarms, in particular in multiobjective optimization [PARS 02] or simply when we do not seek the very best solution at all costs but just a set of acceptable solutions. As we have seen, these types of problems can be treated by carrying out the chosen algorithm several times without re-initializing the pseudo-random number generator, but the goal of multi-swarm techniques is to obtain a better distribution of the solutions obtained.

The general idea is to differentiate the particles by a characteristic ("color" or "charge") and then to define at least a law of repulsion, for example in inverse proportion to the square of the distance between two particles [BLA 02]. Others are of course possible. Thus the one defined in [GAZ 03] induced an attraction at great distances and a repulsion at short distances, which guarantees convergence towards a stable position but goes against what we wish (regrouping of each swarm on an interesting position). In addition we will speak here rather about *color*, because for more than two swarms the literal formulation of the laws of attraction and repulsion can be very simple; for example, particles of the same color attract each other and those of different colors repel each other. Besides, one finds this idea in [BER 03] for an optimization algorithm based on the metaphor of ant colonies.

To add just one law of repulsion is easy to formalize and program, since a sum of additional terms in the calculation of the displacement of each particle will be enough. More precisely, for a particle of given position x, the repulsive contribution of every other particle of position y could be:

– null if the two particles are of the same color;

– equal to $\dfrac{\lambda}{\|x-y\|^2} \dfrac{x-y}{\|x-y\|} = \dfrac{\lambda}{\|x-y\|^3}(x-y)$, where the coefficient λ is positive, if the two particles are different colors.

The experiment shows that the law of attraction inherent in PSO is, moreover, sufficient, provided, obviously, that each particle uses only informants of its own color. Each swarm of a given color tries to converge for its own sake, while being constrained by the others. A disadvantage is that it is necessary to recompute the distances between particles with each iteration, but the principal difficulty of implementation is the estimate of the additional parameter λ. Important theoretical work remains to be done here either to guide the user in the choice of the value of this parameter or, better, to calculate it automatically in an adaptive way, perhaps using a measurement of discrepancy between swarms and measurements of concentration of each swarm. Another possible track would be to take as a starting point the biological phenomenon of speciation and to make the colors diverge from the particles, especially as the exchanges of information between them are rare.

18.4. Dynamic optimization

The rapidity of the convergence of PSO turns it into a privileged tool for dynamic problems, in the sense of a function to be minimized that changes in the course of the search process [CAR 00, EBE 01, HU 02a, PARS 01b]. As we have seen in the applications, the crudest method simply consists of not being concerned at all by the evolution of the function by hoping that it remains appreciably slower than convergence. But it is possible to do better, either by detecting the changes, or by being informed of these changes.

To know if the function was modified, a memory-particle must recompute its value for at least one of its memorized positions (besides, in the simplest case, there is only one of them). If the found value is different from that previously calculated, it is advisable to re-actualize the memories. Some refinements can be brought to this scheme. For example, detection can be done starting from a more or less large number of memory-particles, the two extremes being only one particle (the very best) and all the particles, the first case being obviously the most economical but also the least reliable, in the sense that the detected modification can be only very local and not really requiring a recalculation of all the positions. And also, it is possible to take into account only "significant" variations, i.e. in practice greater than the acceptable threshold of error.

For certain applications, it can be the system optimizing itself that announces its change of state to the optimizer. Or the optimizer may be informed in advance which changes take place at given times, for example in a regular way.

However, the difficulty is not so much in detecting if a change took place or being informed about it, but rather in knowing which strategy to adopt if it is indeed the case. The most radical approach is to recompute the values of the function for all the memorized positions, but it is also possible to do this only for the positions closest to those used for detection. Here again, we are only at an almost completely empirical stage. Even if the results published seem convincing, it would be advisable to make the tool more easily usable, perhaps starting from sampling theory.

18.5. For "amatheurs"

18.5.1. *Maximum flight and criterion of abandonment*

To clarify our ideas, let us examine a very simple canonical system of equations of motion, considering only one particle:

$$\begin{cases} v_{t+1} = \varphi(p - x_t) \\ x_{t+1} = x_t + v_{t+1} \end{cases}$$

It is the recursive representation (iterative). By noting that:

$$p - x_t = p - x_{t-1} - v_t$$
$$= (1 - \varphi)(p - x_{t-1})$$

we immediately deduce from it the direct analytical representation in the case p constant:

$$v_t = \varphi(1-\varphi)^t (p - x_0)$$

With this simple model, convergence is ensured for $\varphi \in \,]0, 2[$. The maximum flight V_t is calculated by:

$$V_t = \sum_{u=t}^{\infty}|v_t|$$
$$= (1-\varphi)^t |p-x_0| \text{ si } \varphi \in]0,1[$$
$$= \varphi(1-\varphi)^t |p-x_0| = v_t \text{ si } \varphi \in]1,2[$$

The radius of the explorable space, centered on the current position, is at most equal to V_t. Let x_{grav} be the center of gravity of the swarm. Let us calculate the pseudo-gradient:

$$\frac{\Delta f}{\Delta x} = \frac{f(x) - f(x_{grav})}{x - x_{grav}}$$

If ε is the acceptable maximum error, our criterion will then be simply:

$$V_t < \varepsilon \frac{\Delta f}{\Delta x}$$

18.5.2. Dilation

We define an initial dilation coefficient ζ_0, a little greater than 1. Let n_{reinit} be the number of re-initializations already carried out. At the beginning, the current dilation coefficient ζ is equal to ζ_0. With each re-initialization, the following operations are carried out:

– displacement of the particle by $x \leftarrow x_{grav} + \zeta\left(x - x_{grav} + \frac{\Delta x}{\Delta f}\right)$;

– recalculation of the current dilation coefficient $\zeta = \zeta\zeta_0$.

The smaller the gradient, the more the particle is moved. The more re-initialization, the more the dilation coefficient increases.

18.6. Summary

Among the many complementary techniques and alternatives of PSO, three are presented briefly: stop-restart, multi-swarm, and dynamic optimization. The last, consisting of tracking the optimum of a function that changes permanently, is undoubtedly the one that has the greatest practical importance. Detailed study of these alternatives is beyond the scope of this book, but the interested reader will be able to consult with profit the references given.

Further Information

To get information, discuss

A good deal of information concerning PSO can be obtained *via* the portal dedicated to it on the Internet: *Particle Swarm Central* (http://www.particleswarm.info). In particular, you will find links there to various bibliographies, downloadable documents, and programs. The majority of the researchers in the field are also referred to there. Many have personal sites that deserve to be visited. They will enrich your documentation and your knowledge of the subject.

There are PSO researchers everywhere: in the United States, of course, the country of origin of the first version, but also in China, Portugal, Brazil, France, etc., even in Fiji! The lingua franca used is often "international" English, but certain researchers also publish in their mother tongue. That is why, when undertaking bibliographical research, it is important not to limit it to English.

As an indication, here are some principal translations of "optimization by particle swarm" in several languages.

English (United States of America)	*Particle Swarm Optimization*
English	*Particle Swarm Optimisation*
French	*Optimisation par essaim particulaire*
Portuguese	*Optimización de enjambre de partículas*
German	*Particle Swarm Optimierung*
Chinese	**粒子群优化算法**

232 Particle Swarm Optimization

PSO in the world. Each dark gray disk indicates the usual place of work of at least one researcher in this field. The American, European, and Chinese schools are particularly active, but many other areas of the world are also represented. The language of communication is often "international" English. Nevertheless, it is worthwhile to make bibliographical researches relating to other languages.

The majority of researchers in the field will be pleased to answer your questions ... provided you take the trouble to write to them in a language they understand! In addition, there is a specific mailing list to which you can subscribe, on the site Computelligence World. The direct link is http://www.computelligence.org/cgi-bin/index.cgi?cat = 80. It is also on the home page of *Particle Swarm Central*.

Test, contribute

All the programs mentioned in *Particle Swarm Central* are in the public domain. If you just wish to use PSO without asking too many questions, you can directly try an adaptive program like TRIBES, but it is much more instructive to start with programs whose code is easier to understand. Remember that there is a very simple one in this book (in Chapter 6).

Those who are users of MatLab® or, better, the free compatible software SciLab (http://scilabsoft.inria.fr/) will be able to use Jagatpreet Singh's PSO TOOLBOX and even contribute to it. More generally, if one day you think you have done something interesting with PSO, send an email to pso@writeme.com, in French or English. The elements you will provide could possibly be put on line, for the benefit of all.

Bibliography

[ANG 98] ANGELINE P.J., "Using Selection to Improve Particle Swarm Optimization", *IEEE International Conference on Evolutionary Computation*, Anchorage, Alaska, May 4-9, p. 84-89, 1998.

[BAR 05] BARITOMPA W.P., HENDRIX E.M.T., "On the investigation of Stochastic Global Optimization algorithms", *Journal of Global Optimization*, 2003. In the press. Available online at http://www.mat.univie.ac.at/~neum/glopt/mss/BarH01.pdf.

[BER 03] BERTELLE C., DUTOT A., GUINAND F., Olivier D., "Color ant populations algorithm for dynamic distribution in simulations", poster presented at European Simulation Symposium and Exhibition, Delft, the Netherlands, 2003.

[BLA 02] BLACKWELL T.M., BENTLEY P.J., "Dynamic Search with Charged Swarms", *Genetic and Evolutionary Computation Conference*, San Francisco, p. 19-26, 2002.

[BLA 04] BLACKWELL T., BRANKE J., "Multi-Swarm Optimization in Dynamic Environments", in G.R. Raidl (dir.), *Applications of Evolutionary Computing, LNCS*, vol. 3005, Springer, p. 488-599, 2004.

[BRA 03] BRANKE J., SCHMECK H., "Designing evolutionary algorithms for dynamic optimization problems", *Natural Computing, Advances in Evolutionary Computing: Theory and Applications*, Springer-Verlag, p. 239-262, 2003.

[CAR 00] CARLISLE A., DOZIER G., "Adapting Particle Swarm Optimization to Dynamics Environments", *International Conference on Artificial Intelligence*, Las Vegas, Nevada, USA, p. 429-434, 2000.

[CAR 01] CARLISLE A., DOZIER G., Alignment changing extrema with particle swarm optimizer, Auburn University, Cse01-08, 2001.

[CHI 98] CHIN T., MITAL D., "Year Evolutionary Approach in Training Feed-Forward and Recurrent Neural Networks", *Second International Conference on Knowledge-Based Intelligent Electronic Systems*, Adelaide, Australia, p. 596-602, 1998.

[CLE 99] CLERC M., "The Swarm and the Queen: Towards a Deterministic and Adaptive Particle Swarm Optimization", *Congress on Evolutionary Computation*, Washington D.C., p. 1951-1955, 1999.

[CLE 02] CLERC M., KENNEDY J., "The Particle Swarm-Explosion, Stability, and Convergence in a Multidimensional Complex Space", *IEEE Transactions on Evolutionary Computation*, vol. 6, p. 58-73, 2002.

[CLE 04] Clerc M., "Discrete Particle Swarm Optimization, illustrated by the Traveling Salesman Problem", in *New Optimization Techniques in Engineering*, Springer, Heidelberg, p. 219-239, 2004.

[COE 02] COELLO COELLO A.C., LECHUGA M.S., "MOPSO: with Proposal for Multiple Objective Particle Swarm Optimization", *Congress on Evolutionary Computation (CEC' 2002)*, Piscataway, New Jersey, p. 1051-1056, 2002.

[CON 02] CONRADIe A.V.E., MIIKKULAINEN R., ALDRICH C., "Adaptive Control utilising Neural Swarming", *Genetic and Evolutionary Computation Conference (GECCO)*, New York, USA, 2002.

[CRI 03] CRICHTON M., *Prey*, HarperCollins Publishers, 2003 (trad: *la Proie*, Robert Laffont, Paris, 2004).

[DAV 92] DAVIDOR Y., BEN-KIKI O., "The interplay among the genetic operators: Information theory tools used in a holistic way", *Parallel Problem Solving from Nature*, Elsevier Science, Amsterdam, p. 75-84, 1992.

[DER 03] DEROÏAN F., STEYER A., Apprentissage social et diffusion de l'innovation: Réseaux critiques et intermédiarité, CNRS, Oses-University of Paris, 2003.

[DOR 04] DORIGO M., STÜTZLE T., *Ant Colony Optimization*, The MIT Press, Cambridge, Massachusetts, 2004.

[DRE 03] DRÉO J., PÉTROWSKI A., SIARRY P., TAILLARD E., *Metaheuristiques for difficult optimization*, Eyrolles, Paris, 2003.

[EBE 95] EBERHART R.C., KENNEDY J., "A New Optimizer Using Particle Swarm Theory", *6th International Symposium on Micro Machine and Human Science*, Nagoya, Japan, p. 39-43, 1995.

[EBE 96] EBERHART R.C., SIMPSON P.K., DOBBINS R.W., *Computational Intelligence PC Tools*, Academic Press, Boston, 1996.

[EBE 98] EBERHART R.C., SHI Y., "Comparison between genetic algorithms and particle swarm optimization", *Evolutionary Programming VII*, San Diego, 1998.

[EBE 01] EBERHART R.C., SHI Y., "Tracking and optimizing dynamic systems with particle swarms", *Congress on Evolutionary Computation*, Seoul, 2001.

[FRI 84] FRISCH K.V., *Life and manners of the bees*, Albin Michel, Paris, 1984.

[GAC 02] GACÔGNE L., "Steady state evolutionary algorithm with an operator family", *EISCI*, Kosice, Slovaquie, p. 373-379, 2002.

[GAZ 03] GAZI V., PASSINO K.M., "Stability Analysis of Swarms", *IEEE Trans. on Automatic Control*, vol. 48, no. 4, p. 692-697, April 2003.

[GLO 97] GLOVER F., LAGUNA M., *Tabu Search*, Kluwer Academic Publishers, New York, 1997.

[GUD 03] GUDISZ V.G., VENAYAGAMOORTHY G.K., "Comparison of particle swarm optimization and backpropagation as training algorithms for neural networks", *IEEE Swarm Intelligence Symposium 2003 (SIS 2003)*, Indianapolis, Indiana, USA, p. 110-117, 2003.

[HEL 98] HELSGAUN K., Year Effective Implementation of the Flax-Kernighan Traveling Salesman Heuristic, Department of Computer Science, University of Roskilde, Denmark, 1998.

[HU 02a] HU X., EBERHART R.C., "Adaptive particle swarm optimization: detection and response to dynamic systems", *Congress on Evolutionary Computation*, Hawaii, p. 1666-1670, 2002.

[HU 02b] HU X., EBERHART R.C., "Multiobjective Optimization Using Dynamic Neighborhood Particle Swarm Optimization", *Congress on Evolutionary Computation (CEC 2002)*, Piscataway, New Jersey, p. 1677-1681, 2002.

[ISM 99] ISMAIL A., ENGELBRECHT A.P., "Training Products Units in Feedforward Neural Networks using Particle Swarm Optimization", *International Conference on Artificial Intelligence*, Durban, South Africa, p. 36-40, 1999.

[JEA 03] JEANNET B., MESSINA F., "Deterministic method of total optimization for the hybrid problems", 5eme *congrès de la Société Française de Recherche Opérationnelle et d'Aide à la Décision (ROADEF 2003)*, Avignon, France, p. 273-274, 2003.

[JEN 96] JENIGIRI S., Comparative study of efficiency of Genetic Algorithms and Particle Swarm Optimization technical to solve permutation problems, internal Rapport, Computer Society of India, University of Mysore, 1996.

[KEN 95] KENNEDY J., EBERHART R.C., "Particle Swarm Optimization", *IEEE International Conference on Neural Networks*, Perth, Australia, p. 1942-1948, 1995.

[KEN 97] KENNEDY J., EBERHART R.C., "A discrete binary version of the particle swarm algorithm", *Conference on Systems, Man, and Cybernetics*, p. 4104-4109, 1997.

[KEN 99] KENNEDY J., "Small Worlds and Mega-Minds: Effects of Neighborhood Topology on Particle Swarm Performance", *Congress on Evolutionary Computation*, Washington, p. 1931-1938, 1999.

[KEN 00] KENNEDY J., "Stereotyping: Improving Particle Swarm Performance with Cluster Analysis", *Congress on Evolutionary Computation*, p. 1507-1512, 2000.

[KEN 01] KENNEDY J., EBERHART R., SHI Y., *Swarm Intelligence*, Morgan Kaufmann Academic Press, San Fransisco, 2001.

[KO 04] KO PC, LIN P.-C., "A Hybrid Swarm Intelligence Based Mechanism for Earning Forecast", *International Conference on Information Technology for Application (ICITA 2004)*, 2004.

[KRA 04] KRAHENBUHL R.A., LI Y., Hybrid optimization for a binary inverse problem, Gravity and Magnetics Research Consortium, Department of Geophysics, Colorado School of Mines, CGEM (Center for Gravity, Electrical & Magnetic studies), http://www.geophysics.mines.edu/cgem/pubs.html, 2004.

[KRI 02] KRINK T., Vesterstrøm J., Riget J., "Particle Swarm Optimisation with Spatial Particle Extension", *Congress on Evolutionary Computation (CEC)*, 2002.

[LAM 04] LAMPINEN J., STORN R., "Differential Evolution", in *New Optimization Techniques in Engineering*, Springer, Heidelberg, p. 124-166, 2004.

[LIT 98] LITINETSKI V.V., ABRAHAMZON B.M., "A multistart adaptive random search method for total constrained optimization in engineering applications", *Engineering optimization*, vol. 30, p. 125-154, 1998.

[LOV 01] LØVBJERG MR., KIEL RASMUSSEN T., KRINK T., "Hybrid Particle Swarm Optimiser with Breeding and Subpopulations", *Genetic and Evolutionary Computation Conference (GECCO)*, p. 469-476, 2001.

[MAU 75] MAURIN J., *Simulation déterministe du hasard*, Masson, Paris, 1975.

[MEN 02] MENDES R., CORTEZ P., ROCHA MR., FIRNS J., "Particle Swarms for Feedforward Networks Training", *International Conference on Neural Networks*, Honolulu (Hawaii), USA, p. 1895-1889, 2002.

[MIR 02a] MIRANDA V., FONSECA N., "EPSO – Best-of-Two-Worlds Meta-Heuristic Applied to Power System Problems", *WCCI/CEC – World Conference on Computational Intelligence, Conference on Evolutionary Computation*, Honolulu (Hawaii), USA, 2002.

[MIR 02b] MIRANDA V., FONSECA N., "EPSO – Evolutionary self-adapting Particle Swarm Optimization", *INESC*, Oporto, Portugal, 2002.

[MOH 01] MOHAN C.K., AL-KAZEMI B., "Discrete Particle Swarm Optimization", *Workshop on Particle Swarm Optimization*, Indianapolis, Purdue School of Engineering and Technology, 2001.

[NIE 86] NIEDERREITER H., PEART P., "Localisation of search in quasi-Monte Carlo methods for global optimization", *SIAM J Sci. Statist. Comput.*, vol. 7, p. 660-664, 1986.

[ONW 04a] ONWUBOLU G.C., "TRIBES application to the flow shop scheduling problem", *New Optimization Techniques in Engineering*, Springer, Heidelberg, p. 517-536, 2004.

[ONW 04b] ONWUBOLU G.C., SHARMA A., "Particle Swarm Optimization for the Assignment of Facilities to Locations", *New Optimization Techniques in Engineering* Springer, Heidelberg, p. 517-536, 2004.

[OVE 03] OVE R., POPPLE R., Sequential annealing – gradient Gamma-Knife radiosurgery optimization, Department of Radiation Oncology, University of Alabama, Birmingham, AL, *Physics in Medicine and Biology*, 2003.

[PAR 1896] PARETO V., *Cours d'Economie Politique*, Rouge, Lausanne, Switzerland, 1896.

[PARS 01a] PARSOPOULOS K.E., PLAGIANAKOS V.P., MAGOULAS G.D., VRAHATIS M.N., "Improving Particle Swarm Optimizer by Function 'Stretching'", *Advances in Convex Analysis and Global Optimization*, p. 445-457, 2001.

[PARS 01b] PARSOPOULOS K.E., VRAHATIS M.N., "Particle Swarm Optimizer in Noisy and Continuously Changing Environments", *Artificial Intelligence and Soft Computing*, IASTED/ACTA Press, p. 289-294, 2001.

[PARS 02] PARSOPOULOS K.E., VRAHATIS M.N., "Particle Swarm Optimization Method in Multiobjective Problems", *ACM Symposium on Applied Computing (SAC 2002)*, p. 603-607, 2002.

[PSC] Particle Swarm Central, http://www.particleswarm.info.

[QUI 93] QUINLAN J., "Combining instance-based and model-based learning", *Machine Learning (Ml' 93)*, San Mateo, 1993.

[RIE 94] RIEDMILLER M., "Supervised in Multilayer Perceptrons – from Backpropagation to Adaptive Learning Techniques", *Computer Standards and Interfaces*, vol. 16, 1994, p. 265-278.

[SAL 01] SALMAN A., IMTIAZ A., AL-MADANI S., "Discrete particle swarm optimization for heterogeneous task assignment problem", *World Multiconference on Systemics, CYbernetics and Informatics (SCI 2001)*, 2001.

[SAN 90] SANDGREN E., "Non linear integer and discrete programming in mechanical design optimization", *Transactions of the ASME, Journal of Mechanical Design*, vol. 112, p. 223-229, 1990.

[SCH 02] SCHOOFS L., NAUDTS B., "Swarm intelligence on binary constraint satisfaction problems", *Conference on Evolutionary Computation (CEC 2002)*, Pistacaway, New Jersey, USA, p. 1444-1449, May 2002.

[SEC 01a] SECREST B.R., Traveling Salesman Problem for Surveillance Mission using Particle Swarm Optimization, Air Force Institute of Technology AFIT/GCE/ENG/01M-03, 2001.

[SEC 01b] SECREST B.R., Lamont G.B., "Communication in Particle Swarm Optimization Illustrated by the Traveling Salesman Problem", *Workshop on Particle Swarm Optimization*, Indianapolis, Purdue School of Engineering and Technology, 2001.

[SER 97] SERRA P., STANTON A.F., KAIS S., "Pivot method for global optimization", *Physical Review*, vol. 55, p. 1162-1165, 1997.

[SET 03] SETTLES MR., RODEBAUGH B., "Comparison of genetic algorithm and particle swarm optimizer when evolving a recurrent neural network", *Genetic and Evolutionary Computation Conference 2003 (GECCO 2003)*, Chicago, USA, p. 151-152, 2003.

[SHI 98a] SHI Y., EBERHART R.C., "Parameter Selection in Particle Swarm Optimization", *Evolutionary Programming VII*, 1998.

[SHI 98b] SHI Y., EBERHART R.C., "A Modified Particle Swarm Optimizer", *International Conference on Evolutionary Computation*, Anchorage, Alaska, May 4-9, p. 69-73, 1998.

[SHI 01] SHI Y., EBERHART R.C., "Fuzzy Adaptive Particle Swarm Optimization", *Congress on Evolutionary Computation*, Seoul, 2001.

[SIL 03] SILAGADZE Z.K., Finding Two-Dimensional Peaks, http://arxiv.org/abs/physics/0402085, 2003.

[SMO 04] SMOLIN L., "Des atomes d'espace et de temps", *Pour la Science*, p. 46-55, 2004.

[STO 99] STORN R., "Designing digital filters with differential evolution", *New Ideas in Optimization*, McGraw-Hill, New York, p. 109-125, 1999.

[SUG 99] SUGANTHAN P.N., "Particle Swarm Optimiser with Neighbourhood Operator", *Congress on Evolutionary Computation*, Washington, p. 1958-1962, 1999.

[TAN 02] TANDON V., EL-MOUNAIRY H., KISHAWY H., "NC end milling optimization using evolutionary computation", *International Journal of Machine Tools & Manufacture*, vol. 42, p. 595-605, 2002.

[TRE 03] TRELEA I.C., "The particle swarm optimization algorithm: convergence analysis and parameter selection", *Information Processing Letters*, vol. 85, p. 317-325, 2003.

[VAN 99] VAN DEN BERGH F., "Particle Swarm Weight Initialization in Multi-layer Perceptron Artificial Neural Networks", *Development and Practice of Artificial Intelligence Techniques (Durban, South Africa)*, p. 41-45, 1999.

[VAN 01] VAN DEN BERGH F., ENGELBRECHT A.P., "Training Product Unit Networks using Cooperative Particle Swarm Optimisers", *IJCNN 2001*, Washington, USA, 2001.

[VAN 02] VAN DEN BERGH F., "An Analysis of Particle Swarm Optimizers", *Department of Computer Science*, University of Pretoria, Pretoria, South Africa, 2002.

[VEE 03] VEERAMACHANENI K., PERAM T., MOHAN C., OSADCIW L.A., "Optimization Using Particle Swarms with Near Neighbor Interactions", *Genetic and Evolutionary Computation Conference (GECCO)*, 2003.

[WAT 03] WATTS D.J., *Six Degrees: The Science of a Connected Age*, Norton, New York, 2003.

[WHI 98] WHITE T., PAGUREK B., OPPACHER F., "ASGA: improving the ant system by integration with genetic algorithms", *3rd Genetic Programming Conference*, p. 610-617, 1998.

[XIE 02] XIE X.-F., ZHANG W.-J., YANG Z.-L., "A dissipative particle swarm optimization", *IEEE Congress on Evolutionary Computation (CEC 2002)*, Honolulu, Hawaii, USA, 2002.

[YOS 01] YOSHIDA H., KAWATA K., FUKUYAMA Y., "A Particle Swarm Optimization for Reactive Power and Voltage Control considering Voltage Security Assessment", *IEEE Trans. on Power Systems*, vol. 15, p. 1232-1239, 2001.

[ZDA 02] ZDANSKY MR., POZIVIL J., "Combination Genetic/Tabu Search algorithm for Hybrid Flowshops Optimization", *ALGORITMY 2002, Conference on Scientic Computing*, p. 230-236, 2002.

[ZEL 04] ZELINKA I., "SOMA – Self-Organizing Migrating Algorithm", *New Optimization Techniques in Engineering*, Springer, Heidelberg, p. 168-217, 2004.

[ZHA 01] ZHANG C., SHAO H., "Particle Swarm Optimisation in Feedforward Neural Network", *Artificial Neural Networks in Medicine and Biology (ANNIMAB)*, 2001

[ZHA 03a] ZHANG W., LIU Y., CLERC M., "An Adaptive PSO Algorithm for Reactive Power Optimization", *Advances in Power System Control Operation and Management (APSCOM)*, Hong Kong, 2003.

[ZHA 03b] ZHANG W., XIE X.-F., "DEPSO: hybrid particle swarm with differential evolution operator", Proceedings *IEEE International Conference on Systems, Man and Cybernetics*, p. 3816-3821, 2003.

Index

A, B

abandonment (criterion of) 226
Ackley 52
adaptation 129
    criteria 129
    frequency 144
    nonparametric 133
    parametric 132, 136
adjusted ellipsoid 112
algorithm
    greedy 203
    of reference 23
"all different" confinement 156
Alpine 10D 57
alternatives 225
apagogy 155
apiarian metaphor 29
backpropagation 174
behavior
    collective 17
    cooperative 31
    individual 17
benchmark set 51
    better parameter settings for 122
    results 147

C

centroid 98
channel of communication 92
chaos 201
circular
    diagram 32
    neighborhood 87
coefficient of
    confidence 34
    constriction 221
collective 17
    behavior 17
    intelligence 13
combinatorial problems 201
comparison
    by pseudo-gradients 147
    direct 147
competence, field of 38
competition 35
confinement
    "all different" 156
    by dichotomy 157
    constraint 151
    granularity 156
    interval 40, 154
    method 203
constraint 151
    by homeomorphism 162
    by penalties 161
    confinement 151
    imperative 153
    indicative 153
    multicriterion 158
    representation of the 152
constriction 220
convergence 220
cooperation 18, 35, 139

D

D-rectangle 16
D-sphere 16
diabetes in Pima Indians 175
dichotomy (confinement by) 157
differential evolution 185
difficulty
    estimate of 26, 56
    intrinsic 26
    measurement 23
discrete variable 154
displacement 31
    strategies of 145
distribution
    bias 45
    isotropic 118
    local 107
    multidimensional 134
    one-dimensional 107
    proximity 103
    random 34
    rectangular 104
    source code 107
    uniform 39, 118
diversity 32, 34
dynamic optimization 228
dynamics of a swarm 211

E

ecological niche 167
effectiveness, criterion of 71
ellipsoidal positive sectors 105
energy
    kinetic 217
    potential 217
error
    acceptable 24
    of follow-up 186
estimate of
    difficulty 26,56
    rate of failure 65
exclusive OR 175
explorer
    particle 89
    swarm 89
explosion 48

F

forced homeomorphism 162
function 30
    Ackley 52
    Alpine 24, 52
    Griewank 52
    parabola 52
    of reference 53
    Rosenbrock 52
    of test 51
    Tripod 52

G

generation of a particle 144
granularity confinement 156
graphs
    of influence 87
    of information 127
greedy algorithm 224
Griewank 52
group
    of information receivers 31
    size 18

H, I

heuristics
    general purpose 190
    meta 190
    mono 190
hybrid JM 173
hyperparallelepid 16
hypersphere 16
I-group 32
independent Gaussian 106
information
    graph 33
    link 30, 33, 38
    path 141
    propagation 34
informant 31, 32
    average number of 49
    best 146
    influence of the number of 93
information receivers 31
initialization 38

interesting site 30
interval confinement 154

J, K, L

KISS 62
link of information 30
list
    not ordered 155
    ordered 155
local optimum 17

M

mailing list 232
memories
    mixing 97
    influence of the number 95
magic squares 170
minimal version 37
mixing of the memories 97
metaheuristic 190
method
    anarchistic 18
    collective 18
    hybrid 14
    iterative 18
mode
    parallel 196
    sequential 196
motion
    equations of 39
moving peaks 185
multicriterion treatment 158
multi-swarm 14, 227
multiobjective 227

N, O

neighborhood
    circular 87
    geographical 87
    social 87
neural network 174
normal law 66
one-dimensional
    distribution 107
    class 161

PSO 13, 18
    adaptive 13
    autonomous 35
    canonical 14, 204
    traditional 40
    history 206
    world 232
OEP 0 (source code) 45, 85
optimization
    algorithm 40
    collective 18
    continuous 190
    dynamics 186, 228
    iterative 17, 31, 43
    linear 151
    canonical representation 169
    stochastic 62, 103
optimal parameter settings 121

P

parabola 54
parallelism 14, 211
parameter setting
    handbook 50, 131
    optimum 131
particle
    bad 142
    best 142
    confined 144
    excellent 142
    explorer 89
    free 144
    generation of a 144
    good 141
    quality 141
    memory 228
    neutral 142
    status 142
    suppression 142
    worst 142
Particle Swarm Central 231
performance
    best 32
    maps 73
Pima Indians 175
pivot 108

Gaussian 111
    with noise 110
polyheuristic 190
possible randomness 113
probability of failure 25
problem
    combinatorial 23
    compression spring 182
    continuous 26
    difficult 23
    discrete 26
    hybrid JM 173
    knapsack 169
    linear 34
    magic squares 170
    nonlinear 18
    pressure vessel 177
    quadratic assignment 171
    traveling salesman 172
    typology 168
propagation 34
proximity
    random 34
    distribution of 42, 103
pseudo-gradient 147
pseudo-random
    number 59
    number generator 27
PSO TOOLBOX 232
Pyramid topology 176

Q, R

quadratic assignment 171
quality
    particle 141
    tribe 141
queen 88
rate of failure, estimate of a 65
recruitment
    direct 92
    by channel of communication 92
    random 99
reference (function of) 57
re-initialization 227
reorganizations of memory-swarm 97
replacement of a particle 131

results
    analyze of the 125
    benchmark set 147
    comparative 98
    comparisons of 113
    first 71
robustness 73
Rosenbrock 54
Rprop 174
rumor, propagation of 30

S

SciLab 232
search
    effort 58
    space 122
selection 18, 35, 131
servomechanism 176
simple program 71
    specific 14
social neighborhood 87
SOMA 179
source codes 15
    dichotomy 162
    KISS 69
    OEP 0 80
status
    particle 142
    tribe 142
stop-restart/reset 224
strategy 17, 30
    displacement 145
    stupid 18
structuring 18
suppression
    particle 142
    tribe 142
swarm
    dynamics 211
    evolution 145
    explorer- 89
    memory 87, 97
    size 30, 37
syncretism 189

T, U

technical terms 17
test functions 51
temporal
    connectivity 99
    decrease 130
    formulas of 135
    weighting with 130
tolerance level 24
topology
    fixed 90, 93
    of problems 168
    Pyramid 176
    random 90, 95
trade-off surface 159
training of a neural network 174
traveling salesman 15, 172, 205
treatment by penalties 174
tribal relationship 141
TRIBES 18, 139, 140
tribe 141
    good 142
    bad 142
    quality 142
    status 142
    suppression 142
Tripod 53

V-Z

velocity 34
    initialization 32
    maximum 48
weighting with temporal decrease 130